The Reality

of the

Message

Psychoanalysis in the

wake of Jean Laplanche

by Dominique Scarfone

and in critical conversation

with Avgi Saketopoulou

Copyright © 2023 by The Unconscious in Tranlation
General Director: Jonathan House
1050 Fifth Avenue, New York, NY 10028
info@uitbooks.com
First Edition

Production: Stephan Trano
Cover art: Vasiliki Kiparissi
Book layout: Thirumoolar Devar

ISBN 978-1-942254-22-5
Library of Congress Control Number: 2023946343

CONTENTS

Introduction

In one of his introductory lectures to psychoanalysis, Freud had this to say:

> "It is in general not such a common thing for psycho-analysis to deny something asserted by other people; as a rule it merely adds something new—though no doubt it occasionally happens that this thing that has hitherto been overlooked and is now brought up as a fresh addition is in fact the essence of the matter." (Freud, 1916-17, p. 45)

The remark applies beautifully to the theory of communication or, for that matter, to the theory of human attachment. Psychoanalysis has nothing to deny in those areas of study, but it has probably something essential to add. For while an indisputable fact about human reality is that of communication and its corollary, making sense of what is communicated, only psychoanalysis takes notice of the particular situation created when communication happens between an adult and an *infans* – literally: the one who does not speak. Nor is it given much attention, even among psychoanalysts, that there is a special "noise" carried over in the channels of communication between the two, a noise resulting from the difference regarding the unconscious sexual dimension, a dimension present in the adult but missing in the *infans*. The noise is of importance at the origin of human sexuality.

Obviously this last view was not likely to gather a general consensus given that Freud theorized an inborn infantile sexuality after he let go of his seduction theory of the 1890s. Laplanche's approach to this "cataclysmic" event (1987), and his efforts to repair the damage which, in his view, it has caused to psychoanalysis, is the backdrop of many chapters in the present book. Here I am referring to Laplanche's General Theory of Seduction (GTS). The theoretical research and the discussions in these pages are an attempt to extend the GTS.

*

This is not the usual collection of papers put in a book format. The chapters *are* reprints of previously published articles (though chapter 5 was not published in English), but they have had the good fortune of being read by a keen-eyed and rigorous critic, Avgi Saketopoulou, who improved them and gratified their author with essential questions and comments. The result is a totally different book than the one Jonathan House and I had intended at first. Each chapter is now followed by a conversation that not only helps highlight the logic of the chapter but updates it and pushes it forward. Each conversation could, I dare say, be considered a new chapter.

The issues Avgi Saketopoulou and I deal with in this book are many, but one could say they gravitate around a number of central themes.

The *clinical significance of metapsychology* is one. It often has been said that metapsychology is the speculative, experience-distant set of concepts and theories which a clinician can ignore without serious loss. I hope that the chapters composing this book and the discussions following each, will convince the reader that it is not so. For one thing, for an analyst who takes seriously the idea of an unconscious, using metapsychology is like Mr. Jourdain's speaking in prose: one does so, whether one knows it or not. However, it is a good idea to know it so as to speak or to make the theory better.

A better psychoanalytic theory is indeed another main goal. Here 'better' does not mean a totally new theory. I have followed Laplanche in his endeavor to give *more solid foundations* to the Freudian edifice. This is why the reader will find Laplanche cited throughout the book, with the unavoidable repetitions due to the independent nature of the original texts. I have chosen not to edit the articles, except for minor stylistic and grammatical changes, in order to give the reader a clear idea of the path that was followed over the years.

Consequently, *the translational model of the psyche* is another central feature. A model that is intimately woven into the General Theory of Seduction and therefore with the origins and the workings of *infantile sexuality*, *repression* and the *sexual drives* whose presence impacts everything human in the individual mind, in society and culture, and, of course, in the psychoanalytic room.

I have tried to use Laplanche's method of critically re-reading Freud while leaning on the Freudian analytic method without hesitating to turn the method around and, when necessary, to use it against the Freudian opus. In my case – and in accordance with Laplanche's wish that his own thinking be put back to work – I also happen to view things somewhat differently from Laplanche.

Acknowledgements

I view the conversations with Avgi Saketopoulou that follow each chapter as an original contribution to the book, so I cannot find satisfactory words to thank her enough for her precious gift. I also wish to thank Jonathan House for welcoming the project of this book from the very start. Katie Hermann has done a splendid work of revision, for which I am very grateful. I wish to also thank another special interlocutor, my colleague and friend Jacques Mauger, for his most attentive listening and his creative suggestions during our long walks on the Olmstead trail, at the very heart of Montreal. My wife Francine Lefebvre has witnessed my shredding numerous drafts of each of the papers published here, always reassuring me that the next one would be better. If this is the case, it is in part due to her constant support. Finally, though they are too many to be named here, I wish to thank the participants in my ongoing seminar titled *Penser avec Freud* (Thinking with Freud) who accompany me, year after year, through the critical re-reading of Freud's writings.

D.S.

A Brief Introduction to the Work of Jean Laplanche[1]

Jean Laplanche died on May 6, 2012, a few weeks before his eighty-eighth birthday. His name is undoubtedly familiar to many psychoanalysts around the world who from time to time must have consulted *The Language of Psycho-Analysis*, an indispensable reference work written in collaboration with Jean-Bertrand Pontalis and translated into many languages. The book includes not only the most reliable definitions of the main concepts of psychoanalysis, but it also—and perhaps primarily—proposes a comprehensive survey of the Freudian sources as well as a critical examination of the concepts, their development, and their place within the whole corpus. This book's ability to account for Freud's ideas with rigor and cogency should not make us lose sight of the other side of Laplanche's work, his "faithful unfaithfulness" to Freud, as he liked to describe it. In fact, Laplanche used his exceptionally deep knowledge of the founder's work as a basis from which to carry out an uncompromising yet appreciative critique of Freud's ideas. Laplanche often specified that he was no "Freudologist" and that his goal never consisted in putting Freud the man on the couch. The only Freud he was interested in was Freud as featured in his written work, work that Laplanche took it on himself to put to the test by "stabbing it with a knife" or "hacking it with a pickax," as he put

---

1 Originally published in a slightly different form in the International Journal of Psychoanalysis 94, no. 3 (June 2013): 545–66. Translated from the French by Dorothée Bonnigal-Katz.

it, to verify the solidity of the Freudian edifice. When this edifice proved to be wobbly in places, Laplanche undertook to consolidate it by working "on the underpinnings,"—in other words, not by destroying everything so as to yield some "new psychoanalysis" but by patiently taking up the research again, by steadying the edifice, providing it, as it were, with new, more solid foundations.

Laplanche did not seek to distance himself from Freud at all costs. On the contrary, Laplanche professed deep admiration for the inventor of psychoanalysis, especially for what he referred to as Freud's "exigency"—that is, Freud's relentless pursuit of his research object, the unconscious, which Freud was compelled to track down despite its enduring elusiveness and, according to Laplanche, at the cost of "going astray." Laplanche used Freud's "goings-astray" as evidence of the need to resume the work of reflection, with great confidence in the fact that, because of his faithfulness to his object, Freud must have gone astray for some definite reason, some reason that had to be identified so that, on its basis, Freud could be put to work again.

Having acquired a solid background in philosophy as the former student of three great thinkers (Jean Hippolyte, Gaston Bachelard, and Maurice Merleau-Ponty), Laplanche undertook an analysis with Jacques Lacan in the late 1940s. Lacan advised Laplanche to embark on medical studies, which he did, and in this context he wrote a dissertation on the schizophrenic poet Friedrich Hölderlin.[2] Laplanche attended Lacan's seminars and, along with Pontalis, started translating some texts by Freud into French. In the meantime, the institutional crisis over Lacan's analytic practice led Laplanche and a few others to break with him at the beginning of the 1960s. As summed up by Laplanche and Pontalis (1985), the main reason for their break was their realization that the "return

---

2 *Hölderlin et la question du père* (Paris : Presses Universitaires de France, 1984). Originally completed as a dissertation in 1961.

to Freud" was in fact a "no return" endorsement of Lacan.[3] Both colleagues did carry out their return to Freud all the same but following a very different path than Lacan. At Daniel Lagache's instigation, they spent several years working on *The Language of Psycho-Analysis*, which was published in 1967. This work, combined with the translation of Freud's texts, endowed Laplanche with deep and intimate knowledge of the *whole* of Freud's psychoanalytic works. Having looked through Freud's corpus from all angles, Laplanche became adept at gauging the equilibria and the breaks, the advances and the dead ends, on the basis of which, as I will expound, he was able to carry out a most effective critique of Freud.

In what follows, I make no claim to account for Laplanche's work in any comprehensive way. Obviously, only the reading of the original texts can adequately convey the wealth of Laplanche's ideas and the multifaceted dimension of his knowledge, as well as the subtlety and rigor of his method. I merely offer here a brief survey, in the hope of arousing the interest of readers who will then be inclined to go and see for themselves.

A Threefold Corpus

Jean Laplanche's impact on psychoanalysis consists in at least three major, highly interdependent contributions: Laplanche firstly designed a rigorous method for a critical reading of Freud's texts; in so doing, he secondly came to ascertain the key role of *translation*, not only for the exploration and the actual translation of Freud's work into French, but also as a fundamental mechanism in the process of psychic differentiation; in the wake of these first two attainments, Laplanche ultimately proposed, through his theory of general seduction, a *refounding* of the whole psychoanalytic field on a new basis.

---

3 "Post-scriptum," in *Fantasme originaire, fantasmes des origines, origines du fantasme* (Paris : Hachette, 1985).

It is very likely that Laplanche developed his original approach to reading Freud's texts in the context of the meticulous research required for the writing of *The Language of Psycho-Analysis*. Indeed, such a comprehensive survey of the founding texts could be carried out only with an awareness of what psychoanalysis has to teach us about "official discourse" and its underpinnings. In fact, psychoanalysts cannot have an innocent reading of psychoanalytic texts, even those written by Freud. Laplanche's undertaking therefore consists in applying the Freudian method to its creator's own work. But to do so, Laplanche had to make adjustments to the psychoanalytic method so as to apply it—mutatis mutandis—to the texts, not the man. Laplanche explains this method in a text that can be seen as programmatic: "Interpreting (with) Freud." The term "with" in parentheses suggests that one must "interpret Freud with Freud." Such parenthesizing, which forces us to read the title twice so as to understanding its full meaning, is indicative of the kind of work that Laplanche set about pursuing—his rule being always to look at least twice to discern, even in the most familiar texts, the detail, the overlooked contradiction, or Freud's second thoughts as they arise within a few lines, paragraphs, or years of one another, and to consider such "accidents" as the textual equivalents of slips of the tongue and other parapraxes in the course of an analytic session. With this approach, the key is to proceed patiently, to refrain from rushing into any interpretation, and instead to map out cross-references and draw comparisons and identify oppositions. Once elements of this sort have been singled out, they may be used as signs marking out the sites of "excavation" where perhaps more serious problems or clues to solutions, until then overlooked, might be unearthed.[4]

As early as during the composition of *The Language of Psycho-Analysis*, Laplanche and Pontalis were able to draw the concept

---

4 Jean Laplanche, "Interpreting (with) Freud," *The Unfinished Copernican Revolution*, p. 57-74.

of primal fantasies from their reading of Freud to develop the implied theory of fantasy in general and to circumscribe its role in the development of Freud's ideas. They also took this opportunity to write an essay providing an enlightening critique of it.[5] Furthermore, *The Language of Psycho-Analysis* itself includes many genuine discoveries, such as, explicitly, the concept of leaning-on (*Anlehnung*, "anaclisis" in Strachey's translation), which had remained ignored until then and was not thematized by Freud himself, despite the undeniable significance of the concept, which is by now impossible to overlook.[6]

Life and Death in Psychoanalysis

As I have suggested elsewhere,[7] Laplanche's research can be said to follow a process of first unfurling Freud's theory—a step that is akin to the analyst's listening with evenly suspended attention— followed by condensing or narrowing the scope, a part of the process during which Laplanche somewhat clarifies matters and draws his own conclusions, even if doing so implies unfurling these conclusions all over again and initiating a new cycle of work. The *Problématiques* series accounted for many years of Laplanche's research and teaching in the context of the University of Paris VII and led to the important volume entitled *New Foundations for Psychoanalysis*.[8] Prior to that, the long research process underlying the writing of *The Language of Psycho-Analysis*, a kind of opening out of all Freud's texts, was similarly condensed, a few years later,

---

5 Jean Laplanche and Jean-Bertrand Pontalis, "Fantasy and the Origins of Sexuality," *International Journal of Psychoanalysis* 49, no. 1 (1968): 1–18.

6 Sigmund Freud, *Three essays on the theory of sexuality*, SE 7:123–246; Sigmund Freud, "On Transience," SE 14:303–7.

7 Dominique Scarfone, *Laplanche. An Introduction.* (New York: The Unconscious in Translation, 2015).

8 *New Foundations for Psychoanalysis*, trans. Jonathan House (New York: The Unconscious in Translation, 2016).

in the form of an important personal book written by Laplanche alone, *Life and Death in Psychoanalysis*.[9] In all these books, Laplanche noticeably applies the method he proposed in his 1968 article, "Interpreting (with) Freud."

Life and Death in Psychoanalysis offers a close investigation of the *Three Essays on Sexual Theory*,[10] the "Project for a Scientific Psychology," "Beyond the Pleasure Principle," and other major texts by Freud. But Laplanche does not merely read. He problematizes Freud's ideas; he examines them critically. The combined chapters of *Life and Death* draw a curve that, starting from the vital order in its relations with the genesis of sexuality, leads to a questioning of the function of the death drive in the general structure of Freud's texts. Laplanche raises the following questions: While Freudian psychoanalysis is in many ways contiguous to biology, can it be reduced to biology? If not, then how is the specific field of psychoanalysis organized in relation to some of the basic notions operating at its borders, such as life and death?

To Laplanche, the first essay in Freud's *Three Essays*, on "sexual aberrations," indicates how psychoanalytic thought has extricated itself from a psychology of adaptation. The sexual drive has little or no relation to the instinct for reproduction. Laplanche suggests that this essay might have been subtitled "The Lost Instinct."[11] But through his discussion of sexual aberrations, Freud does not aim to describe some accidental loss of instinct. On the contrary, as Laplanche clearly shows, Freud's point is to conceive of the whole of human sexuality as devious. The sexual domain in humans is itself an "aberrant" domain with respect to a well-regulated vital order. This is the human exception, and it is the specificity of

---

9 *Life and Death in Psychoanalysis*, trans. Jeffrey Mehlman (Baltimore: Johns Hopkins University Press, 1976).

10 I have retained the first and, in my opinion, correct translation of the title of this work, which Strachey translated as *Three Essays on the Theory of Sexuality*.

11 *Life and Death*, p. 14-15.

psychoanalysis to clearly distinguish the sexual from the domain of adaptation.

The concept of leaning-on, identified by Laplanche and Pontalis during the preparation of *The Language of Psycho-Analysis*, was meant as a notion delineating the difference between the adaptational vital order on the one hand and the drive-related sexual order on the other. It is, however, often misunderstood as establishing the relationship between the psychical and the biological. So, it is important to state that for Laplanche, psychic elements and biological elements operate on both sides of the delineation provided by the notion of leaning-on. At a time when attachment theory was not as popular as it is now, Laplanche never doubted that the adaptational side involved the implementation of some psychological functions. The key here is not to confuse the psychological sphere in general with the psychic sphere as tackled by psychoanalysis. *Psychological reality* can ultimately be subsumed within human or animal brain functioning; *psychic reality*, on the other hand, coincides in psychoanalytic terms with a reality that is strictly human and in which, as I will discuss, the primacy of the other prevails along with the other's message insofar as it conveys, unbeknownst to its sender and in the midst of its well-defined meanings, enigmatic signifiers endowed with decisive importance. Such psychic reality, which Laplanche conclusively refers to as "the reality of the message," will be held as a third category of reality; one in which psychoanalysis is particularly interested, since this is the kind of reality that impacts the body-psyche of the *infans*. As for leaning-on, it does not imply that the psychic sphere should be disembodied; it does not pertain to the relations between psyche and soma. In fact, according to Laplanche, whereas the field of ethology—whether animal or human—is concerned with instincts (*Instinkts*), leaning-on is a first step toward a possible theorization of the emergence of the drive (*Trieb*).

Laplanche later criticizes the concept of leaning-on and upholds seduction as the true story behind it. Yet the study of leaning-on remains a good illustration of Laplanche's work method: it is one of these nodal points that had first to be highlighted in Freud and later to undergo a critique. As Laplanche would put it, it is a concept in relation to which it is easy to go astray.[12] At the same time, it contributes to one's understanding of an important point in Freud's ideas—that is, the delineation of the sexual field (understood psychoanalytically) as opposed to the vital, psychobiological domain. But delineating is not synonymous with finding the origin, and the issue of origin is precisely the premise of Laplanche's critique of the "biologizing" dimension of leaning-on and of his advocacy of a theory of general seduction in its stead (see more on this below).

In *Life and Death in Psychoanalysis*, the critique of leaning-on begins with the discussion of the last of Freud's *Three Essays*, which Laplanche suggested could have been subtitled "The Regained Instinct."[13] For as a natural mechanism, leaning-on soon appears conducive to a view of the sexual sphere and its origin as easily subsumed within the instinctual domain despite their former distinction from it. Laplanche thus underlines how leaning-on fails to account for the origin of the drive-related sexual sphere on the basis of the vital order: Taken as it is, leaning-on gives the impression that sexuality arises from self-preservation rather as the flower blossoms forth from the bud. Yet self-preservation in humans reveals itself to be severely deficient, and this very deficiency ensures that the Sexual takes over.[14] If leaning-on operates, it does so in both

---

12 See *Le fourvoiement biologisant de la sexualité chez Freud* (Paris: Synthélabo, 1993).

13 *Life and Death*, p. 15.

14 Laplanche used the German word *Sexual* to differentiate the object of psychoanalysis from sexuality in general. In keeping with this, throughout this book, when the word "sexual" is used as a noun rather than an adjective (as in "the sexual sphere"), it will be written with a capital *S*, as in "the Sexual" or "the infantile Sexual," to clearly designate the sexual drive and to distinguish it from

directions (from the vital to the Sexual and vice versa) insofar as the Sexual, in its many guises, is led to compensate for the deficiencies of self-preservation. The debility of self-preservation in fact requires the intervention of an other, a helping other (the *Nebenmensch* or "fellow human being" invoked by Freud in the "Project"), hence necessarily giving a prominent role to the Sexual. Indeed, while this other's intervention is attuned, as best as possible, to the needs of the *infans* in a state of radical helplessness (*Hilflosigkeit*), this other is also, inevitably, the bearer of a repressed unconscious that somewhat interferes with the process of mutual adaptation between adult and child. A repressed sexual "contaminant" thus passes through as a stowaway passenger on the carrier wave of the relation of attachment. If leaning-on therefore does operate, as Laplanche suggests, it can do so only as an incidental mechanism occurring alongside the intervention of the helping other. From the simple dividing line between the adaptational and the drive-related sphere (the Sexual) arises what Laplanche later refers to as the "fundamental anthropological situation," the situation in which every human being finds himself or herself inserted by the mere fact of being born in a world saturated with enigmatic signifiers, with compromised messages—compromised, that is, by the repressed Sexual of the other, of the adult. In human beings, the sexual order thus always already overlies the vital order. I will return to this point.

The Ego and the Death Drive

I will further discuss the theory of general seduction, which began to emerge as early as in this 1970 book, later in this chapter. But for the time being, let us focus on two main themes tackled in *Life and Death in Psychoanalysis*.

---

sexuality in general (i.e., sexual behavior).

The Ego

After having related and contrasted the sexual and the vital order, Laplanche sets about locating the ego in relation to the vital order in question. As *The Language of Psycho-Analysis* had already revealed, the ego holds a crucial place in Freud's reflection and, accordingly, in Laplanche's reading. This is especially true of the ego's double status, consisting of an ego standing for the body as a whole and positioned as such before the world (a metaphorical ego) and an ego as a specific agency of the psychic apparatus (a metonymic ego). Laplanche shows that both understandings of the ego can be found as early as in the "Project for a Scientific Psychology." I will not embark on a detailed discussion of the ego itself but will merely stress the fact that, regarding the ego, Laplanche is further developing an argument in *Life and Death in Psychoanalysis* that he introduced in the context of his examination of the Sexual as the buttress of deficient self-preservation.

As stated earlier, where instinct seemingly fails to ensure the survival of the human baby, the helping other and therefore love take over, love meaning the Sexual as tied to the ego. If, at the outset, the ego thus appears as the quintessential representative of the vital order (let us bear in mind that Freud did not distinguish between self-preservation drives and ego drives), the ego also seems to be running on love—that is to say, on libido. Looking at Freud's theory as a whole, Laplanche points out that two sexual regimes are to become distinguished from the vital-adaptational sphere: a drive-related regime strictly speaking, a kind of foreign body experienced as an internal assailant, and another regime representative of the quiescent libidinal cathexis, to use Freud's term. This second regime is the regime of the narcissistic libido, the cement that holds the ego together as a relatively stable structure. The ego thus does not appear as siding with biological self-preservation and the vital order, as Freud first argued, but it appears as invested with libido from the outset, with this narcissistic libido—that is, self-love—

which constitutes the true grounds for human self-preservation. Metaphorically speaking, therefore, the ego presents itself in the form of a living organism, at the pole of life; but it does not blossom forth from biological functions any more than drives do. As Laplanche writes, "It is formed from perceptions and primarily from the perception of a fellow creature, and, on the other hand, it takes over libidinally, as its own, the activity of perception. I perceive, just as I eat, 'for the love of the ego.'"[15]

The Death Drive

Narcissism is so crucial in Laplanche's view because the introduction of this concept in the years 1910-1914 represents for him the great turning point in Freud's ideas rather than "Beyond the Pleasure Principle." A turning point that seems to have been immediately repressed by Freud himself when, soon after writing the seminal paper on narcissim[16], he started writing the metapsychology papers without seeming to take full stock of the impact of his new theorization. Yet posited as the quiescent regime of the libido within the ego, narcissism indicates the form under which the Sexual relays self-preservation to ensure the survival of the individual organism. Laplanche shows, however, that this subject occasions some serious theoretical wavering on Freud's part. In fact, under the generic term of "libido," Freud ends up conflating the drive-related Sexual—that is, the internal assailant—and the narcissistic libido. In other words, under the aegis of Eros, Freud merges the two—once most sharply contrasted—libidinal regimes. The Sexual thus finds itself unified while being viewed as essentially unifying (since Eros is what creates and multiplies links). This dispenses with the "demonic" aspect that Freud had, until then, applied to the sexual drives. Laplanche suggests that this is what compels

---

15 *Life and Death*, 83.

16 Freud (1914) On Narcissism: An Introduction, SE 14:73-102.

Freud, ever driven by the exigency of his object, to find some conceptual balance and posit the death drive opposite Eros. The point is to reintroduce the "demonic" Sexual, which the libidinal "quiescence" of narcissism had overly pacified.

Far from being an absolutely new discovery, the death drive is, in Laplanche's view, a rediscovery of what the great turning point of narcissism had obscured for Freud. As he equates the death drive and the drive-related Sexual, Laplanche proposes the term "sexual death drive." Indeed, there is no point in following Freud in his metabiological speculations as developed in "Beyond the Pleasure Principle." It is only through a metaphoric-metonymic derivation, under the form of the ego, that life, or the vital, partakes in the psychoanalytic domain, which implies that this form of the vital no longer pertains to the one studied by biologists. Similarly, the death drive refers not to biological death but to the process of psychic unbinding generated by the emergence of the drive, jeopardizing the ego's binding action (the nature of this binding action will be discussed later). As clearly implied by the title of his book, Laplanche aims to tackle life and death *in psychoanalysis*, not in general. The "death" in question actually pertains to the differentiation that can be made within the pleasure principle and refers to one of its poles. For as Laplanche reminds us, Freud already viewed the pleasure principle as split in two, distinguishing between the constancy principle (on the side of life drives) and the zero-point energy or nirvana principle (on the side of the death drive).

Seduction, Translation, and
Fundamental Anthropological Situations

A closer look at Laplanche's work reveals how deeply interrelated all its various aspects are, whether Laplanche is reading Freud, theorizing, or translating. Yet translation can be regarded as the leading thread. The reason is that, for Laplanche, not only does translation intervene in the context of the French edition of Freud's texts (Œuvres *complètes de Freud*), but translation also serves as a fundamental model of the constitution and functioning of the psychic apparatus and, consequently, as a key to an understanding of the work of analysis. Let us begin by clearing up a misunderstanding regarding the latter point. When invoking the central function of translation in the psychic apparatus, Laplanche does not imply that the analyst is in any way "translating" on the analysand's behalf in the course of an analytic session. The actual process is rather more complex and in fact implies the exact opposite of what the word "translation" might suggest. It is best, therefore, to follow Laplanche's reflection on the subject one step at a time.

Let me stress, firstly, that Laplanche's metapsychological thought is inseparable from his observations on the analytic situation and on what takes place between analyst and analysand. Having established, in *Life and Death in Psychoanalysis*, the necessary delineation between the vital-adaptational field and the psychoanalytic field strictly speaking (i.e., the drive-related sexual field), Laplanche underlines that such a partition exactly matches the one that the analytic method reinstates with each new analytic session. The analyst suggests that the analysand proceed following the rule of free association and, for his or her part, listens with evenly suspended attention, suspending "conscious purposive aims," as Freud put it[17]. In so doing, the analyst in effect excludes anything that pertains to the discourse of everyday concerns and needs from the frame of the session, allowing the scoria of self-preservation to settle, so to speak, in order to free up the work of the drive-related sphere. Each new session requires such a reinstatement of the analytic space through a subtraction of the adaptational field. Yet the process is less arbitrary than it might seem insofar as it is less a matter of taking anything apart than of remaining consistent with

---

17 Freud (1911) The Handling of Dream Interpretation in Psychoanalysis, *SE* 12 : 94

the fact that, as previously asserted, in humans, the Sexual always already overlies the adaptational field.

The reinstatement of the analytic space is thus not a forced process; it consists, rather, in an acoustic openness to that which remains unnoticed in everyday life. Analysts therefore authorize themselves to hear their analysands statements on a different plane than the plane of "commonsense" motives. For this purpose, analysts must perform some "refusals"—Laplanche's preferred translation of the Freudian term *Versagungen*, often translated as "frustrations." In fact, analysts' *Versagungen* do not consist in frustrations insofar as analysts' refusal to proceed in the vital or adaptational order applies to themselves as much as it applies to analysands. And the first thing that analysts deny themselves is knowledge: the knowledge, for instance, of what is good for a patient or the advance knowledge of the outcome of the analysis. Analysts deny themselves the suggestion, even implicit, of a normative plan of action, however "psychoanalytic" it might be. Laplanche, threfore, challenges the adaptive designs of ego psychology, which Lacan opposed in the 1950s. Yet he equally challenges Lacan's idea that the end of analysis would consist in "assuming one's castration." According to Laplanche, remaining absolutely Freudian implies suspending *any* purposive idea and hence never subjugating the analytic method to any preestablished end whatsoever. As Laplanche upholds, the bracketing of the adaptational end and the refusal to subject the analytic process to any kind of predefined aim goes back to the first meaning of the term "analysis"—namely, "decomposition." Obviously, such a process of decomposition in no way consists in a process of translation; quite the opposite: it can be construed as a process of "detranslation." But what is being "detranslated"? This is where the interrelatedness of the various aspects of Laplanche's work becomes increasingly visible.

As stated earlier, the delineation of the analytic situation effects, for practical purposes, the very differentiation that was pointed out, within Freud's theory, between the adaptational (or self-preservation) and the drive-related (sexual) sphere. But in what way is this differentiation more than the mere outcome of Laplanche's chosen reading of Freud? How can it be said to have an actual premise?

Let us return, at this point, to Laplanche's aforementioned "fundamental anthropological situation." This is the situation of the human baby, who comes to the world in a state of helplessness (Freud's *Hilflosigkeit*), a state that, under normal circumstances, is adequately made up for by the mother or her equivalent. Self-preservation is then somewhat ensured by the nurturing environment within which the by now well-documented functions of attachment operate, along with other functions contributing to the child's integration into the culture of origin. In other words, unless the situation is catastrophic, the self-preservation needs are not the issue for the *infans*. The messages pertaining to the exigencies of adaptation are easily "understood" and are integrated without too much trouble into a context of optimal mutual attunement with an adult. What can, however, fail to be understood and integrated harmoniously into the relational structure is a surplus, an excess, a communication "noise" that stems from the fundamental asymmetry in action between the two members of this pair, however attuned to each other they might otherwise be. Such asymmetry has to do with the Sexual, for which no code of translation or adaptation is available to the *infans*.

A simple illustration of the general process can be given in the context of breastfeeding. If words (in addition to nipples!) could be put in the *infans*'s mouth, they would be: "What does this breast want from me as it gets excited in suckling me and excites me though I cannot understand why?" For as Laplanche points out, it is highly surprising that the basic fact of the breast as a powerfully erogenous zone for the maternal other should have been overlooked in the theory of the mother-child relationship, as well as in the theory of libidinal stages and erogenous zones. Granted, this is but an example, and one quickly gets to the question of what happens when the mother bottle-feeds exclusively. The answer lies in the metonymic displacement and the metaphorical substitution between breast and bottle that is effective in the mother's psyche if not in the baby's. Regardless of the implemented feeding method, the mother interacts with a little subject who, by definition, is intimately tied to her condition as a sexual being, exciting in her (as in other adults) libidinal desires that only effective repression is likely to moderate appropriately.

Let me specify at once that the communication "noise" is unrelated to the child's more or less developed language skills. It is not a matter of linguistic polysemy either. The issue primarily resides in the enigma that is conveyed via even the most articulate messages. Such enigma consists in the adult's repressed Sexual, even when, incidentally, the adult takes care of the child in the most normal way. This repressed Sexual is bound to "contaminate," as it were, the channels of communication, conveying an enigmatic meaning for the child as well as for the adult insofar as the adult is the unconscious source of contagion. Let me also emphasize that this does not imply a transmission of the parental unconscious in the direction of the child's unconscious. The parental unconscious has an impact on the child, in an enigmatic form. Yet it does not flow as such into the child's psyche. The child is on the receiving end of its impact; indeed, he or she is excited by it, but the codes eliciting its translation or the formulation of its meaning are missing. The *infans* must, however, come up with an understanding of this impact, yet this can be achieved only through partial failure. In this case, the adult cannot be helpful in any way insofar as the latter is equally unable to account for the unconscious dimension of communication inherent in his or her attuned care.

Therefore, there is an inevitable failure of translation, which, strictly speaking, denotes a process of repression as understood by Freud in a letter to Wilhelm Fliess on December 6, 1896.[18] In this letter, Freud expounds a theory of the multiple inscriptions of memory. Between such successive inscriptions, translations, or transcriptions, a failure of translation occurs, writes Freud, which corresponds to what we clinically refer to as repression (235). Laplanche returns to this model and applies it to the theory of seduction that Freud abandoned in September 1897. By combining the notion of seduction and the mechanism of translation, Laplanche succeeds in setting up a model of the origin of the unconscious that is precisely premised on a critical reading of Freud.

Conceived of as a failure of translation, repression is characterized by two dimensions: (1) a *translating* dimension thanks to which the child, in keeping with their abilities, produces a version of what affects them in the asymmetrical relationship with the adult (this translation is dispensed to the developing ego) and (2) a *repressing* dimension in which whatever fails to be integrated into the translation process is left behind as a residue, as an "irritative thorn" that will carry on demanding attempts at translation in the child's psyche. Laplanche refers to such residues as the "source-objects" of the drive. According to Laplanche, the human child therefore clearly does not come to the world with a preformed repressed unconscious, and neither are the sexual drives present from the outset. What preexists the child's birth, however, is the adult sexual repressed, whose manifestation— under normal circumstances—is mitigated, "aim inhibited," as Freud put it, but likely to prompt, all the same, the child's perception of a signifier (in the sense of something "signifying to") that necessitates an attempt at translation, at integration. Something akin to excitation is conveyed by the interactions with

---

18 Freud to Wilhelm Fliess, December 6, 1896, in *The Complete Letters of Sigmund Freud to Wilhelm Fliess*, trans. and ed. Jeffrey Moussaieff Masson (Cambridge, MA: Belknap Press of Harvard University Press, 1985).

the adult, and it obscurely disrupts the attachment relation: this is what Laplanche refers to as the "implantation" of the Sexual into the child's "psychophysiological skin."[19] Something is implanted permanently into the child's psyche, something the child must, from then on, try to metabolize to the best of his or her abilities while always leaving out inassimilable residues: foreign bodies, internal assailants resulting from the process of implantation that the adult has unwittingly carried out.

As a result of the attempt at translation and according to the two dimensions of the repression process, the child's psyche splits into two distinct areas. In the dimension of formed (translated) meaning are the nuclei of the ego in a process of gradual integration. (This brings us back to the view of the ego as binding, under the aegis of Eros—see above.) In the dimension of the untranslated residues, conversely, are the source-objects of the drive-related sphere that have become permanent features in the child's psyche. They are foreign bodies that cannot be jettisoned, constant sources of excitation that will be reactivated and intensified by all the other interhuman exchanges of the same order. From the starting point of the fundamental anthropological situation, we are therefore led to the simultaneous formation, in the *infans*, of an ego and a repressed sexual unconscious. The Sexual in question is to be understood in the extended sense Freud endowed it with in the *Three Essays on Sexual Theory*. The unconscious is thus to be understood in a systemic sense—that is to say, as made up of those inassimilable remnants, the residues of the failed translation of the other's message, which, as a result of the failure of translation, defy the laws of common meaning. Such a process of implantation is what Laplanche refers to as general seduction, the inevitable result of the adult-*infans* interaction considering the asymmetry between their respective psychic structures.

---

19 Laplanche, Implantation, Intromission, *The Unfinished Cpernican Revolution*, p. 446

In abandoning—somewhat justifiably—the seduction theory *as the etiologic theory of hysteria*, Freud abandoned, by the same token, the possibility of developing a more general and fundamentally accurate view of the genesis of the individual unconscious. This view is linked to a basic fact that Laplanche underlines, in so doing following in Lacan's footsteps—namely, the primacy of the other in the psychic formation of the subject. Failing to take such primacy into account, psychoanalysis can be said to have partaken in a Ptolemaic view[20]. For just as Ptolemy's astronomical system placed the earth at its center, psychoanalysis, once the seduction theory was rejected, took on as its center the solipsism of a subject that thenceforth had to be endowed, from birth, with an unconscious and with fantasies—preconstituted and already in operation, so to speak. Yet despite its shortcomings, the seduction theory stated something essential: the fact that the unconscious Sexual comes from the other and that it is present long before the advent of biological sexuality. Granted, the seduction theory formulated this fact in a way that now seems overly limited, since its upshot was that there would not be any infantile sexuality without a process of seduction instigated by a perverse adult. In this sense, the *Three Essays* are generally seen as making an advance through their assertion of the existence and decisive role of infantile sexuality. What is objectionable, however, according to Laplanche, is to consider infantile sexuality as a natural, innate constituent of the *infans*'s psyche without understanding how it responds to the inducement sent out unwittingly by the "caring" adult even in the context of the most "normal" of relations. Granted, Freud, in the *Three Essays*, *does* mention that the mother acts as an inadvertent seducer in the course of nursery care, but in his formulation, such involuntary seduction is merely incidental and in no way accounts for seduction as a central and determining fact occurring within

---

20 Laplanche, The Unfinished Copernican Revolution, in: *The Unfinished Copernican Revolution*, p. 3-40.

the asymmetrical adult-*infans* situation. Freud is thus far from conceiving of seduction as a fundamental constituent of infantile sexuality.

The theoretical dead end yielded by the abandonment of the seduction theory is revealed, in Laplanche's view, by Freud's belief that it was necessary to resort to phylogenetics to account for unconscious organizing fantasies. This is another example among many of one of the balancing shifts that Freud was led to make in his theory, but this time Freud was headed for a "biologizing going-astray."[21] The mechanism of phylogenetic transmission became required by the need to solve the new issue of origins that arose from the "innatist" view of infantile sexuality. Freud apparently abandoned what he had viewed as a "real" scene (the scene of perverse seduction), at least as the general model of the origin of the infantile Sexual; yet the fantasmatic scene that replaced it was itself in need of explanation and foundation. Another real scene thus had to be summoned, going back, this time, to prehistoric times: innate primal fantasies entered the theory as a phylogenetic inheritance.

Which Reality?

I previously mentioned an essay on fantasy—now a classic—published by Laplanche and Pontalis.[22] This study highlights the theory of primal fantasies that is featured in Freud but never previously foregrounded explicitly. The essay also occasions a critique of the status of fantasy, especially when it is viewed as inherited through phylogenesis. With the development of the theory of general seduction, Laplanche lays bare two facts: On the one hand, he points to Freud's "exigency"—that is, Freud's unrelenting pursuit of a solid reality behind the psychic facts (e.g., the reality of perverse seduction, then the reality of prehistoric facts, the objects

---

21 Laplanche, *Le fourvoiement biologisant*.

22 "Fantasy and the Origins."

of phylogenetic transmission). On the other hand, Laplanche shows how the sequence of Freud's theoretical development repeats the very sequence of events as experienced by the *infans*. Freud's "going-astray" can thus be understood in the light of the reaction that any psyche has to the impact of the other. The other has primacy and inserts the "irritative thorn" on the basis of which the human child is forced to construct his or her own translations. As stated earlier, this results in a primal psychic split: the simultaneous birth of the ego and of the repressed unconscious. The follows an inevitable process of "Ptolemaic" closure: the advent of the ego and the series of personal "theories" that arise from the child's attempt at translation make up the subjective center that requires, to be indeed established as the ego, that the primacy of the other be essentially misconstrued. Freud's theoretical progression therefore basically follows the same progression as the child's psychic development. His theory, like the child's theories, closes in on itself around a "self-centered" subject, forcing Freud, who pursues the ideal of a scientific account all the same, to trace the "factual" origin ever farther, back to humanity's prehistoric times.

For his part, Laplanche points out that such a giant speculative leap into phylogenesis was not warranted in any way. The reality at stake is here at hand, conspicuously so, provided one bothers to consider the elements of the fundamental anthropological situation, some of which are elements observed by Freud himself over time. Featured among these elements are: the state of "helplessness" (*Hilflosigkeit*) characterizing the *infans* and the necessary intervention of the other (*Nebenmensch*), the necessary "failure of translation" that starts the process clinically known as repression,[23] and last but not least, Freud's creation of the analytic method and frame that, relatively speaking, draws on the elements of the fundamental anthropological situation. What the analytic situation sets up is indeed in many ways akin to the adult-*infans*

---

23 *SE* 1:233–39.

situation. A comparable asymmetry is created on account of the invitation to free associate that the analyst addresses to the analysands. The analysands do not know... that they know, and they are lacking in words (the etymological meaning of *in- + fans*); they credit the analyst with knowledge (the fantasy of the "subject supposed to know" as expounded by Lacan). On the other hand, the analysts' "refusals" ensure that they remain the guardians of the enigma, thus reinstating, for the sake of their analysands, the infantile situation of confrontation with the other's enigma—the enigma that they guard not because they know but because they deny themselves knowledge and offer instead to listen and analyze. The sole reality of the message and its enigmatic dimension, apt at provoking transference, are in this way set as foremost for the efficacy of analysis, as should become clear in the following section.

Filled-In Transference, Hollowed-Out Transference

The theory of general seduction is therefore not a purely theoretical construction; it is a model based on the strong convergence between the analytic situation and the condition of the human baby in the fundamental anthropological situation. This leads Laplanche to a close scrutiny of the pivotal term in any analysis—transference—regarding which he makes important distinctions. Firstly, in keeping with his theory of the primacy of the other, Laplanche does not view transference as some kind of spontaneous production on the part of the analysand. He posits that the analyst provokes transference,[24] which is different from causing or suggesting it. The provocation at stake is unintentional and occurs wherever the elements of the original adult-*infans* asymmetry happen to coalesce—that is, wherever the enigmatic part of the other's message becomes operative. The prominent place transference holds in analysis

24 Jean Laplanche, "Transference: Its Provocation by the Analyst," trans. Luke Thurston, in *Essays on Otherness*, ed. John Fletcher (London: Routledge, 1999), 214–33.

undoubtedly stems, firstly, from the emphasis it has been given by psychoanalysts themselves, beginning with Freud. Furthermore, psychoanalysts are the only ones who have understood the central part played by transference in a relationship where a demand is being made. I think that on this subject Laplanche's view follows that of Lacan and converges with that of Piera Aulagnier[25]—the view that offer precedes demand, whether in analysis or in the mother-child relation.

More importantly, the central place of transference results from the fact that the analyst adopts a position and an attitude based on what could be referred to as an ethics of refusal. By first denying themselves knowledge, analysts, according to Laplanche, offer their analysands a space, a "hollow" in which they may place either something "filled in" or another hollow. Laplanche thus distinguishes two modalities of transference. Filled-in transference consists in "the positive reproduction of forms of behavior, relationships and childhood imagos"[26]; this is transference commonly described as the repetition of archaic situations. Hollowed-out transference, "A hollow is also a repetition, but one in which the infantile that is repeated recovers its enigmatic character."[27] Laplanche specifies that the two modalities of transference inevitably coexist but if there were nothing but filled-in transference—that is, mere repetition—there would be no resolution in sight. Hollowed-out transference, by contrast, "puts the enigmatic messages of childhood back into play, back into question, and back into a process of elaboration; this is due to the analytic situation itself, a situation that tends to stimulate a return to, and a reelaboration of, the enigmatic.." [28] We can see here again that the analytic situation is indeed a

---

25 Piera Aulagnier, "Demande et identification," in *Un interprète en quête de sens* (Paris: Rivages, 1984), 161–98.

26 Laplanche, *New Foundations for Psychoanalysis*, p.184.

27 *Loc. cit.* Translation slightly modified by me.

28 Laplanche, *New Foundations for Psychoanalysis*, 185.

process of reinstatement, this time not simply as the exclusion of the adaptational dimension theorized by Laplanche in *Life and Death in Psychoanalysis* but mostly as a revival of the fundamental anthropological situation. This situation confronts the analysand with the enigma of the other whom the analyst comes to embody, conferring, as was the case for the *infans*, the hollow, the open space where new translations of the enigma may arise so that one is not doomed to the sheer repetition of the same.

The "hollow" offered by the analyst can be seen as an ethical position and attitude on his or her part insofar as the analyst is the guardian of the enigma. As far as the analyst is concerned, "(it) is maintaining the dimension of interior otherness that allows otherness to be brought into play in the transference." as Laplanche notes.[29] This endows the notion of the "neutrality" of the analyst with substance and depth, pointing to a form of "passivity" inherent in analytic listening—that is, an openness bestowed on the other, akin to the kind of passivity theorized by Emmanuel Levinas or, alternatively, to the notion of "passibility" as developed by Jean-François Lyotard.[30] The disposition in question requires that, in the offer of a "hollow," the analyst respect his or her own enigma. The analyst's enigma thus places the analysand in an equivalent position to that of the *infans* in the fundamental anthropological situation, while positing the analyst as the seducing adult. In this sense, the analytic situation is de facto—and inevitably—a situation of seduction.

Laplanche's essay on transference briefly quoted above is one of the best illustrations of what the theory of seduction may have to contribute to analytic practice. It also reveals the extent to which the theory of general seduction is rooted in analytic practice

---

29 "Transference: its provocation by the analyst," [533.]

30 Dominique Scarfone, "In the Hollow of Transference: The Analyst between Activity and Passivity," *Sitegeist: A Journal of Psychoanalysis & Philosophy*, no. 4 (Spring 2010): 7–20.

itself. In fact, in this regard, Laplanche seems fully aligned with Freud, who was able to combine metapsychological, clinical, and anthropological concerns within a single intellectual step. Although such a dimension of Laplanche's reflection must remain unexplored here because of limited space, let me mention that, according to Laplanche, psychoanalysis dwells in at least four sites of experience or domains of practice: (1) the practice of psychoanalysis in the context of the analytic session, obviously, but also (2) the practice of "extramural psychoanalysis," as Laplanche liked to put it, as opposed to "applied psychoanalysis"—that is, the engagement of psychoanalysis with cultural phenomena; (3) the history of psychoanalysis; and (4) psychoanalytic theory itself as a locus and an object of experience, which "is clearly to refuse to give theory a separate and distinct status, whether as a tool (theory is sometimes called a conceptual tool; a tool must be useful for something) or, on the contrary, as a more or less useless superstructure (we can't deny that it was sometimes Freud's affectation to claim that the concepts of psychoanalysis were merely our hobby)."[31]

In fact, for Laplanche theory could be said to be quite "embodied." He shows how various levels of theorization operate within human beings, who are distinct from all other animals in their very capacity for self-theorization. Thus, patients in analysis are the bearers of theories on the subject of their lives, of their histories, of their bodily experiences and of whatever assails them (infantile sexual theories, fantasies, or even delusions). Analysis will be apt at highlighting such theories and at analyzing—that is to say, "detranslating"—insofar as the theories in question arise from the translations carried out when the subject met the other's enigmas during infancy and thereafter. For let us not forget that the child is an inborn investigator and theoretician who develops infantile sexual theories to acquire an acceptable version of the

---

31 *New Foundations for Psychoanalysis*, 16.

sexual enigmas with which he or she is faced. Such theoretical constructions simultaneously make up the framework of the subject's ego and are the organizing principles of his or her lived experience and psychic life. Yet, mutatis mutandis, the same applies to the "patented" theoretician. For Laplanche "to assert that humans are self-theorizing is to say that every true theorization is an experiment that necessarily involves the researcher".[32]

On this subject, Laplanche points out that his model is no other than Freud, and he wonders, when evoking Freud's major texts referred to as "theoretical monuments": "How are these theoretical monuments to be approached if not as exercises in living psycho-analysis?"[33]. This is what authorizes Laplanche to apply his own theoretical practice to Freud's texts, for they are not a superstructure, a backdrop, or a mere tool but sites of experience: "Experiences and experiments that must themselves be analyzed, pushed even further than Freud pushed them; they must be pushed into a corner, even at the risk of seeing them dismantled, seeing them tear themselves apart and put themselves back together "[34]. Theoretical practice is therefore very much like the work in the analytic session: the analyst remains an analyst wherever the work of psychoanalysis justifiably applies, even though the analytic thinking might sometimes move in different directions. This is the case for the analytic session itself, in which the model of translation allocates specific roles: the analysands are the translators, firstly because they come to analysis as the bearers of translations that were already carried out throughout their life—such translations are precisely to be analyzed and hence decomposed—and secondly because, based on the process of analytic decomposition, the analysands carry out new translations. For the analyst's part, he or she works only, in principle, on the side of detranslation.

---

32 *Loc. cit.*, translation modified by me.

33 *Loc. cit.*, translation modified by me.

34 *Loc. cit.*, translation modified by me.

Psychoanalysis and Psychotherapy

Such a view of the work that takes place in the analytic session gives Laplanche a chance to intervene quite elegantly in the perennial debate over psychoanalysis and psychotherapy. Against the grain of all the positions that either radicalize the differences or claim that both are one and the same, Laplanche points out that, in any analytic treatment, the analyst performs a work of analysis in which *the patient is the psychotherapist* as he or she is in charge of the process of recomposition: "*The only psychotherapist is our 'patient' and more generally any human being* who constitutes himself from his first days as *subject of a story,* by temporalizing himself, by memorizing, by 'writing' or rewriting his history in a more or less coherent way."[35]

Therefore, within a session and in the course of a treatment, especially in the analysis of neuroses, psychoanalysis and psychotherapy are involved, but psychotherapy corresponds to what Freud referred to as "psychosynthesis". The synthesis is, in principle, not the analyst's concern, according to Freud, as it is automatically achieved by the patient. Most of the time, in fact, the psychotherapeutic aspect holds center stage in a session, punctuated by proper analytic moments. There is thus no real need to choose between psychoanalysis and psychotherapy: if the analyst analyzes methodically, the moments of analytic detranslation are bound to set off the process of psychotherapeutic retranslation—that is, the patient's work. Naturally, in cases dealing with conditions like of psychosis, for example, one must gauge how permissible such a process of proper analytic unbinding is as opposed to supporting the patient in the work of psychotherapy: "Here the perspective changes radically: the psychotherapist is apparently invited to take part 'creatively' in construction, by bringing his schemas, even his own materials."[36]

---

35 "Gender, Sex and the *Sexual,*" in *Freud and the Sexual: Essays 2000–2006,* trans. John Fletcher, Jonathan House, and Nicholas Ray (New York: International Psychoanalytic Books, 2011), 281; italics in the original.

36 Laplanche *Freud and the Sexual,* p. 291.

Seduction and Psychopathology

Freud's first theory of seduction pertained to the etiology of hysteria and therefore tackled an essentially psychopathological mechanism. By generalizing the theory of seduction, Laplanche goes beyond dealing with the formation of neurosis; he accounts instead for the constitution of the psychic topography itself. The process of implantation and of subsequent translation (along with its inevitable failure) accounts for the advent of primal repression, which begets the differentiation between the ego and the unconscious and instigates the forthcoming differentiation of the psychic apparatus without regard to pathology. The basic traumatic impact of the implantation of the Sexual does not determine any specific pathological development; it is a somewhat "structuring" trauma insofar as it prompts the process of psychic differentiation. Thus, when it comes to theorizing the pathogenic vicissitude of seduction, a variant of the general phenomenon is required, an alternative likely to account for a traumatic effect that no longer structures but cripples development and differentiation.

This is what Laplanche comes to refer to as intromission as opposed to implantation: "Implantation is a process which is common, everyday, normal or neurotic. Beside it, as its violent variant, a place must be given to intromission. While implantation allows the individual to take things up actively, at once translating and repressing, one must try to conceive of a process which blocks this, short-circuits the differentiation of the agencies in the process of their formation, and puts into the interior an element resistant to all metabolizations."[37]

Intromission is therefore the violent variant of implantation. While ordinary seduction implants its enigmatic signifiers into the "psychophysiological 'skin' " and refers to the surface of the body, the perceptive periphery of the *infans*, intromission "relates

---

37 Laplanche, *The Unfinished Copernican Revolution*, p. 447.

principally to anality and orality."[38] By putting in the volume of the body elements that are resistant to metabolization and thus fundamentally resistant to translation, intromission performs a kind of hijacking, crippling the apparatus of translation itself and generating enclaves that will strain the subject's psychic development. Such a crude intrusion on the part of the adult replaces what should have been but a mere "proposition," however unconscious. In this case, the reference to perverse seduction is relevant even if, on a manifest level, there are no instances of sexual behavior as such. In this light, we can see how the theory of seduction might apply to the theorization of borderline phenomena, false-self organizations, frozen affects, failures of mentalization, as well as a number of psychotic states.[39] Let us bear in mind, however, that this violent variant of implantation, which seems fundamentally pathogenic, is not completely at odds with the ordinary role played by seduction. Something akin to this violence is unavoidably operational in the process of normal structuration, resulting in the formation of the superego: "I have no doubt that a process related to intromission also has its role in the formation of the *superego*, a foreign body that cannot be metabolized" [40].

Temporality, Mourning, and the Working Through of the Enigma

From the theory of translation stems one of the key terms in Laplanche's thought regarding psychic temporality: afterwardness[41]

---

38 *Loc. cit.*

39 John Fletcher, "Seduction and the Vicissitudes of Translation: The Work of Jean Laplanche," *Psychoanalytic Quarterly* 76, no. 4 (October 2007):1241–91; Dominique Scarfone, " 'It Was Not My Mother': From Seduction to Negation," trans. John Fletcher, in "Jean Laplanche and the Theory of Seduction," special issue, *New Formations*, no. 48 (Winter 2002–03): 69–76.

40 Laplanche, *loc. cit.*, p. 447.

41 Since the writing of this article, the French expression *après-coup* was ever

(Freud's *Nachträglichkeit;* Strachey's "deferred action") . I've discussed how primal repression, viewed as the failed translation of the enigmatic signifiers, leaves out the "source-objects" of the drive in the form of untranslated remnants. These do not consist in inert residues. The drive-related nature of such residues implies that they operate as constant incentives to translate, or detranslate/ retranslate, former translations. On this basis and in the light of such a translative model, one is well equipped to better understand the inaugural case by which, in his "Project for a Scientific Psychology," Freud accounts for the occurrence of afterwardness. Indeed, in this case, a thirteen-year-old girl has developed a phobia of shops as a result of the rereading she is now able to have of an episode she experienced five years earlier[42]. This new translation has a retroactive effect, leading both lived experiences — which both occurred in a shop, but each lacked sufficient traumatic weight in itself to lead to the later phobia — to become pathogenic through the translative link that conflates them: the young woman now possesses the capacity to comprehend, afterward, the full sexual meaning of the sweetshop keeper's assault that occurred when she was eight. The signifiers left hanging at the time of the trauma therefore acquire their full drive-related force by means of traumatic afterwardness. This prompts the defensive maneuvers of the young woman's ego, resulting in the formation of a phobia with the aim of guarding against the sexual meaning now linked to her desire to go into a shop. This meaning has become an internal assailant, which the young woman's ego's defenses try to drive out and reinstate as external via the mechanism of phobogenic projection.

The theory of general seduction and the notion of a message in need of translation, in close relation to *après-coup* (afterwardness),

---

more used in psychoanalytic writings in English and "afterwarness", which was Laplanche's proposal for the English rendition of *Nachträglishckeit*, does not seem to have taken root.

42 Freud, *Project for a Scientific Psychology, SE* 1:353-356.

furthermore enhance our understanding of the mechanisms of mourning. Let us remember that in "Mourning and Melancholia" Freud uses mourning as the normal prototype in the light of which melancholic depression may be understood; yet, according to Freud, the work of mourning itself requires no explanation since, in mourning, "there is nothing about the loss that is unconscious."[43] In other places, however, Freud states that mourning remains a great riddle and that its painful nature is still to be accounted for. For example, in the "On Transience," he writes: "But why it is that this detachment of libido from its objects should be such a painful process is a mystery to us. . . . We only see that libido clings to its objects and will not renounce those that are lost even when a substitute lies ready to hand."[44]

Laplanche's commentary on the subject starts as follows: "It is a scandal for a realist for whom the dead are really dead."[45] Laplanche then shows how the work of mourning in fact relates to the *message* of the other, of the dead person. The dead go missing, but their messages remain. If one seeks to ascertain the nature of the libidinal ties that mourning works toward unweaving, this is essentially what will be found: "For the person in mourning, [the] message [of the deceased] has never been adequately understood, never listened to enough. Mourning is hardly ever without the question: what would he be saying now? What would he have said? Hardly ever without regret or remorse for not having been able to speak with the other enough, for not having heard what he had to say."[46]

Thanks to the theory of seduction and the model of translation, Laplanche is able to offer a reading of Freud likely to further develop Freud's thinking. On the present subject, some light is shed on the

---

43 SE 14:245.

44 SE 14:306–7.

45 "Time and the Other," trans. Luke Thurston, in *Essays on Otherness*, ed. John Fletcher (London: Routledge, 1999), 250.

46 Laplanche, "Time and the Other," 254.

nature of the reality of the libidinal ties so that the modalities of the work of mourning may be further understood, bearing in mind that it is generally held as the prototype of any form of psychic working through. Mourning requires time and is a painful process because it engages the totality of the ties woven with the lost object. Such ties are communicational; they are the bearers of the other's message, a message laden with meanings in need of translation. Translation is compulsory because the content of the message is that which is spun by the web of relations of tenderness, affection, attachment, but also, at times, passion and violence. Regardless of the emotional charge, the only way the tie can endure beyond death, beyond the loss of the object, of the other, is as a message—a message that remains only partially translated because its enigmatic part was transmitted unconsciously by the lost object. The enigma, Laplanche explains, is an enigma for the transmitter as well.

Repression and the Sexual

Stating a spelling preference perceptible only to Francophone readers, toward the end of his life, Laplanche suggested that the German term *Sexual* be used (as opposed to the French *sexuel*) to refer to the sexual drive tackled by psychoanalysis, the infantile polymorphous Sexual, regarded by Laplanche as one of Freud's greatest discoveries, hence the pregenital Sexual, distinct from sexuality as a repertory of sexual behaviors. With this spelling preference, Laplanche aims to avoid any misunderstanding as to what is at issue when discussing the repressed. As established earlier, repression is featured as one of the modalities of the translation apparatus that the human subject deploys when faced with the enigmatic aspect inherent in the other's message, and Freud himself conceived of the failure of translation as constitutive of repression. In following this line of thinking, it is easier to understand why the Sexual—that is, the infantile Sexual—should be subject to repression. Given the asymmetry inherent in the fundamental anthropological situation (see above) it is inevitable that the enigmatic side of the adult's message will fail to be meaningfully transcribed in the infantile psyche. The hollow in meaning formed by the untranslated residue is what makes up the implant, the "internal foreign body" constitutive of the repressed Sexual. It follows that repression is thus not an ad hoc mechanism applied to some sexual content; from the outset repression works hand in glove with the Sexual insofar as the translation-repression process in fact *creates* the sexual drive.

A lengthy (and impossible in the context of this brief account) digression would be required to clarify Laplanche's original position when, with the concept of Sexual, he intervened in the debate over gender.[47] Let me merely point out that, to Laplanche, gender amounts to an allocation—that is, a primary identification in which the child, rather than identifying as belonging to a particular gender, is rather *identified by the adults*. Subsequently, the discovery of sexual anatomical duality forces the child to interpret (i.e., to translate) the meaning of this allocation according to the binary code of the phallic logic: presence/absence, +/-, 1/0. From this translation/ repression arises the Sexual as "repression-symbolization of gender by sex."[48] Elaborating on the basis of the allocated gender (which can be multiple, polymorphous) and according to the observed fact of sexual difference, the child's own psyche "creates" the infantile Sexual as the residue of what failed to be symbolized. This Sexual will intervene in a variety of ways in the course of the subject's childhood, during the formation of the psychic configurations specific to the vicissitudes of each individual's life.

As we can see, Laplanche proposes a theoretical elaboration that proceeds step by step, methodically, but is not wary of tackling new problems, even if it means broadening the scope in the process,

---

47 "Gender, Sex and the Sexual."

48 Laplanche, "Gender, Sex and the Sexual," 159.

with issues arising from other fields (in this case, gender studies). Along the same lines, there would be cause for an account (again impossible in the present context) of Laplanche's intervention as a third disputant in what appears to him as a false debate or, in any case, as a skewed debate between the advocates of what is referred to as the solipsistic position and the advocates of relational or intersubjective psychoanalysis. To some extent, in the light of the thinking tools bequeathed by Laplanche, psychoanalysis is relational from the outset insofar as it fundamentally takes the other's input into account; yet it does not fully subscribe to the intersubjective trend since it holds as essential, even foundational, the unavoidable adult-*infans* asymmetry which the analysand-analyst asymmetry reinstates. Regarding the so-called "solipsistic" position, we saw earlier that Laplanche considers the "Ptolemaic" closure of Freud's theory to be essentially a reinstatement of the necessary process of subjective closure undergone by the child when it begins to conceive of itself as an "ego." But such a closure is precisely what analysis, if it aspires to be consequential, is led to reopen. Opening and closing are moments featured in an anthropological situation that is bound to evolve. Once it is acknowledged, the "Ptolemaic" closure in no way annuls the primacy of the other; yet if it were not for this closure, there would be nothing to analyze.

Laplanche's Message

When Laplanche published *New Foundations for Psychoanalysis*, his emphasis lay on "new foundations," not on "new psychoanalysis." Laplanche never wished to found a new school. To him, psychoanalysis was first and foremost a procedure invented by Freud, who thus opened up a new domain of knowledge. This domain must, in Laplanche's view, be examined from all angles so that we can catch sight of what necessitates a critique or a revision of its underpinnings and supply it with more solid epistemological foundations; this is what Laplanche consistently did throughout his life as an analyst. His trust in Freud—that is, his belief that the central edifice would not crumble even if it were struck with a "pickax"—underlies his bequest of a psychoanalysis that is more vital and more apt to tackle new questions.

Laplanche's practice, the application of the three main components of his psychoanalytic work (Freudian reading method applied to Freud; theory and practice of translation; theory of general seduction), implies that, in working at the level of the first two components, Laplanche is also a "translator"—in the same way any subject is when finding him- or herself on the receiving end of an enigmatic message. In his turn, Laplanche sets out on a quest for the object that Freud tracked and pursued all his life. Thus, Laplanche's work is obviously not final. He has bequeathed us a myriad of signifiers, couched in his "theoretical messages," which it is our turn to tackle in an attempt to translate them better. Laplanche's transference to Freud's work is transferred in turn: we are now invited to bear the cost, if such is our wish, of this transcendence of transference, of this passing of the baton,[49] as we strive to put to work again not only Freud but also Laplanche himself. This is undoubtedly the best way to pay tribute to him.

---

49 The French word for a relay baton is *témoin*, which also means "witness."— Trans.

Conversation

Avgi Saketopoulou: I am enthralled by the opportunity to have these conversations with you. I expect they will be intellectually riveting and also fun. But before we dive in, might we clarify, for our readers and perhaps also for our own sake, what we intend to do in our exchanges? Here's my version of it: In discussing your forthcoming book, which is awaited with great enthusiasm, we were thinking through the prefatory materials and what we hoped to accomplish with them. You were going to write an introduction, and you had asked me to write a preface. As we talked further, I proposed that we suspend, for the time being the question of how to preface the book. Instead, I proposed we have a conversation after each of your essays as a way to engage your work, to ask for clarifications on the reader's behalf, and to multiply the entry points to your thinking for those interested in it. I imagine that these conversations will work cumulatively, taking the reader deeper into each chapter and also showing your way of thinking not by describing it but by exposing the reader to it "in vivo" (an exercise in "show, don't tell"). Part of what your work has offered me personally, which I hope these exchanges will also convey to the reader, is the sheer pleasure of thinking about theory with you: that it's not a stale or inert process but that, on the contrary, it is an experience in itself.

So much for my general vision of what this series conversations can offer. More specifically now, regarding the structure we have considered for our conversations, after each essay, I will be posing particular questions about the main tenets organizing the paper. Naturally, space limitations mean you won't be able to delve into all questions in equal depth. Given that fact, I imagine that some of your answers will only point us in a direction rather than exhaustively address the issues raised.

Does that accord with what you thought of us as trying to do? What about this vision would you like to edit, and/or what more that you would like our exchanges to make possible?

DOMINIQUE SCARFONE: I believe you've described the idea behind these conversations well, when it comes to both purpose and format. One thing I must add is how grateful I am that you are willing to do this work with me, not only because of the pleasure it gives me to work with you, but also because it provides an elegant solution to a problem I had when it came to writing an introduction. While I thought it might be necessary to write one, I also felt uneasy about it because it was not clear to me what I should put in it that wasn't already in the chapters themselves. I do not like rehashing the same work. So I was more than happy when you suggested that we could instead have these conversations, because I am sure this will give me a totally different outlook on my own work and will enrich the chapters we will be discussing together.

AS: It is clear from this first essay, and from your work in general, that Laplanche is someone you knew personally and knew well. I was wondering if you would be willing to say a bit about him, about what he was like, especially what he was like to think with. For example, he comes across to me as extremely rigorous and extremely imaginative at the same time. Is that accurate based on your experience of him? What was it like to watch him think, and how did he manage disagreement?

DS: Interestingly, this is a question that Laplanche would not have wanted to be asked. As you know, he always insisted that in his study of Freud's ideas, he was not the least interested in "Sigmund." I once proposed to interview him in depth for an intellectual biography I was thinking of doing, but he refused for the same reason: that what matters is the opus, not the author. This also pertains to his conception of theoretical work. He truly held to the idea that theory stands on its own feet—not that it is cut off from practice but that it is in itself a field of practice, of *experience*. Laplanche held to a theoretical praxis which had its own exigencies. And "exigency" is a word that runs throughout his writings but that could also qualify the kind of relationship I had with him and for which I am thankful.

His exigency meant that no complacency was admitted in our discussions, regardless of the affection that from time to time was manifest.

But let me answer your question all the same. I think I knew Laplanche well enough, though I would not say that we were "close," because his stature was really impressive. Around him, I felt I was in the presence of one of the last intellectual giants that the French "*grandes écoles*" such as the Paris's École normale supérieure had produced. He was a kind and warm person but would leave most of the social interaction to his wife, Nadine, whom he always wanted beside him and who eagerly accepted that role. Yet, I have plenty of faxes from the early nineties that end with "*affectueuses pensées*" (affectionate thoughts) just above his signature, "Jean."

AS: You are highlighting something that can be easily overlooked in Laplanche—that for him, theory is not divorced *from* practice but that he regards theory as *expérience*—a word that in French means both "experience" and "experiment." I find that he is very serious about *experimenting*, and maybe this is one way to understand his refusal to give us clinical material that tells us *how* to implement his theory and *what* to do with his ideas. I know that some of his readers find this frustrating—for example, I am often asked by students of Laplanche how one can put to use this or that idea of his. But after the initial frustration wears off, it can also become possible to see how generous and, perhaps more importantly, how respectful Laplanche is to the reader. He does not tell us what to do with the vistas he opens up for us but leaves it to us to venture forth, urging us to invent.[50] In this respect, he reminds me of Foucault's steadfast insistence when he fleshes out how power operates on constituting subjectivities and constellating hegemonies. As for how to change these, he gives us no blueprints. Instead, he famously points us to a horizon of a new architecture of "bodies and pleasures,"[51] leaving us to improvisationally concoct these new ways of doing things, which I think is so much in keeping with Laplanche's approach.

As for the notion of theory as experience, it took me several years of studying Laplanche to come to an appreciation about how matter-of-factly he means that, to realize that it is not simply an idiosyncratic expression. Indeed, if one reads Laplanche rigorously and immersively, one can come to see that he is doing something quite incredible. While he is, indeed, proposing a set of ideas per se, he is offering much more than that: through the ways he is thinking *about* ideas, he is offering an experience *of* those ideas to whomever is able to let themselves be taken over by the text. So I find his writing extremely powerful, not just on a cerebral level. If one gives oneself over to it, it is quite moving and mind-blowing.

DS: You clarify the issue very well, and your parallel with Foucault seems to me quite to the point. One could add Theodor Adorno who, teaching in Germany after the war, would warn his students in these (approximate) terms: "...And don't come asking me how what I just said can be useful to you tomorrow morning."

You are right to point out the dimension of respect for the reader or listener. It is indeed a form of respect not to tell the reader what to do with theory, but perhaps more fundamentally it is a question of being consistent with what Laplanche (or Foucault, or Adorno) taught. Laplanche was, in a way, teaching about the

---

50 Jean Laplanche, "The Kent Seminar," in *Jean Laplanche: Seduction, Translation, Drives; A Dossier*, ed. John Fletcher and Martin Stanton, trans. Martin Stanton (London: Psychoanalytic Forum, 1992), 21–40.

51 Michel Foucault, *The History of Sexuality*, trans. Robert Hurley, vol. 1, *An Introduction* (New York: Vintage Books, 1990, p. 159).

essential freedom of the subject to construe their own meanings. This is not to say that Laplanche's (or others') work is a sort of inkblot on which to project anything that comes to mind but rather that it allows the subject the widest space possible for elaborating their own solution with the tools at their disposal. So it would be totally contradictory to the whole Laplanchean enterprise, based on Freud's analytic method and the translational model of the psyche, to come up with a how-to or a Laplanchean way of doing analysis, as this would influence the reader about how to translate Laplanchean teaching in their own practice.

At the epistemological level, Laplanche also insisted that the person most entitled to describing what went on in the analytic session would be the patient, and even then, the patient would be reconstructing and resynthesizing after the fact what "really" happened psychoanalytically. I have tried to discuss this aspect of Laplanche's thought, though with no direct reference to Laplanche, in an editorial to the *International Journal of Psychoanalysis* bearing the title "Live Wires: When Is the Analyst at Work?"[52]

You captured another essential aspect of this complex issue: the status of theory itself. Laplanche proposed that there are four domains in which psychoanalytic work can be carried out: the treatment of patients, the cultural (or civilizational) domain, history (especially the history of psychoanalysis), and theory. As his programmatic paper "Interpreting (with) Freud" should make clear, theoretical work is itself a domain where the enigmatic is at work, hence where translation and transduction operate.[53] But we should never lose sight of the fact that every transduction or translation is the flip side of repression. This is what justifies applying the analytic method (with the required modifications) to theory itself.

---

52 *International Journal of Psychoanalysis* 92 (2011): 755–59.

53 For a discussion of transduction vs. translation, see pp. 46-47 below.

AS: We will have an opportunity to dive into this last point in great depth later, when we discuss your paper "The Feminine, the Analyst, and the Child Theorist," so I will hold off on that for now.

As someone relatively new to Laplanche, it appears to me that there has been a mounting interest in his work in North American psychoanalysis in recent years. This, no doubt, is partly due to the recent translations of his work in English, for which we have *The Unconscious in Translation* and, specifically, Jonathan House to thank. But I am curious whether it's more than just his availability in English that explains this surge of interest and was wondering if you have any thoughts about why his work has become especially alluring at this particular moment in time.

DS: The wonderful job done by Jonathan House is one important factor we can be sure of, and I hope that my own teaching in numerous North American institutions has also some part in this. But I remember that early in the present century Laplanche's ideas were gaining traction, so to speak, in the US. My hypothesis is that his way of revisiting Freud does in fact effectively provide new foundations to psychoanalysis so that through Laplanche we rediscover Freud but without any worship of his word. Laplanche shows us how to critically reexamine Freud's theories, how "to take Freud to task", as he often said. So, I guess there is a triple bargain in following Laplanche: one part of it is rediscovering Freud, another is seeing that Freud can be put back to work on very contemporary issues, and the third is that Laplanche bequeathed us a formidable tool for critically studying not only Freud, but also Laplanche and other major authors as well.

AS: Reading Laplanche, as you have written, demands a really solid foundation in Freudian metapsychology. I find that such a sturdy Freudian scaffolding is not always offered in psychoanalytic institutes. I have taught, for example, fourth-year candidates who have not studied even a text as fundamental as the *Three Essays* in

41

depth. In your published work, you are especially crisp and clear in tracking what Laplanche is doing with Freud's ideas, something that can be very grounding to a newcomer to Laplanche—and I say this having myself found my way into Laplanche through your exegesis of Freud's work. I have also observed this: when I reread a paper by Laplanche, even a paper I thought I understood relatively well, I recognize that, in my effort to grasp him, I had previously contorted some aspect of the novelty of his ideas into something I already knew. This tendency to understand something new on the basis of the familiar is not unique to reading Laplanche—or to me, I hope! Still, I find that I have to do more work on helping students resist this pitfall with Laplanche than with other thinkers (such as, say, Klein, Winnicott, or Kohut). Is this something you have encountered when teaching Laplanche, and if so, why do you think it happens? What do you find to be the aspects of his work most vulnerable to such appropriative readings?

DS: Yes, I think that, as you say, this is a very natural response to the novelty contained in Laplanche's work or in any comparable work. On the other hand, Laplanche's method also plays a part in this. I get the impression that major psychoanalytic authors relate to Freud in a few standard ways. At one extreme, you have those who praise Freud for his pioneering work and then radically part ways with him, proposing a new brand of psychoanalysis and throwing away what Freud considered the pillars of the discipline, such as repression. At the other extreme, one could put Lacan, who believed in a "return to Freud," something he certainly fostered for many years, but then turned away from Freud, surreptitiously offering strictly Lacanian ideas, yet under the label "Freudian." In between, there are authors who develop their own ideas and models but who avowedly cannot speak in Freudian terms even if many of the developments they bring are rooted in Freud. To give a brief example, I think of Winnicott's idea of the mother-infant unit, which was clearly prefigured in Freud's paper on the two principles of mental functioning.[54] Obviously, Winnicott's experience as a pediatrician and child analyst pushed him, quite naturally, in that direction, and I don't mean to minimize his merit. I'm just highlighting what Winnicott himself stated in a letter— that if you "cornered" him, he would declare himself a Freudian. Finally, there are authors who stay with Freud without adopting a critical method.

Laplanche did none of these things. He stated from the start that he would turn Freud's weapons (i.e., the Freudian method) against Freud's theories, thus offering a critical view of Freud's text thanks to a staunch Freudian way of working. I believe that this results precisely in the experience you reported, of readers sometimes not noticing what is truly new in Laplanche. In a way, this would please Laplanche because the last thing he wanted was to propose a "new psychoanalysis." He thought of his work as that of a construction worker who aimed to give the Freudian edifice stronger foundations and who needed to test the solidity of the building. Hence, you will always recognize in Laplanche the Freudian stamp, so to speak, even when he frontally challenges Freud's theory and even when he sometimes takes a firm stand against certain Freudian ideas.

AS: Your work is rooted in Laplanche and very influenced by his thinking, and we see this not only in terms of your ideas but also in *how* you work on them. You are not just theorizing but also theorizing about theorizing, which is a quintessentially and uniquely Laplanchean methodology. In that sense, you take quite seriously his invitation for us to put to work not also Freud but also himself. At the end of this essay, you write that "Laplanche's work is obviously not final. He has bequeathed us a myriad of signifiers . . . which it is our turn to tackle in an attempt to translate them

---

54 "Formulations on the Two Principles of Mental Functioning," *SE* 7:213–26.

better. . . . We are now invited to bear the cost . . . of this passing of the baton, as we strive to put to work again not only Freud but also Laplanche himself."[55] This makes me think of the modification you have helpfully introduced to the notion of translation by pointing out that the term "transduction" might best render what Laplanche describes as "translation."[56] My understanding is that you propose this because "transduction" is less likely to lead *us* astray by making us think that translation involves a search for an accurate rendering. Could you say a bit about putting Laplanche to work in your own thinking?

DS: Generally speaking, I would repeat what I stated in the paper—that there are three main dimensions to Laplanche: the methodical and critical reader of Freud, the translator of Freud's opus, and thirdly, the author of the General theory of seduction. I stand by my statement that the first of these three dimensions is the most important one, in part because starting from it, you eventually encounter the other two. Hence, my way of "using" Laplanche is to try and apply his method, be it when reading Freud and thereby trying to prolong Laplanche's own critical study or when reading Laplanche or Winnicott for that matter. But then what you get is that the concepts themselves start blinking,[57] so to speak. And one central concept is certainly that of translation, much too important

---

55 See p. 35 above.

56 AS: I note for our readers that references to this distinction can be found in your book *The Unpast* and in your paper "The Feminine, the Analyst, and the Child Theorist" and that the matter has also received some attention in the seminar *Penser avec Freud* that you run in Montreal.

57 AS: I don't want to take us too far afield, but I can't resist asking about your formulation that when you subject concepts to the Laplanchean method, they start to "blink." Can I ask you to say a bit more about it briefly here?
DS: It is a matter of letting things wave at you, so to speak, in the sense that you are not proceeding "by design" from a preconceived idea. The Laplanchean method of reading is the analog of the analytic method in that you try to "listen" to the text with an evenly suspended attention, not expecting something in particular, and then your attention is forcefully attracted to something you had not foreseen.

to be left unexamined since it is just as central in Freud. So when you start to make a theory of psychoanalysis rest on a pillar such as translation, you'd better make sure that it will "pass the test."

While I kept using the term "translation" in its generic sense, from early on I realized there was a problem with it.[58] The term is so widely used in other domains—by linguists, translators, and laypersons as well—that it is easy to lose sight of its strictly metapsychological significance. The linguist Roman Jakobson identified three sorts of translation: intralinguistic (saying the same thing in other words within the same language), interlinguistic (what we usually refer to as "translation": translating from one language into another), and intersemiotic (translation between two different sets of signs, say, between icons and words). What is common to these three forms of translation, is that they suppose a preexisting code, either conventional or designed in such a way that the meaning of the signs can be intuitively guessed (think of the icons on your computer's desktop, for instance). But if you consider what the infant's psyche is required to do when confronted with the enigmas traveling within the parental messages, you realize that none of the three sorts of translation applies. The enigma is an enigma, says Laplanche, in that it is enigmatic for the adult emitter as much as for the child at the receiving end. It is not formulated either in words or in icons. It is best conceived as an event that excites the infant's body-psyche and provokes it into trying to make sense of it, except that there is no pre-established code for how to do this. Obviously, the child uses some "tools" such as its bodily experience and the elements of communication provided by the adult caretakers in their ordinary exchanges. But these are not about the enigmas in the message, since they are enigmas, as we saw, for the emitters themselves.

---

58 Dominique Scarfone, *Oublier Freud?: Mémoire pour la psychanalyse.* (Montreal: Boréal, 1999).

Hence, I propose "transduction" as a more appropriate term, as it describes a transformation from one domain or energy type to another, totally different domain or energy type, such as happens, for example, in the retina, where the energy of photons is transduced into nervous influx. This means that transduction allows the infant to formulate a first "meaning" that is truly original and thus, strictly speaking, not a translation. Of course, the tools I mentioned exert some constraint, so there is no infinite freedom in formulating a first transduction. But certainly, this means that there is no good or bad transduction of what was experienced at the receiving end of the enigmatic message; within a range limited by the bodily parameters and the other elements provided by the adult environment, the child can make its own unique interpretation.

In proposing "transduction" I may seem to be overly concerned with terminology, but I believe this has implications not just in theory but also in analytic practice. It matters, for instance, that preverbal and nonverbal experiences cannot be translated as if they were already formatted in a linguistic code.

AS: I have learned from Laplanche, though not only him, that being overly concerned with terminology—with what we call things, with why we call them what we call them, and with the implications of those namings—is quite consequential. So I appreciate your precision. And I find helpful your clarification about how "transduction" captures something about the economics of the process that the term "translation" does not as readily accommodate.

But here's a question that I have been wondering about— and that perhaps will interest our readers as well. While you've introduced the term "transduction" in your writing and have before, as you have done now, explained its utility and what it can offer us over and beyond translation, you have also been somewhat hesitant to completely substitute it for "translation." You are always very intentional about your language, so I suspect that there's more to it than just not having gotten around to it. I would love to hear your thoughts on that.

DS: Perhaps what we have here is another example of the insuperable ambiguity of psychoanalytic terminology, not because the theory is ambiguous, but because it is destined to account for the human condition, which *is* truly ambiguous. Maybe I should write a paper discussing transduction versus translation at greater length, because as our discussion goes on, I'm prone to relativize what I've been stating about transduction versus translation. At the economic level, "transduction" is inarguably preferable for the reason you mentioned. However, "translation" is closer to the actual experience of the analysand because it comes into play in the *après-coup* fashion, resuming the process in terms that are compatible with the representational aspect of the psyche. The psyche certainly uses transduction when confronted with the "stowaway" transported by the message of the other, but when the transduction is done and one looks back, it looks as if the resulting meaning had always been there and was simply translated. This leads me to consider that transduction is what happens at the level of the primal (Laplanche's *originaire*) whereas translation has to do with the ulterior elaboration of the results of transduction.

AS: This is incredibly interesting because I had, so far, understood you to be saying that "translation" as a term is an inadequate, if not perhaps misleading in that it implies the possibility of a determinate transcription, and that you had argued in favor of the term "transduction" as a way of more accurately capturing the economic shifts that occur in the churning of something less bound (the enigmatic dimension of the message) into something more bound (meaning). But it now seems that you are developing your thinking about transduction by adding that the job of translation is to make the process look like a mere discovering of something that was already lying in waiting but hidden. And that translation is able to do this work because transduction has already economically transformed the unbound (enigma) into something that could be psychically handled. Am I understanding you well?

DS: You are indeed. And the same can be said regarding unconscious fantasies. It has been pointed out—correctly in my view—that there is no way of knowing if a fantasy that emerges during the analysis was already there, waiting to be uncovered, or was created in situ. Philip M. Bromberg, for instance, argues that it is created there and then.[59] This is a false solution in the sense that if the fantasy was created there and then, it has necessarily been motivated or triggered by something that requires being represented by that fantasy. Creation on the spot does not avoid the question of what requires—and what it takes to arrive at— that creation. I think it is more consistent to suppose that, as for everything else regarding the unconscious, there is a transduction of something really extraneous to the representational mind. And when the transduction is done, the representation may seem either to have always been there or to have been created a moment ago. Winnicott's paradox of the found/created applies here beautifully in my view.

AS: There is so much you say here that, were time and space unrestricted, I would want to follow up on—your points about Philip Bromberg, for example, which would interest relational analysts very much. But also, about what you are gesturing to in relation to what is extraneous to the representational mind: at the risk of sounding too linear, I'd say you are suggesting that transduction has to come first, effecting an economic transformation that will, in turn, make it possible for a translation to be experienced as if it carries the heft of "truth."

---

59 " 'Grown-Up' Words: An Interpersonal/Relational Perspective on Unconscious Fantasy," *Psychoanalytic Inquiry* 28, no. 2 (March 2008): 131–50.

Your deepening of our thinking about translation and transduction makes me want to ask you this: Laplanche is insistent that he is not working toward a "new psychoanalysis" but toward "new foundations."[60] To me it seems, though, that these new foundations, even though they come out of his return to Freud and his mining Freud's "going-astray," do ultimately yield a new psychoanalytic focus of sorts. New not in object, as the object always remains the exigency of the unconscious, but in the sense that these newly scaffolded foundations give us substantially different inflection points when it comes to theory and open up different vistas for clinical technique. For example, as you note in this paper, Laplanche moves away from neurosis to think about the institution of psychic topography;[61] he introduces a strikingly new way of thinking about mourning;[62] and he argues, unlike thinkers in most other schools of analysis and unlike Freud himself, for the importance of the analyst abstaining from interpreting to the patient. Some contemporary Freudian analysts[63] and relational analysts[64] have themselves argued against interpreting, but Laplanche was writing about this decades before these more recent contributions. So while we see him go back to Freud to pick up where he thinks Freud went astray—which he brilliantly does in proposing his General theory of seduction as opposed to restricted seduction (i.e., childhood sexual abuse)—the theory he offers us develops well beyond Freud. He revisits Freud but lands in a different place, following a spiral movement. So it is increasingly appearing to me

---

60 See p. 34 above.

61 See p. 28 above.

62 See p. 30-32 above.

63 E.g., Bruce E. Reis, *Creative Repetition and Intersubjectivity: Contemporary Freudian Explorations of Trauma, Memory, and Clinical Process* (London: Routledge, 2020).

64 E.g., Amy Schwartz Cooney, "Vitalizing Enactment: A Relational Exploration," *Psychoanalytic Dialogues* 28, no. 3 (May 2018): 340–54; Donnel B. Stern, "How I Work with Unconscious Process: A Case Example," *Contemporary Psychoanalysis* 55, no. 4 (2019): 336–48.

that Laplanche's claim that he is just pursuing Freud's object is not entirely accurate; and yet he is adamant about it. I wonder how you understand that. Is it modesty? Is there something else he worries about that he tries to ward off with his insistence that he is not founding a new school?

DS: Your question is important, and answering it requires clarifying certain aspects of Laplanche's ideas. He does not claim to have introduced a new psychoanalysis, because he stands firmly by Freud's definition of analysis as first and foremost *a method*—of investigation and of treatment. As already mentioned, it is the very method he employs—mutatis mutandis—in exploring Freud's opus. So in that respect, he could not invoke a new psychoanalysis, since the fundamental method stays the same. What you are pointing to are the consequences of heeding Laplanche's version of the seduction theory, but I would say they have to do not so much with technique as such as with the analyst's ethical stance, if we agree that "ethics" refers to an inner disposition more than rules of conduct.

As for changing the way of working with the theory, yes, Laplanche certainly changes that aspect of psychoanalytic praxis, something that can be done only *after* Freud and that Freud himself could not do, because he was busy creating the method and the theory. So the essential Freudian method remains, nudged here and there by the attention paid to the corollaries of the General theory of seduction. For example, if we acknowledge that the analyst provokes transference, then we cannot make an as liberal use of projection as is usually made to account for what goes on transference-wise in the analytic room. One could say that Laplanche mostly displaces the accents in Freud's texts and only rarely rewrites them. But displacing accents is like transposing the notes in a musical piece: the end result can differ significantly from the original. As I write this, I am also thinking that this is exactly what the Freudian evenly suspended attention does: displace the accents in the patient's discourse so as not to adhere to the ego's melody line—that is, to what the patient's ego would like the analyst to hear.

AS: I hope you will permit me to push a bit harder here. Isn't a transposition of accents precisely how something new gets churned out of something old? Isn't it the case that, to some extent, the crafting of everything novel involves a recycling or reordering of old materials? I still, I guess, see what Laplanche does as revitalizing psychoanalysis.

DS: Absolutely. One needs to think here of what the "evenly suspended attention" (a.k.a. "freely hovering attention") recommended by Freud actually requires. This recommendation stems from the fact that the patient's discourse is that of the ego, which is concerned with coherence, civility, correctness, obedience. This implies that whatever transpires from that discourse that belongs to the unconscious can be given access to consciousness only if one does *not* follow the patient's prosody. That prosody is directed at emphasizing some parts of the patient's discourse and downplaying others, attracting the analyst's attention to x or diverting that attention from y. The prosody therefore produces a wavelike pattern, with spikes and troughs representing changes in the tone of the voice, for instance, or in the number of details. The analyst's evenly suspended attention is directed at "flattening the curve" so that the analyst is not captive of the ego's intention. So when I said "displacing accents," I should have added that the new disposition of accents is a *result* of the evenly suspended attention and not something the analyst creates on purpose. The difficult task of the analyst is not to heed any accent whatsoever until some unforeseen pattern imposes itself. In saying this I am aware that one could consider this an impossible task and thus not to be even attempted. But I beg to differ: just as with the patient's free associations, the analyst's evenly suspended attention is needed to put speech and listening under a certain tension. What matters most is what we learn from the *resistance* encountered during the effort to implement both of these practices. It may turn out that when such resistance is worked through, what we get is the same content but with accents distributed differently, hence with a quite different meaning.

AS: I have always been very taken with the centrality of his notion of "going-astray," which involves his methodology of putting Freud to work, tracking the inconsistencies in his theory, and subjecting the theory (not Freud himself) to a Freudian reading. The notion of going-astray, however, also implies by its very wording a deviation, a deviation from a path that should not have been deviated from or a deviation that was not marked as such. And yet Laplanche would be the first to argue against such a path: one follows not a path but follows—or perhaps "is carried by" would be a better way of saying it, by the exigency of the unconscious. Is this phrasing and its implication of a deviation Laplanche's own "going-astray," a Ptolemaic closure that, like Freud, he, as a human being, cannot entirely step out of?

DS: I don't know how much clarity I can bring in response to this question, but let me try. The most blatant case of Freud's going-astray (*fourvoiement*), according to Laplanche, is his biologism. For Laplanche, resorting to biology was a mistake on Freud's part in more than one way: for one thing, it meant misconstruing psychoanalysis as a natural science based on biology, which it is not; also, the biology itself that Freud invoked was already obsolete. For instance, phylogenetic transmission of fantasies, by which Freud explained what he believed were inborn primal fantasies, makes no sense in the Darwinian evolutionary theory. But this is a too-simple rendition of what the strayings are really about, and you're right in pointing out that Laplanche would be the first to reject the idea of a "correct path." Laplanche's idea is not that Freud should not have gone in a given direction; it is rather that he went where he went for a reason, even if the road taken led to a dead end. What Laplanche admired the most in Freud was that he relentlessly searched for better access to the unconscious, and this is why his "strayings" are still instructive—in that, despite their being missteps, they show us Freud at work.

Things get a bit complicated here, so please bear with me. I wish to make it clear that with this criticism, Laplanche is not pointing his finger at Freud's strayings to show how mistaken he was and then propose a Laplanchean alternative. Laplanche takes Freud's research as his object of study and looks at how his thinking evolves from his early theory of seduction to its abandonment and its replacement with the theory of inborn fantasies. In so doing, he realizes that Freud's theory building followed, unbeknownst to him, the same pattern as the evolution happening in the child's psyche: the primacy of the other (seduction) is followed by a "Ptolemaic closure" that negates the primacy of the other and replaces it with inborn fantasies. So just as the child naturally becomes ego centered, so does Freud's theory. Here it is important to mention that this Ptolemaic closure, in the psyche and in theory, is unavoidable; it is a normal penchant, because it is not bearable to constantly stay in the decentered position entailed by the primacy of the other.

As we see the official Freudian process of theory building having itself something of the infantile theory building, we are reminded that, as analysts, we are continually exposed to the risk of mistaking the theories we find in our patient's minds (infantile theories, fantasies) for psychoanalytic theory itself. This is as if anthropologists who hear myths reported to them by members of societies they are studying adopted those very myths as their official theories of how those societies works. In a paper on the feminine in psychoanalysis,[65] I tried to show how Freud fell prey

---

65 See chapter 4 below.

to that type of mistake by elevating the infantile theory/fantasy of castration to the status of a psychoanalytic theory about the actual status of female subjects. So when Freud writes that at some point the young female child "discover[s] that she is castrated,"[66] he does not mean she forms the *fantasy* of being castrated; he means it is a painful discovery of the truth. Whereas in the male child, Freud simply describes the *fear* of castration.

To return to the strayings: After having replaced the primacy of seduction with the theory of inborn fantasies, Freud needed to account for the origin of such fantasies, and this is where biology stepped in—namely, with the theory of phylogenetic transmission. So, the strayings in question, according to Laplanche, are not so much about Freud having taken the wrong psychoanalytic route; rather, it's about his having begun basing his ideas on an unnecessary and, what is more, outdated biology (Haeckel's law). But the problem is not biology itself. Freud could have resorted to sociology or historiography, and the problem would have been the same: that of abandoning the metapsychological, or more accurately, meta-anthropological point of view on the theory of seduction and searching instead for an empirical, factual foundation. Forced to forgo the idea that actual abuses were always a material fact in individual life, he hypothesized the same abuses, this time in the prehistory of the species, and therefore needed to invoke a phylogenetic transmission of the scenes related to those prehistoric events.

AS: We will be discussing an entire essay you wrote on this topic later in this book, so this whets my (and I imagine the reader's!) appetite. So, more on your point about "mistaking the *theories* we find in our patient's minds (infantile theories, fantasies) for psychoanalytic theory itself" soon! Right now, what you are

---

66 Freud, S. "Femininity," in *New Introductory Lectures on Psycho-Analysis*, SE 22, p. 126

illuminating for us is the fact that Laplanche feels that it is expectable, perhaps even inevitable, that this Ptolemaic closure happens in our theorizing, right? And, if I am understanding you correctly, you are clarifying that going-astray is not about a deviation from a "right" theoretical path but about the closing-up operations of the ego itself on the level of theory. In this sense, going-astray would make one feel quite at home.

DS: You just made things much clearer. I think it is obvious that Freud's strayings were inevitable because no one can stay forever in a decentered position. It's worth mentioning that in addition to meaning a negatively connoted closing off of what was open, "closure" is the word we use for what we wish for after a significant loss, because without closure we are left in a state of turmoil. It is also worth considering that, in his 1915 paper "The Unconscious," Freud himself wrote that every progression to a superior level of organization entails a new censorship. Already in his letter to Fliess of December 6, 1896, he posited that every translation – we could say "every closure"– leaves a repressed residue in its wake. Similarly, every progression in our theory leaves out something for the sake of coherence. The end result is precisely what you describe: feeling "quite at home."

AS: Laplanche is not alone in arguing that psychoanalytic work needs to be freed up from all "purposive ideas,"[67] but it does seem to me that he is unique in *how* he proposes that be done: the analyst should not synthesize and interpret but side with detranslation. Even those analysts who are pushing back on interpretation do not go as far as to orient the analyst's attention to the work of delinking. Reorienting the analyst to understanding his or her work not as synthetic but as working *toward* lysis contests a certain orthodoxy in psychoanalysis: we are not the ones to be making the links. To some degree, of course, this is aspirational, as every intervention,

---

67 See p. 56 above.

even those not intended to synthesize or forge propositional links, can have an unmitigatedly binding dimension. But the assertion that it is the patient, not the analyst, that is the hermeneutic agent in the clinical situation is quite consequential. From that angle, even the seemingly neutral aphorism "First do no harm" becomes a purposive idea that should be resisted. This delinking of the analyst's goal from *any* purposive idea is freeing but also—and I think this needs to be said—unsettling for the analyst. Would you agree with that? If so, can you help us think about the analyst's anxiety in working without a magnetic north?

DS: I understand your point as being: do not forget that your job is essentially to *analyze*. But I don't know if I would go as far as saying that the rule "First do no harm" should be resisted. After all, analysts do provide a setting that feels secure enough for the patient to dare to go to places in their mind where they never went before. Now, as you know, the setting is made first of all of the analyst's capacity to "contain" (as in "containing a crowd") and supposes the reliability of that function. So I believe that analysts are also required to contain their own eagerness to analyze or unbind, inasmuch as they feel that the situation or the timing do not warrant the optimal conditions for that "lysis."

AS: The Hippocratic "Do no harm" maxim opens up to a larger discussion that I'd like to return to later in our talks.[68]

For now, let me move to a different direction, a question that, in fact, preoccupies me whenever traversing Laplanche's oeuvre and to which I am returned in rereading the chapter we are presently discussing. It's a hard one, but I want to see if we can approach it, even if sideways, because it troubles many of us who try to think with his theory. As you explain so lucidly, the part of the enigmatic message that does not get translated becomes repressed, forming the sexual unconscious. You insist here as well as in the paper we

---

68 AS: See the conversation on chapter 4.

will discuss next ("The *Three Essays* and the Meaning of the Infantile Sexual in Psychoanalysis") that the repressed is not the Sexual in the sense of sexuality per se. Why does Laplanche nevertheless insist on calling it the Sexual, inviting, thus, confusion? My sense is that it has to do with the body's excitability and with the economics of psychic energy, but is that enough to call it the Sexual? To put it differently, why does he want us to be thinking of that as sexual even as it's not about sex or sexuality as such?

DS: As you often do, you are pushing me toward stating my personal views, which, though largely inspired by Laplanche, may not faithfully represent his own. Moreover, you are addressing the exact point that (as we write) I am working on as I reflect on the question with the Laplanche meeting of October 2021 in mind[69]: What exactly are we talking about with the term Sexual if it is not sexuality?

To get to a clear answer to this, we first have to look at how psychoanalytic concepts are created. In the case of the Sexual, it started with what we could call Freud's empirical theory of seduction, when he believed he had discovered the "*caput Nili*" — the true origin of hysteria in actual cases of sexual child abuse. For him, this meant that sexuality was brought to the child from without, implanted as a foreign body, the memory of the related event being repressed. When Freud realized this did not hold up, in the sense that not every patient had in fact been sexually abused, he gradually resorted to the theory of inborn infantile sexuality, with atavistic imprints of prehistoric events being present in the form of "primal fantasies." This represented at once progress and a problem. Progress in that Freud had introduced the concept of psychic reality—that is, a third domain between material or outer reality and imagination pure and simple. A problem because with

---

69 Referring to conference titled "Laplanche in the States : The Sexual and the Cultural" that, due to the Covid pandemic, took place online on October 2-3, 2021.

the theory of primal fantasies —of seduction, castration, and so forth—, Freud, as we just saw, was just sending back to earlier times, to the prehistory of mankind, that which did not hold up in the infancy of the individual. Yet the problem of validation or falsification remained the same.

I follow Laplanche in thinking that "primal fantasies" cannot be inborn, phylogenetically transmitted remnants going back to the primal horde—and Freud himself conceded at one point that the primal horde with the totally narcissistic father was a "just so story."[70] But in our practice we do encounter fantasies related to seduction, castration, the primal scene. Discussing their apparent universality would require another long digression. For now, I will simply signal that even when they cannot be ascertained as memories of actual events, they do not operate as pure imagination. For instance, they do serve as templates of sorts, organizing the subject's symptoms and/or their basic stance in their love life. This, to me, is an aspect of what Freud introduces in the last few pages of *The Interpretation of Dreams* as "psychical reality," which must not be mistaken for the ordinary subjective opinion or point of view on self and the world.[71] Psychical reality is an effective operator in the mind of the subject, independent of their subjective preferences and often inflecting these against the subject's would-be rational choices. In other words, it is the unconscious as we come to know it in our clinical work.

What I just laid out allows us to distinguish between sexuality and the Sexual. A subject's *sexuality* is indeed, developmentally speaking, of one or the other "official" orientations while inflected by the psychic reality that operates in terms of certain unconscious schemes or scenarios that we "unearth" in analysis as unconscious fantasies (or phantasies, if you prefer). Why are

---

70 *Group Psychology and the Analysis of the Ego*, SE 18:65–144.

71 DS: See also the conversation following chapter 5 in the present volume.

these ph/fantasies related to the sexual dimension? Because they result from the work of transduction/translation done by the infant on the "compromised messages" emanating from adults. What "compromises" or, as I prefer to say, contaminates the messages in question is the sexual dimension in the adult's body-psyche that, in turn, excites the infant's body-psyche enigmatically—that is, in excess of what it can make sense of. This means that the infant is thus involuntarily seduced by the adult caretakers, and such seduction, operating through ordinary care, progressively draws the sexual geography on the child's body-psyche. To give a general example: the erogenous zones are not inborn as erogenous zones, but they develop on the loci of significant exchanges between adult and child, so they arise as erogenous through the cathexis at work during those exchanges. As for the child, it will be brought to make sense of all these excitations by elaborating its own infantile sexual theories, which we analysts later uncover as fantasies in our patients' heads.

So the genesis of *sexuality* is closely linked with the process of seduction/transduction, but we can see that the process provides only the raw elements of sexuality—elements that are in themselves impervious to any process of maturation or integration into the structure of the ego. Hence, we can say that both *sexuality* and the Sexual have their roots in the excitable body-psyche. Yet the mere excitability of the body-psyche could not by itself entail the rich and intricate texture of infantile sexuality. That requires the complex exchange taking place in adult-child communication and the asymmetry that lies therein. I must add that not only do these implanted elements not themselves mature, but they also are cause for a sort of permanent "trouble at the borders," so to speak. They are factors of unbinding because their load of raw energy was not totally dissipated by the process of transduction; it was merely contained by the forms that were found in the process. I believe this is a possible version of what Freud meant by the term "countercathexis."

AS: You have clarified and once again stimulated my and the reader's appetite!

In this paper, you also flesh out for us Laplanche's critique of Freud's introduction of the notion of narcissism, tracking how he explains that Freud ended up having to posit a death drive as a corrective to his defanging the Sexual of its demonic force. This is an important reminder of how the sexual drive is a complex force that does not only aim at binding or self-love; rather, it ontologically contains both binding and unbinding forces. I think, however, that it can be difficult to discern how consequential this theoretical move is because after Freud argues that the erotic can pair up with aggression, we do have (in Freud) a way of thinking of the commerce between sexuality and aggression.[72] It's not as if Freud has made a full return to his earlier understanding of the Sexual as also involving unbinding elements, but he does seem to be backtracking from the cleaning out of the Sexual effected by the introduction of narcissism. Arguably, thus, we have in Freud a way of thinking about the two (sex and aggression) operating jointly. From that perspective, what does Laplanche's insistence that the sexual drive includes both binding (life) and unbinding (death) forces add to our thinking that Freud did not cover in speaking about a primary erotogenic masochism?

DS: This is a difficult question, and I will again ask you to bear with me while I go into the meanders of metapsychology created by the notion of a "death drive."

Narcissism itself is not the problem. On the contrary, Laplanche believed that the "great turn" in Freudian thinking was not "Beyond the Pleasure Principle" but the introduction of narcissism. The "defanging," as you so aptly call it, of the Sexual happened when Freud considered that the main conflict was now the one

---

72 "The Economic Problem of Masochism," *SE* 19:155–70.

between ego-libido (narcissism) and object-libido—that is, it was not a question of free versus bound libido (i.e., sexual drive vs. ego) but a question of where libido was to be bound: in the ego or in the object. In either case, it was a matter of bound or "quiescent" libido, and this is what resulted in Freud's placing the sexual drives under the aegis of Eros, the creator of links. Laplanche reasoned that, Freud being Freud, he could not let go of an unbinding factor—a role that until then had pertained to the sexual drives. Hence, Freud introduced the death drive to account for unbinding effects.

AS: If I may interrupt you for a moment, what is "quiescent libido"? I have understood it to be bound libido. Is it not?

DS: Indeed, it is bound libido. I call it quiescent because it has not the "imp" of the drive.

AS: And can you clarify what the difference is between ego-libido and object-libido so that we may follow along?

DS: I am simply using Freud's terms. Ego-libido is the libido invested (cathected) in the "good form" represented by the ego; it is the necessary narcissistic libido, the love for the ego's image that keeps the ego going. At one point, between 1915 and 1920, Freud entertained an unofficial second topography where the ego was considered the great reservoir of the libido, part of which was invested in its objects. It's the same libido but invested differently. So we see something of a problem here, because the ego's libido was postulated as quiescent libido; therefore, the object invested with that libido was not the object of the *drives*, the drives whose libido was certainly not seen as quiescent. This temporary, somewhat covert model is possibly one of the things that forced Freud to look for the demonic part that had been thus lost to view, leading him, according to Laplanche, to the postulation of a death drive.

So here we are with Freud installing a death drive at the center of the psyche, with deflection of destruction to the outside being possible only thanks to the "mixture" of life and death drives. But Freud had also posited that the ego is in fact the first object on the path traveled by drive energy. In that case, if we wish to think of the mixing of life and death drives in a more clinically significant manner, we need to situate the ego in its fundamental masochistic position—a position, that is, where the ego manages to bind the destructiveness by finding pleasure in suffering. That is very clever and appears to make sense, but it has all the characteristics of a metaphysical speculation. We have no idea what a "death drive" is like, unless it simply means the biological and psychological version of the second law of thermodynamics: the growth of entropy or disorder. But if this is so, do we really need a special drive to account for something so universal? So, Freud being Freud, one has reasons to believe that he is thinking of something else. But this something else encounters another serious problem: Freud had stated that the death drive has no energy of its own and that it can manifest itself only by using the energy of life drives. Except that he is hard pressed to account for how the energy of *life* drives, which is none other than libido, can be put in the service of hate. So when he addresses the issue in chapter 4 of *The Ego and the Id*, fully aware of the conundrum he's in, he feels obliged to invoke some "neutral energy"—that is, nonsexual, nonlibidinal energy. And to answer the question of where to find such energy, he invokes the process of desexualization of libidinal energy. As for the problem of how desexualization is achieved, he answers that it is through sublimation, itself arrived at through binding the libido to the ego— that is, producing narcissistic libido. But if you ask what narcissistic libido is, well, it's . . . desexualized libido! We've come full circle and have explained nothing.

The fact is that you would need no explanation of that kind if you simply referred to the sexual drive as having two possible regimens: that of "life sexual drive," concerned with finding objects for long-standing linking (in other words, love objects) and that of "death sexual drive"—that is, the demonic Sexual of old, whose concern is finding the shortest route possible toward release of tension, hence possessing an unbinding effect. Primary erotogenic masochism is still accounted for as a last post form of binding: running against the grain, so to speak, it means for the ego resorting to the enjoyment of pain rather than leaving the scene.

AS: So masochism, in this way of thinking, would itself amount to a binding of sorts as opposed to being the manifestation of the death drive. Is that what you mean?

DS: It is a binding made necessary as the last possibility left to counter the unbinding effects of the death drive. So you could see it also as a *compromised* manifestation of the sexual death drive.

AS: Psychoanalysis, you write, "is relational from the outset."[73] You have in mind not relationality in the conventional sense of the word—that is, as interrelatedness or intersubjectivity—but a different kind of relationality, one that has more to do with the mystery of the other, the part of the other in ourselves that is not accessible to us. This is an important point that runs through your work. Would you, nevertheless, say a bit more now about how you use the word "relational"? I think it will be clarifying for all our readers and especially for relational analysts, who seem to be taking a great interest in Laplanche and your work.

DS: I may seem to use "relational" in a very specific way, and I will say more about this in a minute, but I would say that I use it in a very generic way all the same. I base myself on the fact that nothing can be known, in any kind of knowledge, except from interacting with it—that is, having a relation to it. The specific aspect you ask me about concerns what we are able to know about the other human being and, through this other, about ourselves. In this regard, I certainly state the obvious if I say that there is no human being outside of a relation to others or that the other was there for

---

73 See p. 34 above.

me even before I was conceived, as when my mother dreamt of having a child. The problems that I have with some aspects of the relational point of view have to do with when it fails to consider the *asymmetrical* nature of the relationship that occurs in the most central aspects of human life, starting of course with infancy. So here we are brought back again to the centrality of seduction in that it unmistakably rests on the relational nature of human beings but more specifically creates an irresolvable gap inside the human psyche, leaving a part of us eternally *in-fans* and thereby open to the effects of the asymmetry in question. This runs contrary to any hope of a symmetrical kind of relationship in analytic therapy; indeed, if, by pure hypothesis, the analyst succeeded in establishing a symmetrical relationship with the patient, then the infantile would not show up in the analytic session. This has to do with our conception of what is transference and what is transferred in the course of analysis.

AS: Many analysts would agree that there is an asymmetry in the mutuality of the caretaker-infant relationship. But by "asymmetry" here, I think you mean something more than just the fact that the adult is more developed psychically or that they have at their disposal language or cognitive and psychic capacities the child does not: you foreground the fact that the adult has a sexual unconscious while the child does not (yet). This particularity of how you (and Laplanche) use the word "asymmetry" freights the term "relational" because it refracts it, we might say, through the Sexual. Relational, as you use it, thus does not mean interactive on the level of a subject-subject relationship—that is, when you say that "psychoanalysis is relational from the outset," you mean something more specific than "we are always in relation to the patient/the analyst," and you are not speaking about intersubjectivity, is that right?

DS: You are right in recalling that the asymmetry I'm speaking of concerns the Sexual; this is the fundamental discrepancy existing between adult and infant. But regarding the patient-analyst relation, one could object that in that case both partners are equally endowed with a sexual unconscious; so where is the asymmetry? The answer is in the analytic method and the analyst's stance, by which the primal asymmetrical situation is reinstated. The stance I refer to includes free association and evenly suspended (or freely hovering) attention but just as importantly what Laplanche called the analyst's "refusals," such as the refusal to know, the refusal to play at the level of ordinary reality, in order to work as much as possible with psychic reality. The infantile Sexual, which is at the core of psychic reality, emerges in the transference that the analytic situation and the analyst's stance provoke.

Does this differ from intersubjectivity? It all depends on how we conceive it. Intersubjectivity appears tricky to me. In a paper on subjectality,[74] I highlight the fact that the victim of abuse so well described by Ferenczi—but this could also apply to a member of a sect—operates in a fully intersubjective manner; their subjectivity is therefore not destroyed but subjugated.

AS: When you say "intersubjective" here, however, you don't mean it in the sense that there is respect for the victim's subjectivity-is that correct ?

DS: I mean that intersubjectivity in itself is a state of fact occurring spontaneously and outside any critical examination. In everyday situations we find intersubjectivity at work all the time, for instance in the uncritical sharing of mainstream opinions. Given this perspective, elevating intersubjectivity to the dignity of the method does not seem to me to go beyond stating the obvious—we are intersubjective beings. The sharing that occurs intersubjectively is in no way a guarantor of the truth. Quite the opposite in

---

74 Scarfone, D. Trauma, Subjectivity and Subjectality, *American Journal of Psychoanalysis*, 81 ((2021) : p. 214–236.

fact. Unconscious collusion between patient and analyst is an intersubjective event just as much as is the shared elaboration of an unpleasant truth. What I mean is that intersubjectivity in itself has no special virtues. Hence, I was very happy to discover that we could think of another term, "subjectality" (and its corollary "intersubjectality"), which I use as the name for the "critical moment" within subjectivity or intersubjectivity. Subjectality both contains subjectivity and lifts it to another level, temporary as that may be.

The *Three Essays* and the Meaning of the Infantile Sexual in Psychoanalysis

The psychoanalytic domain is traversed by many different and contrasting currents, with debate and disagreement occurring at every turn, but I believe that nothing has sparked as much discussion and dissent as the place and role of sexuality in psychoanalysis.

Having been invited to write about the significance today of Freud's *Three Essays on Sexual Theory*,[1] I cannot avoid taking a personal stand on the subject. I will contend that in spite of their many limitations and defects (with which I will not deal here), the *Three Essays* are still highly significant today because they have brought to light a whole new way of considering human sexual reality—a conception that we should put our efforts into constantly rediscovering.

Freud accomplished this monumental achievement merely by applying to sexuality the same method he had used and developed in *The Interpretation of Dreams*.[2] In other words, Freud did nothing other than *analyze* human sexuality—that is, *decompose* it into more elemental forms. The analysis carried out by Freud inevitably required a methodological reduction, but it did not result in philosophical or theoretical reductionism. Quite on the contrary, psychoanalytically breaking down the notion of sexuality allowed

---

1   SE 7:123–246. Title translated in *The Standard Edition* as *Three Essays on the Theory of Sexuality*.

2   *SE* 4–5.

for an *extension* of the sexual domain—an extension that is truly specific to psychoanalysis as much as it is truly specific to the human being.

For Freud, analyzing human sexuality was necessary for various reasons, first among which were his previous abandonment of the seduction theory of hysteria and the end of his long relationship with Wilhelm Fliess. In the last years of the nineteenth century, Freud had been writing *The Interpretation of Dreams*, whose last chapter can be seen as the purely psychological version of many ideas contained in the unpublished neuropsychological "Project for a Scientific Psychology."[3] As we know from his correspondence, Freud had expected Fliess to simultaneously come up with the biological counterpart to the dream book. But it happened that, when *The Interpretation of Dreams* was published, the relationship with Fliess had started to unravel, ending in a quarrel and a final rupture in 1904.

The *Three Essays*, published a year after this dramatic turn of events, appears in this context as Freud's effort at complementing his book on dreams. In a way, his research for the *Three Essays* can be seen as aimed at identifying the biological, embodied motivational force behind the psychological mechanisms that the study of dreams had allowed him to formulate.

This was rendered all the more necessary after, for a number of empirical and epistemological reasons, Freud had resolved in 1897 to abandon the seduction theory, by which he'd thought he had identified the first motor that put the hysterical psyche to work. Freud had until then firmly believed that perverse seduction by an adult abuser was the crucial causal factor in every case of hysteria or obsessive neurosis.[4] In the period after his private abandonment

---

3   *SE* 1.

4   Letter of September 21, 1897, in *The Complete Letters of Sigmund Freud to Wilhelm Fliess*, trans. and ed. Jeffrey Moussaieff Masson (Cambridge, MA: Belknap Press of

of the *neurotica*, Freud devoted himself primarily to the study of dreams and memory.

Thus, the seduction theory, with all its sexual underpinnings, was left in limbo, with no major rival theory to take its place. It is commonly believed that the seduction theory was replaced by a theory centered on fantasy, but the latter was itself in need of a *primum movens*, since the causal "fact" behind the fantasy was still evading Freud's grasp.

The *Three Essays* of 1905 appears, therefore, as both a strong *overt* marker of the turn that Freud had secretly taken in 1897 and the formulation of a biopsychological theory to account for what puts the psyche into motion. The *primum movens* that in the previous theory was the seduction of a child by an adult pervert is here replaced by a basic driving force, the *libido*—the equivalent for sexuality of hunger for the feeding instinct.[5] Infantile sexuality is, from this point on in Freud's thought, not an extraneous element imposed on a sexless child by an adult abuser, but something that grows from within, although in normal situations it is elicited or "awakened" by an unintentional seducer—the mother or her substitute—in the course of ordinary caregiving. In a way, what we have here is a "soft" version of the seduction theory in which involuntary and benign seduction is the ancillary process while the inborn sexual drives are the main fulcrum.

The *Three Essays*, however, provide more than a replacement for the seduction theory. Since the seduction theory does not so much disappear as become reframed in a more general theory, and since acts of perverse seduction are still acknowledged by Freud as playing a role in pathogenic effects, what is really new in the *Three Essays* is that Freud turns his attention to the perversions themselves. He does so not with an exhaustive psychopathological

---

Harvard University Press, 1985), 264ff.

5   *SE* 7:135.

study in mind but by decomposing human sexuality into its discrete and unconscious components. Neurosis is now seen as "the negative of perversion."[6] This, as Freud writes in his preface to the fourth edition of the *Three Essays*, was the result of strictly psychoanalytic research,[7] and the author clearly states that "it is impossible that these *Three Essays* . . . should contain anything but what psychoanalysis makes it necessary to assume or possible to establish. It is, therefore, out of the question that they could ever extend into a complete 'theory of sexuality,' and it is natural that there should be a number of important problems of sexual life with which they do not deal at all."[8]

What the psychoanalysis of human sexuality allows Freud to extract is what we could call the generality of the Sexual, embodied in the drives and playing a central role in the psyche. But that remains an incomplete picture. The Sexual in question is generalized and decomposed by Freud into its pregenital components, those that, when they persist, form the perversions. Moreover, he discovers that something of the pregenital drives does persist, even in ordinary adult sexuality (as attested to by sexual foreplay, for instance), and that neurosis is the result of the repression of pregenital, perverse elements of human sexuality. Thus, not only is the Sexual now located internally, but it also will reveal itself to possess an inherently perverse slant.

In the *Three Essays*, Freud starts, indeed, by examining sexual aberrations—that is, deviations from a norm that is instantiated by heterosexual genital union. However, instead of strictly separating the said aberrations from normal sexuality, he posits a continuum between normality and pathology. Freud thereby takes a clear stand against the theory of degeneracy, be it in relation to homosexuality

---

6   *SE* 7:165.

7   *SE* 7:130–31.

8   *SE* 7:130.

("inversion") or the perversions. Even when he acknowledges that aberrations can take clearly pathological forms, he mainly uses pathology as a magnifying glass for the study of normal processes.

This will have important consequences, for if perverse sexuality is at the root not only of neurosis but of sexuality in general, then the norm from which "aberrations" deviate seems to be vanishing from view. Now, this is more scandalous—today no less so than in Freud's time—than, say, the idea of infantile sexuality. In fact, as Freud turns to infantile sexuality in the second essay, it is not simply to assert the existence of sexuality in children, nor for that matter to reassert the centrality of the "sexual factor" in the causation of the neuroses. The true scandal resides in Freud's *extension* of the notion of sexuality to children's activities that were thought to have nothing sexual in them (e.g., the baby's oral activity) and, through such extension, in the assertion that the infantile Sexual has much to do with adult perversions.

Moreover, in denying that "inverts" and "perverts" are degenerate and in asserting on the contrary that one can find "sexual aberrations" even among the greatest contributors to civilization, the *Three Essays* points to the generalized presence and action of the infantile, potentially perverse sexual factor in human activities of all kinds. Not only is infantile sexuality a source of pathology, that is, but it is also a contributing and perhaps decisive factor in the most elevated cultural accomplishments, attained via what would later be invoked as the mechanism of sublimation. With these ideas, Freud was completely upsetting the moral and intellectual order of the day.

Perversion or Polymorphism?

The fading out of the norm is implicit in Freud's notion that adult sexuality, even in its most standard forms, rests on a rather strong armature of pregenital sexual excitement in which oral and anal mucosae, as well as partly voyeuristic, exhibitionistic, fetishistic, and sadomasochistic components, can and frequently do play a role in the foreplay of—and the forepleasure (*Vorlust*) experienced by—the most ordinary sexual partners. The child is said to be "polymorphously perverse," a qualification that is still today an eyebrow raiser for those who do not understand that the key word is "polymorphously," not "perverse." The polymorphism in the child makes this quite the opposite of a truly perverse attribute, since pathological (or "true") perversion rests on the rigid *fixation* on a repetitive pregenital scenario.

Consider, for instance, this passage in which Freud ends up formulating a quite astonishing idea: "The conclusion now presents to us that there is indeed something innate lying behind the perversions but that it is something innate in *everyone*, though as a disposition it may vary in its intensity and may be increased by the influences of actual life. What is in question are the innate constitutional roots of the sexual instinct."[9] In other words, in spite of their innate biological baggage, human beings are nevertheless responsive to their environment and their personal experience. This, by the way, is an example of Freud's concept of "complemental series," which he used profusely—although not always overtly—in his etiological theories, thus avoiding the either/or alternative between endogenous and exogenous factors.[10]

In the *Three Essays*, Freud clearly invokes the complemental relationship of innate disposition with the intervention of the other. On the matter of the polymorphously perverse child, a close reading reveals that Freud's conception is far from being as simplistic as it is often purported to be. Consider, for example, the following passage: "It is an instructive fact that *under the influence of seduction* children can become polymorphously perverse, and can be led

9 *SE* 7:171; italics in the original.

10 See Jean Laplanche and Jean-Bertrand Pontalis, *The Language of Psycho-Analysis*, trans. Donald Nicholson-Smith (London: Hogarth Press, 1973).

into all possible kinds of sexual irregularities. This shows that an aptitude for them is innately present in their disposition."[11] The words I have italicized show that the theory of seduction was still active in Freud's thinking but also, and most important, that at this point he had inserted it into a more complex dynamic process. The passage could be read as follows: "Human beings are biologically predisposed to be influenced by cultural factors!" Though this idea may have sounded contradictory a few decades ago, at a time when quite a rigid conception of genetic predisposition reigned and was used to dismiss Freudian views, today we can appreciate how it easily it converges with modern conceptions, such as the epigenetic mechanisms in biology.[12]

What such a modern view does not satisfactorily account for, however, is *why* and *how* seduction can make children polymorphously perverse and why such an inherently perverse factor can later entail psychopathological formations. One way to answer those questions has been to say that the child and the adult do not speak the same language. This was the view expounded by Sándor Ferenczi in an important contribution. But while Ferenczi's paper is highly useful and explanatory at the clinical level, it fails to identify what it is in the adult that speaks with the "language of passion" while the child speaks the "language of tenderness." Ferenczi simply invokes psychopathology or intoxication in the adult, stopping short of thinking psychoanalytically about what it was in the abuser that had not sufficiently matured and had turned them into a perpetrator.[13]

---

11 *SE* 7:191; italics added.

12 See, e.g., Eva Jablonka and Marion J. Lamb, *Evolution in Four Dimensions: Genetic, Epigenetic, Behavioral, and Symbolic Variation in the History of Life* (Cambridge, MA: MIT Press, 2005).

13 S. Ferenczi, "Confusion of the Tongues between the Adults and the Child— (the Language of Tenderness and Passion)," *International Jouranl Psychoanalysis* 30 (1949): 225–30.

Picking up where Ferenczi left off, we are drawn back to the idea of a distortion that must have occurred in the abusive adult's infancy, thus invoking a pregenital factor in the perpetrator; the only other option would be to reinstate the pre-Freudian theory of degeneracy. It soon becomes obvious that the only adequate, though necessarily generic, answer to what pushes abusive adults to commit their deeds is their infantile, inherently perverse sexual constitution—a complexion whose pathological outcome should, of course, be subjected in each individual case to a detailed investigation.

Whatever the specific personal factors, it seems legitimate to conclude that it is the infantile that operates in the adult, through what I have called elsewhere the "Ferenczian chiasm"—the child is traumatized through the effects of the indomitable infantile Sexual in the adult. The infantile, therefore, reveals itself as that part of the Sexual that is passed on from one generation to the next, be it through ordinary or perverse seduction, without ever maturing.[14] Such transcendence of the infantile entails a very different way of considering the Sexual in psychoanalysis, as I will try to explain.

What Is Infantile in Infantile Sexuality?

In a paragraph of the second essay of the *Three Essays* (titled "Infantile Sexuality"), Freud equates polymorphism with the "infantile disposition,"[15] and this induces me to examine what specific meaning the word "infantile" assumes in psychoanalysis. To put it differently, the assertion of the existence of infantile sexuality was not really a revelation in 1905 Vienna—if it meant only that there existed a sexuality of, in, or among children. Parents and educators were clearly aware of the fact—as suggested, for

---

14 Dominque Scarfone, "Sexual and Actual," in *Infantile Sexuality and Attachment*, ed. Daniel Widlöcher, trans. Susan Fairfield (New York: Other Press, 2002), 97–110.

15 *SE* 7:191.

instance, by the many moral and "medical" precepts against children's masturbation—and needed no Freud to teach them about that matter. More challenging for the social *doxa* was to think of an infantile sexuality in which "infantile" qualifies not the age of the subject but the sexuality itself.

Before going any further, I will add a few words regarding methodology. Just as in every other field, in psychoanalysis concepts do not *directly* result from empirical observation. They have their roots in empirical facts, to be sure, but they are constructed in a way that must take into account what is specific to the psychoanalytic domain: mainly, the experience of analysis itself and the effects resulting from the "force of attraction" exerted by the unconscious.[16]

Consider, for example, the concept of libido introduced in the first of the *Three Essays*. Freud starts by stating that libido is in the sexual realm what hunger is in the domain of nutrition. But the parallel is short-lived. Whereas hunger is self-regulated and guides the hungry subject into a specific behavior, libido has a very peculiar and unpredictable way of securing its satisfaction. It turns out that the nutritional instinct and the sexual drive are not relatives after all; while the former craves the appeasing food, the latter craves ever more excitement because its satisfaction is always incomplete. Later on, Freud even asserts that there seems to be in the sexual drives something "unfavourable to the realization of complete satisfaction."[17]

The same reasoning applies to the concept of the object of the libido. Whereas in the self-preservative domain, the object is readily conceivable as that which provides satisfaction (e.g., food is the object of hunger), in the sexual domain, the object soon starts drifting away from such a simple relationship: the sexual object

16 Jean-Bertrand Pontalis, *La force d'attraction* (Paris: Seuil, Librairie du XXe siècle, 1990).

17 "On the Universal Tendency to Debasement in the Sphere of Love (Contributions to the Psychology of Love II)," *SE* 11:188–89.

can be another person, a body part, a fetish, one's own self-image, merely a fantasized object, and so on.[18]

Turning now to the concept of the infantile, I would suggest that we can see it drifting in a similar fashion in Freud's theory and practice. Let us begin by analyzing its very name from an etymological point of view. We will soon be struck by the fact that "infantile," which is obviously derived from the Latin *infans*, meaning "unable to speak," has something in common with a neurological condition that had interested Freud in the early 1890s: the aphasias. *Infantia* is the exact Latin equivalent of the Greek *aphasia*.

There is more to this than just a linguistic coincidence. In addition to the irony of Freud's leaving behind the neurological aphasias only to turn to another state of speechlessness, there is something here that may help us characterize in more specific terms the infantile Sexual in psychoanalysis.

What the etymology of the word "infantile" alerts us to is the truly speechless nature of the infantile Sexual—as it refers not to sexual behavior but to a sexual reality that cannot be put into words. And as a consequence, it cannot be integrated into the conscious mind. The infantile escapes mastery on the part of the subject. It is therefore not a single theme among others in psychoanalysis. Rather, it is woven into the very fabric of the unconscious inasmuch as the unconscious is that which has not yet been transcribed and registered in the symbolic structure of language and consciousness.

Psychoanalysis, as we know, is a talking cure in more than one sense: not only does it proceed through verbal exchange; words are also what, when added to unconscious material, give it the necessary

---

18 Jean Laplanche, *Life and Death in Psychoanalysis*, trans. Jeffrey Melmahn (Baltimore: Johns Hopkins University Press, 1976); Laplanche, J (1971) The Derivation of Psychoanalytic Entities in *The Unfinished Copernican Revolution, Selected Works, 1967–1992*. New York : The Unconscious in Translation, 2020, p. 157-176.).

quality for becoming conscious. With this in mind, "infantile" can just as well be used to refer to the unconscious as a system—that is, not simply what is not conscious, but also that which is not capable of becoming conscious until the words to say it are found.[19]

One could argue along these lines that anything not yet formulated in words could be deemed "infantile," so I must now discuss in what way the Sexual is intrinsically *a-phasic* or *infantile*—or in what way the infantile in its more specific sense is precisely the unconscious Sexual. It is worth noting that an aspect of the infantile that could be used to trivialize it has to do with its temporal profile. The term "infantile" can be used merely to qualify a stage in the course of the development of the personality. In that sense, it designates a phase that is bound to be superseded one day by maturation or integration into an adult form, with puberty intervening as the decisive maturational step. Freud clearly sees it in this way in the last of the *Three Essays*.

But insofar as our analytic experience attests to the persistence of the infantile Sexual in the adult, it follows that a distinction must be made between, on the one hand, a maturational infantile sexuality— by which we mean sexual interests and manifestations in children that will evolve toward adult sexuality—and, on the other hand, an infantile Sexual that does not evolve or mature, remaining as the unconscious core of adult sexuality (the transcendent infantile Sexual that I evoked earlier).

Jean Imbeault detected in Freud's writings these two sorts of "infantile," which he dubbed the "small" (*petit*) and the "big" (*grand*) infantile.[20] The small infantile is the observable infantile sexuality, the one that eventually goes through stages, tending toward something like an adult organization, with its objects and its preferential modes of satisfaction. As for the big infantile, it is

---

19 See Marie Cardinal, *The Words to Say It* (London: Women's Press, 2000).

20 "Petit et grand infantile," *Le fait de l'analyse* 8 (Spring 2000): 23–43.

not recruited by any integrative or organized structure; in fact, it resists such maturation or integration and is "the contrary of a being-for-the-future,"[21] thereby constituting a kernel of pathological organization. Pathology, in this sense, is to be conceived as a resistance to becoming, to moving toward maturity, where maturity is meant as the capacity to deal with the sexual impact of the other.

The big infantile is not directly observable as infantile sexuality is in the maturational sense. It must be extracted through analysis, writes Imbeault, from a number of clinical impressions[22]—as it was extracted by Freud from Dora's coughing, for instance.[23] The big infantile may therefore not immediately be seen as sexual or for that matter as infantile—if the word means "pertaining to the child." The psychoanalytic concept of infantile, though starting from empirical observation of infantile sexuality, is constructed in a way that soon "deports" it, so to speak, and transfers it to a very different realm of signification. Infantile in that sense becomes a foundational concept in psychoanalysis whose status we must now try to legitimize.

The Always Already-Deviated Character of the Sexual

We are thus drawn to conclude that the nonmaturational infantile Sexual identified by Imbeault is precisely the kind of "perverse" Sexual of which, according to Freud, neurosis is the negative. Freud was probably also pointing to this sort of infantile Sexual when he stated that the symptoms of neurosis are the sexual activity of neurotics. For it does not come naturally, except after a long-enough clinical experience, to associate neurotic symptoms with sexual activity, and psychoanalytic theories such as this are often

---

21 Imbeault, "Petit et grand infantile," 31; all translations of Imbeault are my own.

22 "Petit et grand infantile," 29.

23 "Fragment of an Analysis of a Case of Hysteria (Dora)," *SE* 7, 1-122.

met with understandable skepticism by clinicians who remark that their patients are capable of having intercourse and attaining orgasm, for instance, thereby apparently contradicting Freud's thesis. But no contradiction occurs if one makes a clear distinction between *sexuality* as an observable set of behaviors and the *infantile Sexual*, conceived as that part of the sexual drives that resists being integrated into a psychic or biological maturational process. With this distinction in mind, it becomes easily conceivable that neurotic patients are capable of ordinary sexual activity; what clinical experience shows, however, is that their sexuality can itself be diverted or disturbed to various degrees by conflicts concerning the repressed infantile Sexual.

The reason that the infantile Sexual cannot be integrated into a maturational sequence was elegantly theorized, in my view, in the general theory of seduction.[24] While Freud reframed the seduction theory by inserting it into the general sexual theory of the *Three Essays*, as we have seen, Laplanche proposes neither a return to the original theory of seduction nor a mere reframing of it. His is actually a *generalized* conception of seduction, a seduction occurring within the most ordinary adult-infant relationship (although it can of course give way to severely pathogenic variants).

Although Laplanche's conception is compatible with Freud's ancillary use of seduction within the new framework of the *Three Essays*, it is much more comprehensive and actually reverses the order of events. Seduction, in Laplanche's theory, does not merely *elicit* an inborn sexual potential; it is the process by which the Sexual is actually *implanted* in the infant's psychobiological apparatus.[25]

---

24 Jean Laplanche, *New Foundations for Psychoanalysis*, trans. Jonathan House (New York: The Unconscious in Translation, 2016); see also chapter 1 above.

25 "Gender, Sex and the *Sexual*," in *Freud and the Sexual: Essays 2000–2006*, trans. John Fletcher, Jonathan House, and Nicholas Ray (New York: International Psychoanalytic Books, 2011).

Ordinary bodily care, identified by Freud as a way of "awakening" the sexual drives, is for Laplanche but one instance of the seductive process. The process of seduction is put in motion through the unconscious emission of enigmatic or compromised messages on the part of the adult—compromised, that is, by the adult's own repressed sexual unconscious.

Laplanche theorizes that, while attachment is a normal biological or ethological phenomenon, it also serves as the carrier wave for what emanates from the adult's unconscious desires and fantasies, and it necessarily affects the child, a child who is unable to integrate the compromised part of the message for lack of a proper code of translation. The child's limitations in that respect are due to what Laplanche calls the "fundamental anthropological situation" into which each of us is born.[26] This situation is marked by the unavoidable discrepancy between the adult and the child in terms of psychosexual constitution. Regardless of the adult's efforts to adapt as completely as possible to the infant's needs, there is indeed one domain that escapes such seemingly preprogrammed adjustment, and this is the sexual domain.

The adult's world, into which the child is born, is therefore replete with sexual facts and meanings that may not be conscious for adults themselves. The child, at every stage of their progress toward maturity, is unavoidably confronted by these, which for the child represent a mostly enigmatic reality—a noise, as it were, in the otherwise clear channels of communication and of mutual adjustment with caregivers.

It follows that, for Laplanche, there is no inborn unconscious; the unconscious is *constituted* through the mechanisms activated by the sexual gradient existing between adult and child. The enigma conveyed in the adult's communication is in itself seductive and

---

26 *New Foundations for Psychoanalysis.*

triggers a response in the infant that will initiate the psychic scission, producing the system unconscious (primal repression). The mechanism for this psychic split is simply the child's own effort to *translate* the enigmatic message.

It is worth noticing that, in proposing a "translational" mode of functioning for the psychic apparatus, Laplanche was inspired by none other than Freud himself and more precisely by Freud's letter to Fliess of December 6, 1896, in which memory traces—that is, the traces left by perception—are described as undergoing a series of successive transcriptions or translations, with *repression* being defined as a failure occurring in one of these translations or transcriptions.[27] For Laplanche, this primal repression, this partially failed translation, accounts for the split between a "translated" and therefore integrative element of the child's psyche that produces the kernels of the ego and the untranslatable residues that install the nuclei of the unconscious, dubbed "source-objects"—sources of the sexual drives[28]. So the structuring of the mind and the differentiation between psychic agencies are the result of the translational mind affected by seduction.

One can see how Laplanche's theory expands and at the same time remains firmly connected to Freud's views in the *Three Essays*. We have indeed seen the sexual being conceived by Freud as inherently perverse. In Laplanche, what the ordinary mother or caregiving adult cannot integrate into an otherwise well-enough-adapted relationship is this inherently perverse—hence, repressed—side of their sexual complexion. And this is also what the child cannot adequately translate and integrate. The infant's efforts at translating the enigmatic part of the adult's message—

---

27 Freud to Wilhelm Fliess, December 6, 1896, 264-266.

28 Laplanche, J. (1984) The Drive and its Source-Object: its Fate in the Transference, in *The Unfinished Copernican Revolution, Selected Works, 1967–1992*. New York : The Unconscious in Translation, 2020, p. 293-311.

that is, at making sense of and integrating it into an ego-centered area of meaning—are therefore doomed to fail, at least in part.

It follows that "sexual" and "repressed" actually refer to one and the same thing when it comes to the enigmatic or compromised character of the messages that flow from adult to infant or child. Children can adjust to almost everything that the ordinarily devoted mother is capable of offering, but children have no way of responding appropriately to what affects them in the sexually enigmatic or compromised part of the communication, nor will development allow for a final adjustment to this discrepancy. When biological sexual maturation arrives at puberty, the infantile Sexual will have long since set up occupancy on the premises, so to speak, so that puberty brings only an additional impetus to what was already implanted and was always already "deviated" from the biologically adaptive aims of sexuality.

Positing that this deviation is already present in the adult, one could ask whether we are not dealing here with a case of infinite regress: deviation implanting deviation, with no idea of where or when the deviation originally began. Laplanche avoids this logical trap by arguing that what is implanted in the child's psyche is not the adult's unconscious sexual phantasm itself; for Laplanche, there is no direct transmission form the adult's unconscious to the infant's. Something in the adult's message affects the child, but the child is ultimately solely responsible for the progressive structuring of their internal fantasy world through their own work of translation. The templates for the fantasies under discussion are found by the child translator in the child's own bodily experiences—giving way to the various infantile sexual theories—and in the basin of mytho-symbolic expressions and representations provided by cultural surroundings, elements that each individual child will use in an idiopathic way.

The Sexual in Psychoanalysis

We have seen that in the *Three Essays*, Freud begins by dismantling the idea of a normative sexual constitution in the human being. Yet in the third essay, he seems to reinstate a normative view when introducing the changes brought about by puberty. We get a sense that, in the end, Freud reconnects with a kind of natural "master plan" that must ultimately lead to the primacy of genital sex.

The return of the apparently normative instinct in the third essay is in a way inevitable after the fragmentation of the Sexual performed in the first two parts. Freud's writing, too, after all, is subject to the unifying work of Eros, whose role is to unite, to create larger and unified structures after the disjunctive consequences of analysis. When we think about it, isn't this also the actual movement of every analysis? We dare analyze inasmuch as we know that eventually the patient's psyche will do the work of recomposing, hopefully achieving a new, more flexible, and more inclusive synthesis.

In the *Three Essays* as in psychoanalytic practice, therefore, what matters is that there was an *analytic moment* that disentangled the knots to allow for a more favorable rearrangement. The question, of course, is whether this better rearrangement actually occurred in the *Three Essays* or if the analysis of sexuality operated by Freud simply had no effect whatsoever against the popular view that he had criticized in the first pages of the book. The answer is clear. While the last essay may seem less analytical and more normative than the first two, the *Three Essays* as a whole has created an irreversible change in our way of thinking about human sexuality. Reading the essays as a unit and from up close, we undoubtedly obtain a new way of understanding the role of the Sexual in psychoanalytic thinking and practice.

The reading of the *Three Essays* that I have been doing here implies an idea of the Sexual that is specific to and foundational for psychoanalysis. Our discipline has often been blamed for its so-called pansexualism, accused of explaining everything solely by the sexual factor. And this criticism has come not only from the outside; it has also flared within our own ranks, as mentioned in my opening remarks, giving way to harsh debates—and even to theoretical and sometimes organizational splits. Such criticism, however, is deserved only to the extent that we conceive of the Sexual in psychoanalysis as something to which nonsexual elements can be brought back or reduced. Now, this is precisely the idea that my reading of the *Three Essays* incites me to revoke.

We have witnessed, in the first and second essays, the extension and *generalization* of the notion of sexuality. The question now becomes: What can be made of such generalization? In my opinion, it does not amount to saying that everything is driven by sex in the same way one would say, for instance, that politics are driven by money—that is, by one factor that takes precedence over other, possibly legitimate factors. The sexual dimension in psychoanalysis is not something that must be adjoined, put in competition with, or substituted for other, nonsexual factors. I wish to insist that the Sexual, in the psychoanalytic sense, is inextricably woven into the very fabric of the repressed unconscious and, in fact, into everything specifically human.

Laplanche once wrote that the pansexualism of psychoanalysis comes down to this: not everything human is sexual, but the Sexual is in everything human. As he put it, *"Pansexualism is a state and a movement of human reality before being an aberration attributed to Freud."*[29] Obviously, I am not arguing that this is also what Freud explicitly had in mind while writing the *Three Essays*. What I have been doing here is combining Freud's generalization of human sexuality with the consequences of Laplanche's general theory of seduction. The former states that many more things are sexual in human affairs than is usually thought; the latter asserts that,

---

29 · Jean Laplanche, *Nouveaux fondements pour la psychanalyse* (Paris: Presses Universitaires de France, 1987), 63; my translation; italics in original.

in human communication, the "noise" produced by the sexual contaminant in the adult's messages received by the infant has a decisive consequence—the creation of a repressed unconscious. The two ideas combined mean that psychoanalysis is primarily concerned with the Sexual as the specific anthropological dimension in which the human psyche is constantly bathing.

The human psyche swims or drowns in a sexual sea. It is because of the sexual incongruence occurring in the otherwise well-adjusted relationship between child and caregiver that a repressed unconscious is formed at some point during infancy. As a result, there is no need to look for a *sexual meaning* of psychic productions. It would be more appropriate to say that everything in the psyche has a *sexual lining*, so to speak, a character that is sexual in the extended sense proposed by Freud. The Sexual in the psychoanalytic sense is thus like the air we breathe; it is so omnipresent that one loses awareness that it infiltrates everything human—and is therefore also part of whatever has to do with the repressed unconscious. This means that what we need to do in analysis is not to discover hidden sexual meanings but to uncover the personal equation by which individual analysands deals with their sexual complexions.

To go back to the example of Dora: It was certainly a progressive step in our knowledge when Freud was able to understand the sexual meaning of Dora's cough or of her rhythmic insertion of her finger into her purse. This provided material in support of his discovery that what mattered in neurosis was the Sexual. But that was only a preliminary step: the crux of the matter, which Freud himself did not clearly understand at the time, was Dora's *disposition* and *attitude* toward the sexual demands that were made on her—in her childhood as much as during her adolescence—an attitude that Dora eventually reproduced in the transference, a reproduction that eluded Freud's grasp.[30]

---

30 Freud (1905) *op. cit.*

This is where we stand now: Having benefited from Freud's early discoveries and from his later understanding of what goes on in the transference, we no longer have a need for proof of the sexual meaning of symptoms, dreams, slips of the tongue, and so forth. Our task is rather to help analysands bring to light how they have been responding to the sexual enigma of the other and how this response has led them to the existential or symptomatic impasse that motivated the analysis. By analyzing (decomposing) an analysand's personal equation concerning the impact of the other, the analytic process allows a new configuration to emerge, which is elaborated in the course of analysis itself through the living experience of the transference. Let me note in passing (although I cannot go into it deeply here) that this way of conceiving and of clinically utilizing the psychoanalytic theory of drives is quite . . . relational.

For lack of a clear distinction between, on the one hand, the discovery and generalization of the Sexual in psychoanalysis and, on the other hand, its use in understanding and treating our patients, we expend much ink and much saliva in discussing whether this or that has a sexual meaning or if it has instead an aggressive meaning, and so on. And it has become a sort of dogma to see today's psychopathology as having little to do with the sexual "complexes" described in Freud's time. I believe that this kind of divergence is pointless if we think of human relations as intrinsically sexual in the generalized sense discovered by Freud and if we situate them within the framework of the fundamental anthropological situation in which, according to Laplanche, generalized—or for that matter perverse—seduction occurs.

Discovering a sexual meaning in a symptom has little or no effect, and in the framework that I am proposing here, it has little or no relevance either. Yet the Sexual remains what the analysand has been defending against. The predicaments in which our patients find themselves are the results of the responses that they were able to formulate to the enigmatic messages of the other. Obviously, there are all sorts of possible responses, and there are perverse and destructive variants of seduction, leading to severe psychopathology. This leads me to observe, however, that there is no reason to distinguishing pathologies related to the Sexual from others supposedly not related to it. The scripts guiding individual responses—at least if we consider their most psychically elaborate forms—are manifestations of the infantile sexual theories that psychoanalysis uncovers *in the minds of analysands*.[31] These infantile theories are therefore a result of the impact of the "transcendent," "aphasic" Sexual—the infantile in the sense of that which does not evolve (the "big" infantile)—and they should not be mistaken for psychoanalytic sexual theory itself.

---

31 This is not the place to discuss forms of pathology resulting from an inability to develop working infantile theories or other sorts of failures in the psychic response to perverse or violent seduction.

Conversation

AS: This is a remarkable essay for neophytes and experienced analysts alike because it touches on some aspects of Freud's *Three Essays* that are really hard to grasp. And it flings open the doors to so much! My plan for our conversation today has, thus, multiple goals: I want to clarify some of your ideas, to ask you questions about places where I might be too quick to think I know what you mean and risk missing your points, and to try, as much as I can, to anticipate where analysts of different theoretical affiliations might have inquired for clarification or challenged you. Last, one of the things I am often struck by in your writing is that you make some brilliant points quite modestly, without emphasizing how consequential (and exciting!) their ramifications might be. So I am especially eager to slow us down around those nodes to mark and briefly think through some of their implications.

Let me start with a bird's-eye view of sorts. One of your main goals in this essay is to flesh out that the infantile Sexual is ontologically immature and that its immaturity does not index pathology or developmental arrest. To explain to us why that is the case, you call on the distinction between the actual infant and the *infans*. And, also, you draw on the condition of aphasia to highlight that the *infans* is speechless not because they predate language acquisition (a developmental factor) but because their speechlessness has to do with the very process by which the unconscious gets instituted: as precisely that which escapes transcription. Through the fundamental anthropological situation (FAS), the infantile is installed in us as that which cannot speak — and which, to some degree, will never speak.

DS: You understand correctly, and you highlight a central aspect of the paper, though I don't know if I would use the term "immature," because it seems to point to a defect that maturation is called to correct. Perhaps we could agree that the infantile is "nonmaturational"? Whatever term we use, this is an idea that was brought into daylight by my colleague Jean Imbeault (whom I cite in the paper), an idea that clarifies so much in terms of what we are looking at and that relegates pathology not to the infantile Sexual itself but to the subject's difficulty evolving by, say, building around it through various maturational processes of the personality. These processes, however, do not exhaust the energy of infantile sexuality itself.

AS: When you say "evolving," I imagine you are referring to the energy of the infantile Sexual becoming bound by being coated in some representational form. Is that correct? If so, how does the maturational process fit into that? I am asking because Laplanche's theory is not an attachment theory, nor is it a biological one—and yet he denies the role of neither attachment nor biology. It might be helpful, then, if you could explain to us if by "maturational processes" you are referring to either of these and, if so, how.

DS: Yes, as the subject evolves the energy is bound in the sense that a link is created between the Sexual and a number of representations that give it a certain "coating." This representational cover is what matures. It does so through learning—that is, attaching new and more elaborate forms to the always-more-complex situations encountered as the child grows up. For all we know, though, the core element, that which we call the repressed Sexual or the infantile, does not evolve or mature. This is how we account for the basic irresolvable conflictuality in human beings. But I find it useful to remind myself from time to time that what we separate in theory is a single process in real life. So we could say that what we call attachment is the aspect of the adult-child relationship that displays a maturational process, but looking at it that way, we risk missing the nonevolutive Sexual, until, that is, we examine things from up close with the analytic tools.

AS: In theorizing the infantile, you write that the term "can just as well be used to refer to the unconscious as a system—that is, not simply what is not conscious, but also that which is not capable of becoming conscious until the words to say it are found." After this statement, you refer readers to Marie Cardinal's book *The Words to Say It*, a novel well known in Europe but perhaps not as familiar to readers elsewhere. To summarize, in this novel, which is autobiographical, Cardinal recounts her analytic journey with Michel de M'Uzan: she starts out with a medically inexplicable somatic symptom (profuse menstrual bleeding), and we observe the tedious psychic work involved in her processing of her early sexual abuse. I read this book as a teenager and remember marveling at the notion that words could be found to say unsayable things. But as an analyst, and especially as someone influenced by Laplanche, I am uncertain if I am reading you correctly as saying that the words to say "it" can always be found. Doesn't the very nature of the infantile imply that words cannot always say "it"?

DS: Absolutely. This is why I used the expression "building around it." I believe indeed that, as can be seen in Freud in many guises, there is a generic structure of psychic reality made of an "actual" kernel or "thing"—foreign to representation, let alone to discourse—and a representational envelope that is wrapped around that kernel or "soldered" to it, as Freud says somewhere about the meaning of Dora's symptoms.[32] The importance of finding the words is not diminished by this, but we must accept that the best we can hope for involves at least two components: first, finding optimal *forms* capable of channeling and dissipating the energy of the "thing" into representations, fantasy scenarios, and ultimately discourse; second, a capacity of these forms to evolve, to be revised as new situations may require. Pathology is a fixation on one or a few immovable forms.

AS: What are we left with, then, when we are not in the province of words?

---

32 *SE* 7:41.

DS: Well, the forms can be many. Closer to the kernel and besides the discovery of discursive forms (i.e., transduction and translation), there are "seeds of affect" that Michel de M'Uzan discovered in Freud's writings;[33] these will develop concurrently and may or may not be attuned to discourse. It is a common experience that affects exceed the capacity of words to "say" them. Affects can be so overwhelming as to drive the subject to discharge them by the shortest route, be it a muscular, motor discharge, as in acting (*Agieren* in Freud's language), or an internal discharge, such as the somatization you recalled in Marie Cardinal's case. Fortunately, there are other channels, such as those afforded by sublimation: creative expressions in crafts and in the arts, to name the most obvious ones. Literature is a special case in that it pertains to the domain of words but not in the same way as ordinary discourse: literature, I believe, is what it is because it captures and conveys much more that ordinary discourse ever could, by finding forms that transcend the words or the phrases themselves.

AS: These are indeed quite different domains. Poetry comes to mind as a version of literature where we see especially clearly the distinction between words and ordinary discourse.

I have heard you say explicitly—and we'll encounter this assertion again shortly—that Laplanche's theory is not a developmental one. The infantile Sexual's nonmaturational quality is partly the reason, in that we never quite outgrow infantile sexuality's grasp on us. Nor can interpretation in the analytic context or self-understanding exhaustively account for the infantile so that it may be eliminated or entirely processed.

By saying that this is not a developmental theory, you are referring, I believe, not only to the fact that the infantile Sexual never matures but also, perhaps, to the notion that implantation

---

33 "Affect et processus d'affectation," in *De l'art à la mort*, Collection Tel 84; Paris: Gallimard, 1977 (my translation).

is not a chronologically fixed process either—that is, as Homay King also points out, it does not happen just in childhood, settling our subjectivation once and for all, but it continues throughout our life-span.[34] Do I understand that correctly? If so, I have a question to ask: In infancy it is the asymmetry between the adult's sexual unconscious and the infant's radical helplessness that accounts for the enigmatic surfeit of the message and its implantative impact on the receiver. What would the equivalent be for an adult on the receiving end of an implantation, since the adult already possesses a sexual unconscious?

DS: You have well summarized the reasons Laplanche's theory is not developmental. But I believe your question is all the more important because it invites an additional distinction that I will address in a minute. First, I want to acquiesce to your summary by underlining the fact that if seduction were a one-time, chronologically fixed event, psychoanalysis would not be possible. The analytic setting, indeed, is precisely a reopening of the fundamental anthropological situation (FAS) that we have already mentioned. The asymmetry within the analytic dyad recaps the one encountered in the FAS, which, it must be stressed, pertains not to chronological time but to the category of the *primal (originaire)*. The primal designates not a beginning or a first occurrence but something that is always present, or "actual," as I often say. As Laplanche insisted, the analytic setting (and we could perhaps add the analyst's desire to analyze, though Laplanche does not put it in those terms) operates a seduction that provokes the analysand's transference. And by the way, seduction of the generalized kind is present wherever an asymmetry exists between two persons, inducing transference: doctor and patient, professor and student, priest and parishioner, tennis coach and tennis trainee, and so forth. The difference is that outside psychoanalysis such inherent

---

34 *Lost in Translation: Orientalism, Cinema, and the Enigmatic Signifier* (Durham, NC: Duke University Press, 2010).

seduction and the transference that ensues are not noticed and not put to any use (except, perhaps, by a psychoanalytically informed physician or in the service of abuse).

The distinction your question invites me to make, which had never crossed my mind before, is that perhaps we could say that, yes, *seduction* is happening all the time when a situation akin to the FAS exists but that the *implantation* of the Sexual could be dated back to the chronological time we call infancy. As you may notice, I say "perhaps" and "could," because I never thought of this before, and I don't remember having seen this in Laplanche, so I need to think it over. But I can already see that a strong caveat is in order, because this issue is quite complex. It is indeed reasonable to posit that implantation occurs in discrete, potentially datable events. But what is implanted, as indicated above, possesses a peculiar time dimension: it belongs to the primal, which must be distinguished from the primary and even more so from the idea of a chronological first time. Because of what is implanted—the Sexual—the infant's mind cannot fully process the message of the other, and the part that cannot be transduced/translated (i.e., that which is repressed) does not enter the flow of time. Hence, there is a sort of transcendence of the Sexual, which I described in a paper of some twenty years ago as operating simultaneously within and outside of chronology. At the time I compared it to the transmission of the leaven in the artisanal process of baking bread: every baking was a datable event, but there was a part of the dough that never ended up being baked, because it was put aside to become the sourdough for the next baker. Using this analogy, we could say that every implantation could, in principle, be dated but that what is implanted never itself enters the flow of chronology.[35]

---

35 Scarfone, "Sexual and Actual." DS: Here is the full discussion of that analogy in the paper:

In some villages of southern Italy, before the "economic miracle" of the second half of the 20th century, but also during part of it, women used to bake their bread in the communal oven, a wood-burning oven that was heated from the inside by

The immediate usefulness I see in the distinction we came across is that it helps answer the last part of your question, when you ask: "What would the equivalent be for an adult on the receiving end of an implantation, since the adult already possesses a sexual unconscious?" I would be tempted to say that the presence of a sexual unconscious implies that the Sexual was indeed already *implanted*; hence, we could say it needs not be reimplanted. Implantation is what causes the primal split in the psyche, resulting in the ego-unconscious duality and the "commerce," as Freud

---

setting fire to some branches. Once the fire was consumed, the ashes were removed and the burning slabs that formed the floor of the oven were quickly washed, and the loaves of bread that the housewife had prepared at home were placed to bake. I describe all this not without thinking of the quantity of associations that come to mind and which undoubtedly belong to the inventive and playful domain to which the analytic conception of infantile sexuality refers. No doubt any child in the village could be provoked to fantasize by the vision of this bulging belly (the oven was a kind of dome) which was the exclusive business of the women and inside which burned a fire which, once extinguished, made it possible to "grow" the breads that these women had previously kneaded in the privacy of their home. However, to illustrate the notion of "the actual," I wish to dwell on another aspect of this story of bread, though aware of the limits of any metaphor when it comes to speaking about a subject as difficult as the primal (*originaire*). This other aspect is that of the leaven. The successive productions of bread made by the women of the village always had a link between them: she who had just kneaded her dough would obligatorily put aside a part of it, which she did not make rise, but which she let sour under the shelter of a vine leaf, then passed on to a neighbor, a relative or friend who would use it as leaven for the making of bread the next day; the neighbor, in turn, would leave a part aside for sourdough. . . . In short, there was a part of what belonged to the most ordinary activity that never reached the end of its normal course, but remained as a germinative residue, destined to "contaminate" the dough of the next kneading. So, this part circulated ceaselessly, from hand to hand, without the chain ever breaking.

Interestingly, when the women of this village were asked about the origin of the first piece of sourdough, they answered with a myth: In times immemorial, women did not know how to make bread rise and therefore had to rely on the Sibyl who jealously guarded the secret. But one day a young girl named Maria (some women said it was the Holy Virgin herself), whom her mother had sent to buy a loaf of bread, found the Sibyl kneading the dough. So when she absent-mindedly left her kneading to go and get the loaf to sell, Maria swiftly dropped a piece of the dough under the table on which the Sibyl was kneading. Later, during night-time, she went back and recovered the dropped part. This stolen piece of dough would henceforth circulate indefinitely among the women.

would say, between the two, with its intermediate formations such as fantasies, the ulterior differentiation of the agencies, and so on. So in the adult, its work is done and has had irreversible consequences. What the reopening of the FAS operates then is perhaps not a new implantation but certainly a renewed seduction creating turbulence at the borders between the psychic agencies, a stirring or reawakening, as it were, of the primal processes of transduction/translation. This, by the way, also implies that the analytic process, in which *detranslation* occurs, actually challenges and even disrupts to a certain extent the borders in question, forcing the psyche into recomposing itself and, in so doing, eventually finding new forms.

AS: You are suggesting that the reopening operates on the site of the original implantation, as opposed to its being a new seduction itself that is freshly implanted. In that sense, the reopening would work mostly by scratching at the scab of the wound of implantation, would it not? I am kind of stumbling over my words here because, if this is the case, I would personally be hesitant to think of it as a reopening; a reopening implies a closure that gets opened up again, while implantation refers to something being " 'stuck' in the envelope of the ego like a splinter in the skin"[36] — which means that the wound never quite closes.

DS: I am saying that the reopening exerts a new seduction but based on the grounds of the *primal* implantation. To be more precise, we could let go of the spatial metaphor of site or grounds and bring up another temporal feature: that of *après-coup*. Implantation is the first "blow" (*coup*), and the reopening of the FAS is one of the many "after-blows" ("after-blow" being the literal translation of *après-coup*). Each new "blow" reopens the FAS; it may be felt as genuinely new, but it resonates with the preexisting blows in an unending spiral reinstating the *difference* that was created by implantation.

---

36 Jean Laplanche, "Masochism and the general theory of seduction," trans. Luke Thurston, in *Essays on Otherness*, ed. John Fletcher (London: Routledge, 1999), 209.

But then, it is true that the term "reopening" suggests a previous closing of the wound. This, in a way, seems accurate if we think of the "Ptolemaic closure" of the ego, by which the ego becomes the experiential center of the subjective world. Except that this closure does not eliminate the implanted irritative spine. With the closure of the ego, the psyche encloses the "foreign body"—the Sexual—in a more structured manner. I mean by this that the durable investment (cathexis) of the ego forms a more or less coherent network, a pole of relative stability that "situates" and "engages" the chaotic unconscious within a permanent ego-unconscious conflictual relationship. In this, the unconscious remains the unconscious, of course, but it is not some general and vague domain of non-consciousness; through its conflictual polarization with the structured ego, it becomes the specific psychic reality of the individual.

AS: "Reopening," then, would be an "accurate" description of what happens in analysis but only if its seen from the viewpoint of the ego. The ego, that is, considers itself healed, restored to its original state, which it narcissistically understands as enclosed to begin with. Is that consistent with what you mean?

DS: Yes, it is consistent with the fact that once the ego exists as an agency, as a differentiated structure within the psyche, its first concern is defense, about how to perpetuate itself. This concern goes hand in hand with a self-mythification—that is, a narrative in which things were always what they are now, as if the ego has always existed. Now, this myth is possible because, as we know, the terms "ego" and "self" can designate the agency we are talking about, but they can also designate the whole organism, regardless of its subdivision into different agencies. This is yet another ambiguity of the human condition. So in a way, the sense of a reopening resonates with the retrospective sense of a lost unity.

AS: These are important clarifications and open up the way to thinking much more deeply about a consolidated sense of self not only as a way of feeling "at home" with oneself but also as an organized resistive network of sorts.

I want to turn now to your insistence that seduction, in the Laplanchean sense of the term, "does not merely *elicit* an inborn sexual potential" but is how the infantile Sexual is "actually *implanted* in the infant's psychobiological apparatus."[37] This statement cannot be repeated often enough, and it is what makes Laplanche's theory a very embodied one. But because the theory is highly abstract in its theorization of enigma, it can also come across as overly cerebral. Can you give an example or an illustration that can help us see the potential of the theory for thinking about embodiment?

DS: I am indeed often asked a question such as: Where is the body in Laplanche's theory? I believe the term "message" used in the general theory of seduction may seem to suggest that it is a question of semantic information or communication, hence a "cerebral" matter, as you say. In fact, it's quite the opposite, as I will now try to explain. The body is central to the process for many reasons, the first one being that the psyche we talk about is not synonymous with the intellect; it is the embodied psyche. Secondly, the "message" in the expressions "enigmatic message" or "compromised message" used by Laplanche is not necessarily verbal; actually, if we consider the mother-infant situation, we see that it is largely *nonverbal*.

Freud himself, in the *Three Essays*, recognizes that an involuntary seduction is operated by the mother merely attending to the child's bodily needs. From this *anecdotal* version of seduction, Freud, a few years later, postulated an inborn psychosexuality—that is, not only an excitable body, but a whole psychosexual *program* with phylogenetically inherited primal fantasies, and so forth.

---

37 See p. 79 above.

One root of that theoretical development is Freud's notion that the libido (a.k.a. the Sexual) emanates from the erogenous zones in the same manner as, say, bile is secreted by the liver. The mother is then seen as simply pulling the trigger, so to speak. While this has the merit of signaling that seduction occurs to a large extent through bodily contact, Laplanche makes things clearer by suggesting that the seductive function of these contacts is not mechanical. There is conscious and unconscious excitation, fantasy, desire on the adult's side; there is a special interest in the bodily areas that will be *defined* as erogenous zones by the very interest the adults show toward them and the somewhat "troubled" relation they have to them. I think here, for instance, of a mother who took every precaution to avoid touching her little boy's penis for fear of exciting him sexually, so she never washed it under the uncircumcised foreskin, which led to an infection and the need for medical attention. This example illustrates how without her touching her child's genitals, the mother's negative attention all the same delineated them as a special zone, loaded with enigmatic aspects going back to the mother's own fantasies about bodily contact. So the body is implicated even when one tries to avoid touching it!

I must stress that the compromised message theorized by Laplanche is not a cognitive phenomenon; what matters most is that it contains a sexual element that affects the child's body-psyche as a whole.

AS: This was a very succinct and clear explication of Freud's understanding of libido. Thank you for that!

What you say makes, in my mind, a significant intervention and issues a corrective to the notion of the message's excess. "Excess" is a term that Ruth Stein (2008) brought to her reading of Laplanche from her encounter with the work of the philosopher Georges Bataille. She used it to discuss the excess of excitation, the excess of the other, and the plenitudes more generally that accompany the asymmetry in the caretaker-child dyad. This reading has canonized, at least in North America, a particular reading of Laplanche: that the other's excess on us is, in some way, too much. Jonathan House has also noted that the other's "too little" can also be enigmatic and in that sense have an implantative effect.[38] Your example here underscores that even absence can implant enigma, without being excessive in and of itself.

DS: If we speak of "excess" conveyed by the message, it is always an excess in the sense of what the infant's psyche can translate, make sense of. The term says nothing about the intensity of the message or its positive (presence) or negative (absence) form. An absence, or a silence, or the like, is still a message in the sense I mentioned above: it affects the child all the same.

AS: That an absence involves an enigmatic dimension is an important point because it helps show us that the enigmatic surplus is not a "surplus" in the sense of an excess of something added—for example, the child who is purposefully starved by the mother is in lack, but wouldn't you say that too is a seduction of sorts? Though perhaps not in the usual way we think of "excess."

DS: Yes, exactly. . . . Perhaps you could call it a "negative seduction" but a seduction all the same in the sense that, in your example, the child is thrown out of the narcissistic bubble it should normally form with the mother in the attachment relationship and becomes the mother's part-object on which she exerts her sadistic impulses.

AS: There is a rather remarkable line in your essay that I think our readers may want to know more about. You track how Freud remained ambivalently attached to his theory of seduction long after he had (ostensibly) renounced it. You quote a passage from

---

38 "Après-Coup," in *The Unconscious: Contemporary Refractions in Psychoanalysis,* ed. Pascal Sauvayre and David Braucher, Psychoanalysis in a New Key (New York: Routledge, 2020).

the *Three Essays* where he writes that the fact that children can become polymorphously perverse under the influence of sexual abuse indicates that an aptitude for sexual irregularities is innate in their disposition. I know that you are not yourself inclined to think that our biological substrate fully determines psychic life and that you are more of the mind that the facts of organismic life become psychic by becoming subject to our own theorizing of ourselves. In thinking this through, you write that we can read Freud as saying, "Human beings are biologically predisposed to be influenced by cultural factors!"[39] This is a fascinating claim, especially at a time when so many analysts are working hard to think about how to theorize the way in which the social gets structuralized into the psyche. In some instances, those theorizations appear to me slabbed on, as if we could explain the complex imbrication of the psychic and the social by proposing that considerations of, say, race or ethnicity could just be layered atop an already theorized subject. However admirable the intent, I find such formulations to be somewhat impoverished efforts to account for how the cultural syndicates with the psychic. The notion that we are predisposed to be influenced by culture interests me as a possible pathway to addressing the complexity of their entwinement.

DS: To elaborate around on this idea, I'll need to make a long detour, which I believe is worth doing so as to give a fuller view of what is at stake. A quick response to your comment, however, would be that the psyche is always already social in that it exists as a system that has to interact with its surroundings—that is, with other systems, either with those at the same level of organization or with superordinate systems such as family, group, society. The primacy of the other—the fact that the individual enters a social environment from its birth—speaks of the social nature of the psyche as we study it psychoanalytically. The individual psyche

---

39 See p. 100-101 above.

and society as a whole belong to the same domain of meaning. Hence, the psychic is always social, and we could say that the social necessarily entails the psychic.

Obviously, the domain of meaning itself contains differences and contradictions. There would be no meaning without difference. For instance, when society establishes norms, these will eventually clash with the idea that the pregenital Sexual is always already perverse. A reading of the pregenital made from the social point of view will eventually clash with what we can say from a metapsychological point of view; but this clash is not different than the one between metapsychology and the point of view of the ego, which we could call a psycho-ideology.

Another aspect of the social nature of the psyche is that the social we speak of in this case is not the social of norms, governance, rules, and morality but the social in the sense of the presence of otherness in each individual, a social matrix resulting from the primacy of the other. So it's not a question of how to introduce the social into the individual. The social other is there from the start.

The claim, which we arrive at if we follow Freud's reasoning through to its logical conclusion, that "human beings are biologically predisposed to be influenced by cultural factors" is, of course, not a teleological one. Biology cannot be said to "predispose" humans to culture; it so happens that because of some fluke of evolution, humans found themselves to be cultural as much as biological beings. My statement is then somewhat ironic and intended to counter both the "everything biological" and the "everything cultural" views, both reductionistic in their own way. Rather than speaking of nature versus culture, I find myself ever more inclined to speak of *living systems* and more precisely autopoietic (self-creating) living systems theorized by Francisco Varela and the sociologist Niklas Luhmann.[40] The expression "living system" should not

---

40 Varela, *Principles of Biological Autonomy* (New York: North Holland, 1976);

be limited to strictly biological—that is, chemically structured—entities. It requires only that such a system be autonomous, which means possessing an "operational closure" that actively and constantly differentiates it from its environment, hence allowing it to function according to its internal laws. A system such as this can be one that is implemented biologically (e.g., a cell or a whole organism), socially (e.g., any human society), or psychically. As for the latter, Freud clearly had a something like this in mind for his "soul apparatus" (*Seelenapparat*) with the three-tiered model of conscious/preconscious/unconscious or the so-called "structural model" of id/ego/superego. Thus, he insisted that what is central to the unconscious system is not the lack of consciousness but its functioning in the primary process mode (i.e., its specific laws). But the model applies to the whole psyche as well, so that we have a complex psychic system with subsystems that interact with one another, one representing the environment for the another.

Thanks to the notion of a system/environment unit, we are not settling for a purely biological or a purely psychological or sociocultural conception; the biological body, the psyche, and human groups are all systems in their own right, and each can be looked at as an environment from the point of view of any of them. Hence, the somatic entity can be seen as an environment for the psyche, just as social groups are environments for the somatic bodies and the individual psyches, and within the psyche, the repressed is an environment for the ego, and so on. Saying this, I must immediately clarify one point: I am not speaking of concentric circles where, say, the unconscious is the center and the ego surrounds it, as we imagine when we say that we have to "dig deep" to reach unconscious material. The point where the whole somatopsychic organism meets the world of the other is a point where all the subsystems (ego, unconscious, soma) also meet.

Luhmann, *Introduction to Systems Theory*, trans. Peter Gilgen (Cambridge: Polity Press, 2013).

This is most important for the understanding of what happens in trauma, for instance. What indeed is traumatized? Is it the ego or the whole psyche? I would like as much as possible to do without diagrams, but this one may be useful in that it may make things easier to grasp:

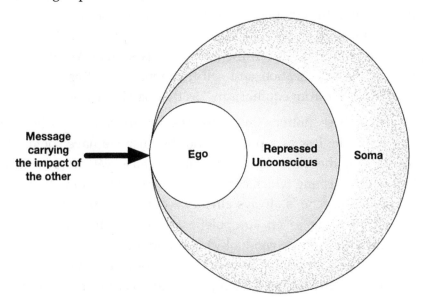

The diagram presents a somewhat differentiated apparatus in which the impact of the other operates at the point where every substructure of the psyche is reached. There is no way of affecting one element without also affecting the others. Note that in this diagram, unconscious refers strictly to the repressed unconscious and not the larger nonconscious domain.

A central idea in this way of looking at things is that the environment—the surrounding world that the system dwells in and feeds from—is also a threat to the system, unless a manner of "coupling" is found such as exists, for example, in the mother-infant relationship. No destructive intention is implied in this threat. The threat simply results from the fact that, left alone, the general entropic tendency in the universe would draw every system toward dissolving into its environment by abolishing the gradient between the two—a gradient that is actively maintained by the operational closure that works against the entropic tendency. This is true of the single biological cell with its membrane pumping electrolytes in and out of the cytoplasm, for instance, as it is of the ego actively maintaining its closure, its difference (or *différance* with an *a*, as Derrida would say) from the unconscious system. What matters then is the self-creation and self-maintenance of this difference, operating "far from equilibrium," as they say in thermodynamics.

With these notions in mind, the nature/culture dichotomy appears to be less of a problem, not because we have solved the mystery of the birth of culture, but because we don't need to bother establishing which came first, the individual or culture: the individual psyche is always already a cultural entity. The psyche came into being as an autopoietic system, as did societies and biological cells, so we can look at them not as hierarchical systems but as living systems that present to one another as environments— and thus potential threats—simply because each of them needs to be able to preserve its internal logic, which is by definition different. Still, for all its threatening difference, the environment is inseparable from the system and is necessary for the system's survival, hence the inherently conflictual relationship between them.

Going back to issue you raised, we see that the cultural environment is not superimposed or layered on the biological or the psychical; it is plainly a different system, yet interacting with the individual psyche as one of its environments, both nurturing it and threatening it, as we just saw.

AS: Your description in this essay of pathology as residing not in specific behaviors, fantasies, or actions but as being "a resistance to becoming" is extremely expansive and inspiring.[41] It is not directly put in conversation with Deleuze and Guatarri's notion of becoming, but it seems to me that there is a synergy between these ideas, especially because you offer us a refreshing angle from which to think, suggesting that it is the sclerotic ego, not the deviation from a norm itself, that should alert us to pathology. I am thinking about gender as an example—about how, for instance, even normative gender positions can become pathological if they become too rigid because of their very resistance to becoming; this is a position that feminist theory and trans studies have been arguing for a while, but it has not appeared in more Freudian psychoanalytic thinking. For example, masculinity that is rigidly defended against feminine strivings to the degree that it becomes a caricature of itself, or masculinity that too ardently tries to separate itself from anything that resembles the feminine would be pathological in your thinking. So toxic masculinity is pathological precisely because it's become too inflexible. Same with the sclerotic aspects of White domination, where lording over the non-White other becomes a cohering center to the White subject's psychic life to the point of pathology. I am curious what you think about this way of utilizing the attention you draw to "resistance to becoming."

DS: With the proviso that, as already mentioned, I borrowed this idea from Jean Imbeault's very useful distinction between the "small" and "big" modalities of the infantile, I think I can subscribe to the way you formulate things, though I would probably not use the term "pathological" when referring to social phenomena. If I can use one of your examples, when masculinity becomes a caricature of itself by way of too rigidly defending against the feminine, it is actually limiting its own experience, its own becoming, and hence its own liveliness. And given the sociopolitical context in which this happens today, it is literally "reactionary" in that it reacts to—and

---

41 See p. 78 above.

resists—both the evolution of society and that of the individual psyche. This immediately evokes for me another important point that I have touched on only in passing in my paper on subjectality:[42] that the sexual drive and the drive for mastery over the other (Freud's *Bemächtigungstrieb,* briefly discussed by him in the *Three Essays*) also are inseparable and are perhaps two sides of the same coin. In that sense, rigidified masculinity is also a masculinity stuck, so to speak, at the level of the phallic expression of the drive, unable to proceed from there to the discovery of the other as another subject. The other is therefore seen as merely the instrument at the service of one's power and enjoyment. The sexual drive and the narcissistic stance go, here, hand in hand, and the patriarchal status quo counts on this sexual/narcissistic duo to, among other things, maintain itself. In other words, the dominant ideology *selects* from the infantile theories within the individual psyche those that best serve its perpetuation (for example, the theory of phallic hegemony). The infantile theories are thus elevated to the dignity of social norms. Going back to the question of social versus individual, here is then one more reason why they need not be seen as layered: the individual psyche is as much the scene of social and ideological struggle as society is the scene for the struggle to get beyond the infantile.

This should serve as a cautionary tale: every one of us should beware that we should not conflate our infantile theories with the theory guiding the struggle at the social level. I mean by this that sclerosis can happen to any position that ends up being rigidified after having been revolutionary. I hear of instances of the same resistance to becoming when in the name of "diversity" we end up with the opposite—that is, a plethora of rigidly identitarian positions that seem to contradict both the idea of diversity and

---

42 AS: The reference here is to the essay "Trauma, Subjectivity and Subjectality," *American Journal of Psychoanalysis,* 81 (2021): p. 214–236.

the idea of "gender trouble," to quote a famous title.[43] Whatever the case, the central idea is indeed that the only norm from which pathology deviates is that of staying alive and hence of permanently becoming.

AS: In keeping with this point, in discussing the polymorphously perverse, you place your emphasis not on perversity but on *polymorphousness*. Pathology, you write, is a "fixation on a repetitive pregenital scenario."[44] I am with you on the matter of fixation (that is, on the idea that the absence of polymorphousness can be a problem), but why would "repetitive" and "pregenital" be the terms that are asked to carry the weight of pathology? For instance, in your own thinking, you speak of repetition as potentially being our greatest ally,[45] so why distinguish it here as the marker of something going awry? Are there, perhaps, specific kinds of repetitions you have in mind that you would single out as more likely to be problematic?

---

43 Judith Butler, *Gender Trouble: Feminism and the Subversion of Identity* (London: Routledge, 2006).

44 See p. 72 above.

45 Dominque Scarfone, "Repetition: Between Presence and Meaning," *Canadian Journal of Psychoanalysis* 19, no. 1 (2011): 70–86.

DS: I think that what you are highlighting with your question is the need to consider two types of repetition. Michel de M'Uzan distinguished between repetition of the same and repetition of the identical[46]. Repetition of the same could be figured in the form of a helicoidal movement, with each cycle of the helix presenting a similarity with the previous one but also a difference, as in this figure:

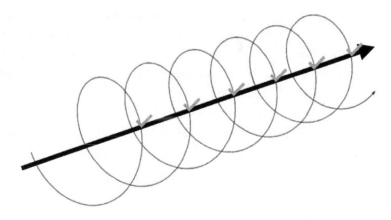

The marks on the helix indicate the crossing of a similar, though not identical, coordinate as the movement continues; there are cycles, to be sure, but within a movement forward (or upward), a becoming. Repetition of the identical would look more like a single vicious cycle with no progression in view.

AS: Are you saying then that as long as repetition is repetition of the same (allowing, that is, for some generative difference), repetition is welcome and that in the phrase "repetitive pregenital scenario," what concerns you is repetition of the identical? Is repetition of the identical ever possible, though? Don't all repetitions, to borrow Deleuze's terms,[47] repeat with a difference? Relatedly, I would

46 Michel de M'Uzan (2007) The same and the identical, *The Psychoanalytic Quarterly*, 76:4, 1205-1220.

47 Gilles Deleuze, *Difference and Repetition*, trans. Paul Patton (New York: Columbia University Press, 1994).

like to linger a moment longer on your formulation that pathology is a "fixation on a repetitive pregenital scenario" to ask why we would think of pregenitality as a problem. I am a bit surprised by that because the pregenital is also the source of multiplicity in your thinking, no? If so, why would it be listed on the side of the potentially pathological?

DS: You are right to ask about repetition of the identical. In a paper on repetition, I explained why, in my view, it is not possible.[48] But I consider it as an asymptotic reference point against which to think of the kind of repetition that, in contrast to repetition of the same, does not offer a perspective for change. But this actually rests on the analyst's passibility toward seeing difference. Yet in "fixation on a repetitive pregenital scenario," the key terms are "fixation" and "repetitive," not "pregenital." Pregenitality in itself, in its polymorphism, has nothing pathological in it. (We inherited the term from Freud's *Three Essays*, so it is difficult to shed it despite its implicit reference to "libidinal stages," which is not the way Laplanche or I use the term.) As discussed above, fixation—that is, the lack of evolution, of elaboration, and hence of openness to difference—and the squalid repetition of a petrified script is the problem. This brings back the question of *living versus inert* systems. The rigidly repetitive scenario is perhaps not totally inert, but it is certainly not full of life either. What is more, the requirements of rigid repetition cannot help but instrumentalize the other, encasing them in one's repetitive script, stifling their personality, their difference, and their own becoming.

AS: For Laplanche, attachment is the "carrier wave," as you have so beautifully described it,[49] on which the "noise" of the adult's infantile Sexual travels. Even though he is by no means an attachment theorist, this makes attachment relevant in his thinking.

---

48 Scarfone, "Repetition," 31–51.
49 See p. 80 above.

Still, his project is organized around an entirely different axis: not the order of self-preservation (in which attachment also belongs) but the evolutive—or nonevolutive—course of drive movements. Many analysts, however, who think from a developmental perspective worry that this minimizes the vicissitudes of the attachment relationship and their impact on the child. For instance, what about parental neglect? The ways in which parental trauma infiltrates the parent-child relationship unbeknownst to the parent? Or the question of how intergenerational trauma sediments in the infant, bypassing conscious registration as an "event"?

DS: Perhaps what is needed here is a renewed emphasis on what is meant by "message" and "the reality of the message." In Laplanche's thinking, a message is whatever signifies *to* someone. Early in his theorizing, Laplanche spoke of "enigmatic signifiers," an expression he later replaced with "enigmatic messages" and finally "compromised messages." All three expressions are acceptable but, in my opinion, not wholly synonymous. Indeed, the term "signifier" smacks too much of linguistics and what is more of Lacanian *linguisterie*, therefore exposing the theory to being labeled "cerebral," as we discussed above. Then the term "enigmatic" also poses a certain problem that made Laplanche always have to add that the message is enigmatic also for the emitter (the adult in the infant's case). The notion of enigma summons up the idea that there is a key to it, a solution that needs only to be found, whereas the idea is really that there is "noise" in the channel of communication. Hence my preference for "compromised," which speaks more to the fact that there is something in excess of adaptive communication, something that travels on the wave of open communication but challenges the receiver's capacity to make sense of it. I like "compromised" for another reason as well: in the optimal situation, the message's form and content is also "a compromise," as it were, between tender attachment and the manifestation of the Sexual.

In any case, the message carries *information*, but its "enigmatic" or "compromised" status makes it impossible to completely metabolize. If we stay firmly grounded on this notion of "message," it soon becomes clear that any parental difficulty with attachment, any occurrence of parental neglect, is also a message; the parent's absent-mindedness in the presence of the child sends a message, and this is all the more true in the case where the parent's struggle with their own traumatic experiences is responsible for such "absence". I would say that Laplanche's theory agrees with the basic idea that, in principle, you cannot not communicate. Hence, the difficulties in the process of attachment, far from representing an exception to the theory, are exemplary of what Laplanche means by a compromised message. The child, who cannot possibly understand what goes on in the parent's mind, since the parents themselves are not fully conscious of what they emit, is nevertheless impacted by the message and, even more so, by the "noise" surrounding the "signal" in the message. The situation gets still more complicated if we consider that the same parent is also the primary provider of the forms (linguistic, semiotic, or in some way expressive) with which the child will try to make sense of the murky message. As Piera Aulagnier has theorized, the transmission of these cultural elements carries a primal, unavoidable violence of its own, but the transmission can take the form of a secondary, excessive violence that imposes a strict code of translation[50]. Here again, this can be done positively or negatively—that is, either through the exertion a direct imposition of certain meanings or through the absence of certain elements that would be needed by the child to make its own translations. Though I am not an expert in the domain of transgenerational transmission, I think we have here some keys to understanding how it happens.

---

50 Piera Aulagnier, *The Violence of Interpretation. From Pictogram to Statement.* (Transl. Alan Sheridan), London, Routledge, 2001.

AS: There is so much here that I want to ask you about, but let me first say how important I find your reminder that Laplanche's notion of enigma does not operate on the model of a "puzzle," to use his term, as if a piece is missing that should—or could!—be filled in thereby completing the puzzle. And it makes me want to ask you about Aulagnier, about intergenerational transmission, and about the role of translation in all this. I thus hope you'll permit me to slow us down some.

Let me start with the question of where intergenerational transmission fits in Laplanche's theory, which is a question I find comes up often. Most frequently, I hear colleagues discuss it in the context of enigma, misreading enigma as carrying a meaning-ful trace of the generational past—say, the trauma of slavery—that is then transmitted from one unconscious (the adult's) to the other (the child's). Because trauma arrests representation and because of its monstrously upsetting nature, this line of reasoning goes, it can be transmitted only inchoately—not as content per se but as something that is not represented and yet sneaks into the child's psyche. How would you think about this kind of formulation?

DS: This question indeed comes up often. I can give only my personal view as I don't remember Laplanche addressing it in his writings. We can start from what I know for sure Laplanche would say, to which I subscribe: that there is no direct communication from unconscious to unconscious. The idea of direct communication is frequently invoked, and some even cite Freud's metaphor of the telephone to support it. But for one thing, a close reading of the telephone metaphor shows that Freud did not mean a direct transmission. The passage of Freud that is often cited in support of this idea is: "To put it in a formula: [the analyst] must turn his own unconscious like a receptive organ towards the transmitting unconscious of the patient. He must adjust himself to the patient as a telephone receiver is adjusted to the transmitting microphone."[51] But note that Freud immediately adds: "Just as the receiver *converts back* into sound waves the electric oscillations in the telephone line which were set up by sound waves, so the doctor's unconscious is able, *from the derivatives of the unconscious which are communicated to him*, to *reconstruct* that unconscious, *which has determined the patient's free associations*."[52] Hence, when he mentions that "the receiver *converts back* into sound waves the electric oscillations in the telephone line which were set up by sound waves," Freud is describing an actual example of transduction! There is converting and converting back; there is change of medium (sound waves to electric oscillations to sound waves). This is easily lost to view, I believe, because the reader represents themselves as one of the *persons* at either end of the telephone connection and forgets that Freud is saying that the analyst must "adjust himself . . . *as a telephone receiver*" and not as a telephone user. This may seem to be pushing the metaphor quite far, but I think it is important to read Freud carefully, especially since this passage is often quoted to invoke Freud's authority on the subject of direct transmission from one unconscious to another.

Having said this, let me now return to intergenerational transmission of trauma and hence of content. If anything of that sort is transmitted, it cannot happen directly via the "noise" in the message. Yet the noise is certainly modulated by what Laplanche calls the mytho-symbolic elements that the child finds in their surroundings—that is, in the culture in general and the parental subculture in particular: the words and phrases that are said in a certain tone, those that are omitted because of their emotional load, and so on. In this case we are talking about signifiers that populate the family's discourse, blanks included. I recently read an interview with a French novelist who recounted that he had started writing

---

51 "Recommendations to Physicians Practising Psycho-Analysis," *SE* 12:115–16.
52 *SE* 12:116; italics added.

poems at the age of six, and his poems were mainly about trains leaving.[53] At that age, he said, he was not aware of belonging to a Jewish family or that his grandparents had been deported by train and murdered in a Nazi death camp. I can only speculate here, of course, but I believe it is plausible that the signifier "train" was evoked more than once as he was growing up in his family but with a certain inflexion in the voices or with some elliptic expressions in order not to scare the child, strategies that nevertheless did attract the child's attention to it.

AS: So you are suggesting that "train," for this poet, was a signifier whose deep significance was unknown to him as a child but, nevertheless, circulated in the family and that the adults might have uttered the word in a fashion that in some inchoate way marked its significance in the family's history even as the family tried to cover it. To continue with my question about your thinking in relation to intergenerational transmission, if the mere utterance of the word "train" carries, unspoken, the horrific history of forcible deportations and death, couldn't it be said that the aura of the word conveys this information to the child? That the word "train" has, somehow, packed into it the history of Holocaust trains carrying people to their deaths? And if so, how would that not imply that the meaning of "train" is enigmatically conveyed *to* the child poet, even if in nonverbalized ways?

DS: I very much like the term "aura" that you introduce here. It reminds me of Walter Benjamin, who uses the word in his essay on "The Work of Art at the Time of Its Mechanical Reproduction."[54] Discussing Benjamin's use of the term would require a long digression, but let me try to say a few things in a concise way. Benjamin deplores that the massive reproduction of a work of

---

53 Interview with Ivan Jablonka, Le Monde, April 11, 2021.

54 In *Illuminations: Essays and Reflections*, ed. by Hannah Arendt (New York: Schocken Books, 1969), 217–51.

art deprives it of its "aura," which he at one point defines as "the unique phenomenon of a distance, however close it may be."[55] Now, this, I believe, applies to the type of aura you introduced in our discussion of transgenerational transmission. To say it in a simple way, and at the risk of oversimplification, the word "train" could have been repeated in innumerable ways in the family we are speculating about, yet it retained an unspoken reference to something both distant from and very close to home. We can imagine that it would still have been "loaded" with an energy that the child poet could obscurely *sense* but not *make sense of*. It was a live wire in the family narrative, even if, as we may suppose, the word could be spoken without constant awareness of the tragic story it referred to. Saying that it conveyed something enigmatic, therefore, needs some qualification. The word "train," obviously, has nothing enigmatic in it. It works as an index pointing at an untold (to the child) story whose affective charge could not but transpire, conveying a "something" that made of "train" a constant theme of the poems the child composed. To summarize: what makes the signifier "train" enigmatic is its "aura," which, in the *après-coup*, can be seen as an index of something "distant" (i.e., not easily reachable and translatable) and yet much "closer" than the child could suspect.

AS: This is delightful. Thank you! I appreciate you bringing in Walter Benjamin here, since when I used the word "aura," I wasn't thinking of it in that particular context. Your response makes me think about how he formulates his polemic about what is unique in original art as opposed to reproductions: what specifically furnishes the art with its aura, he writes, is its "presence in time and space," including the "changes which it [the art] may have suffered in physical condition over the years as well as the various changes in its ownership."[56] We may think, thus, that there is a

---

55 "Work of Art," 222.

56 Benjamin, "Work of Art," 220.

chain of custody, so to speak, in the aura that subtends the word "train" as it gets passed down through the generations, that this particular presence in time and space etches in it an originality that is nonreproducible. That, it seems to me, might be connected to what you are describing when you write that the untold story of the trains has a trail that follows the word. In that sense, not only does the word "train" haunt enigmatically, but also (bringing Benjamin and Laplanche together) the "aura" of the word train cannot be reproduced. The word can be, of course, repeated, but its "presence in time and space" and the condition it has suffered over the years cannot be explained to the child poet (or by the child poet to his analyst, if we imagine a clinical situation).

DS: What you are introducing is important in that it dispels any "mechanical" idea regarding the enigmatic message and its translation. The form in the overt message (e.g., "train") is obviously not just any form. It belongs to a large set of forms and signifiers that together weave a unique story, hence the aura. It is important to underline this fact, lest we end up believing that form is secondary. In a way, since the unconscious kernel itself cannot be grasped, all we have is forms. I would introduce here a notion upheld by Laurence Kahn who, in a book about analytic listening, begins by stating that form "is not a state separate from the act; it is the act. . . . It is that with which the analyst works."[57] I would combine this with what you say about the aura and suggest that the aura cannot be reproduced, because it is the very active element in the form.

AS: The distinction you draw between what the child poet may have *sensed* about the word "train" and what he would not have been able to *make sense of* is illuminating. From that perspective, the aura of the word "train" is what points to the something more and

---

57 L. Kahn, *L'écoute de l'analyste: De l'acte à la forme*, Paris: Presses Universitaires de France, 2012, p. 1 (my translation).

is, at the same time, an obstacle to further elaboration—because it has, as you said, nothing seemingly enigmatic about it. Is that a correct understanding of the distinction you draw?

DS: The signifier "train" is indeed both an index of something else and, secondarily, an obstacle. I say "secondarily" because it is not meant to be an obstacle. Like any other psychic representation, it both points at something and hides something. It is in the nature of representation to simultaneously represent and repress. This is a basic law of psychic functioning that we can draw from Freud's translational model of repression, which I've already referred to.

AS: This is a really important point—that representation both symbolizes and represses, both brings forth and, at the same time, obscures. It connects to the idea that every translation simultaneously occasions a repression. But the larger, bird's-eye-view kind of implication is that anything that is organized into psychically meaningful mental systems both conveys and works to obscure; and this notion, which you explore in greater depth in *The Unpast*, is especially important because it puts under pressure the conventional ways in which psychoanalysts emphasize understanding (of the patient, the dream, the symptom, genetic links, etc.) Your approach to representation stands to disabuse us of the notion that organizing meaning is an illuminative process, a process that reaches for a final clarity; in other words, it puts pressure on the notion that we can exhaustively understand a patient's symptom by tracing it, say, to the Oedipus complex or to x traumatic event.

DS: The psyche is a living system, always evolving, constantly enriched and modified by the ongoing experience of being alive. It follows that psychoanalysis—the discipline but also the individual treatment—is itself an open-ended venture; it is meant to untangle some knots that are impeding evolution and to let the life processes resume a freer course. For this reason, there can be no "final word" on anything. Searching for the ultimate explanation in analysis is not only a waste of time — as no ultimate explanation really exists — but also antithetical to the open-ended nature of psychoanalysis. I guess every analyst has experienced the fact that any construction that was reached at some point in analysis will be modified or even contradicted by something that shows up later in the process. This is not a problem; it does not point to a mistake or failure. It simply shows that the mind is alive and constantly recomposing itself. Obviously, discoveries are made in analysis; new and more encompassing views about one's life do emerge, but it would be a mistake to think that these are the truths the analysand should from then on cling to. Rather, the process is like moving from a tiny space to one that is bigger but a somewhat limited space nevertheless. The most important benefit of analysis is the regained capacity for movement, not reaching a final destination.

AS: Can we also switch gears for a moment to move to thinking about Ferenczi's work on the "confusion of tongues" that exists between the adult and what Laplanche, and you, have to say about it? I have in mind a brief clinical story to ground my question. For a few years, I worked in a maximum-security psychiatric facility treating adult sex offenders, including pedophiles. Some of them had been convicted of confirmed sex crimes against children, some in triple-digit numbers. They were held in a psychiatric facility (as opposed to serving a prison sentence) precisely because they had been found to have committed their crimes *on account of their psychiatric disturbance*. A patient I saw multiple times weekly for a while had the following theory about his behavior: He explained that his father was an alcoholic who had abused him and that he had been severely neglected by his mother. As a result, he felt, he never quite learned how to establish developmentally appropriate relationships, often finding himself in the company of minors whom he could easily impress — with his car, his record collection, and his clothes, all of which left his adult peers indifferent. But once he "befriended" these children, this man recounted, he'd lose track of "what's what" (that was his phrase), confusing the closeness he felt to them and the friendship they signaled to him with sexual attraction and invitation. This, according to him, was the point when he'd usually capsize the "friendship" into molestation. This hits all the Ferenczian marks: there is a confusion of tongues between adult and child as well as psychiatric pathology. And yet I never felt that his theory, which seemed reasonable enough to him, or his mental illness, from which he demonstrably suffered, fully explained what would come over him in the moment of the molestation. Unlike other patients I treated, he did not plan the abuse or groom his victims in the way that some pedophiles do.

So it seems reasonable, with Laplanche, to assume that the pregenital factor, the adult's own perversity, which is not ontologically pathological per se, was also at work here.

DS: Your example is a good case in point to illustrate how the seminal paper by Ferenczi requires some revision. It is a very rich paper in most of its components, and I make a constant reference to it in my understanding of what the term "trauma" refers to psychoanalytically. An important aspect, however, is surprisingly missed by Ferenczi regarding the etiology of the adult's behavior. Whereas his description is impressively rigorous and, I believe, speaks to every clinician, Ferenczi nevertheless falls back on an incidental or anecdotal form of causality when he invokes psychopathology or intoxication in the adult as the single element explaining abusive behavior. Certainly, psychopathology and/ or intoxication play a part, but what is it in the adult that takes advantage of this weakness in the ego and results in the abusive behavior? What is the drive involved if not the infantile Sexual itself? So we have here a confusion that is not merely at the level of how to interpret the signs; the confusion is also at the level of *what in the psyche is doing the interpreting*. I proposed two decades ago that we have here what I call a "Ferenczian chiasm," in the sense that on both sides of the abuser-abused dyad, it is the *infantile Sexual* (hence, the pregenital) that operates.[58] At the risk of oversimplifying, I would say that the abuser you describe is motivated by the same kind of drive that is at work in the child. Except that the child—inasmuch as it has not been already perverted—expresses the drive's momentum in terms of infantile sexual playfulness. As for the adult abuser, he is, as an adult, equipped with a biologically mature body, with hormones and all; the abuser is thus infantile in desire but adult in means. I can see how simplistic this may sound, given the numerous variables that enter the equation (personal history, family and social conditions, etc.), but I hope it helps clarify the issue.

More importantly, in my view, abusers make use of their victims, exploit them for their own enjoyment, instrumentalizing them and negating their status as subjects. The importance of this cannot be overstated, and by the way, this is what "pregenital" means in this context—not a developmental stage but a mode of relating to the object of one's desire in which the object in question is an instrument and not a subject. When interacting with a child subject, we need to consider that this is a subject who cannot interact sexually at the same level as an adult, because their infantile Sexual is not shrouded, so to speak, into the personal, more autonomous forms of being of an adult subject.

AS: In this way of thinking, though, what is it that distinguishes the adult whose perversity is not directed toward a child from the adult whose perversity victimizes a child? Don't we have to return to matters of pathology anyway to account for that distinction, which is what Ferenczi advised? And if so, why does it help us to keep in mind the adult's perversity as a normal part of the infantile Sexual if it is ultimately pathology that tips the scales toward a violation?

---

58 Scarfone, "Sexual and Actual."

DS: Let me say with other words what I tried to formulate in my previous reply. We should not think in terms of essence—normal essence, pathological essence. The pregenital Sexual is a dimension of the relation to the other. What seems the most important feature of the pregenital is that it is not addressed to another subject (as attachment behavior, for instance, is); the object of the pregenital is the part-object. A part-object need not be a part of the body (even though the concept was drawn from the idea that the child first relates to the breast, then to the whole mother). A part-object is an object solely meant to satisfy the drive. It is, one could say, a disposable object and not an object of love, if we agree that love means a durable relation. Hence, the perversity I refer to describes the sort of relationship established, its lack of mutuality, or, as I came to think of late, its lack of intersubjectality.

AS: When I read older work of mine, I sometimes find myself wishing I'd said something differently or wishing I'd understood something about my own thinking more deeply then. Of course, this is how thinking proceeds—not linearly but in a scrambled way. But it makes me want to ask you: This essay that we are discussing was written in 2014, which is not a very long time ago. In looking at this essay today, is there something that you would like to state differently or something you would like to edit?

DS: If I had a long time ahead of me and a greater power of concentration, I would probably rewrite all of my papers and books, even the most recent. I think I am not alone in seeing my own writing as work constantly in progress, without any formulation that I would carve in stone. This is why I enjoy so much the work we are presently doing together, the questions you ask me that require new thinking on my part. My wish is that my papers induce in readers a personal reflection, that they help them connect some dots differently. I am not, therefore, looking for the final word on anything, even if, of course, I hope I haven't written things that are totally mistaken. Just as I was going to answer this very question, I received an email from a colleague who had attended a weekend seminar organized around some of my papers. The email said that the discussion that followed had helped him make connections between two phases of his intellectual life that he had until then considered separate. This is certainly the kind of result I hope for in publishing my work.

You may have guessed by now that I am not inclined to reexamine this paper with the intent of rewriting it—not because I find it perfect but because it is not an element of some "master plan" into which a rewriting would make it fit better. The paper is what it is, warts and all, as they say. It was a paper that I was invited to write by the editors of the *Psychoanalytic Quarterly*, who wished to assess the relevance of the *Three Essays* one century later. Perhaps your question reflects that my motivation in writing it was not as "internal" as it was for other papers? I cannot say.

The Sexual and Psychical Reality

What place should we give the sexual drives in psychoanalysis today? Where is the sexual drive in the session, and what is its role? These are important questions, and I am grateful to the organizers for having asked me to address them[1].

What place indeed? Shall we put the sexual drives on an equal footing with other concepts, or shall we follow Freud, who conceived of psychoanalysis as a kind of building with repression as a main pillar? Opting for the latter view, we shall find that Freudian concepts come in clusters, and I'll address what, in my view, is the main cluster, containing repression—inseparable from translation, *Nachträglichkeit* (or *après-coup*), resistance, and transference—and having at its center the Sexual.

As we know, the original Freudian story about the Sexual was based on a misconstrued vision. Freud's initial empirical stance had led him to believe that all neurotics were once victims of infantile perverse seduction, a theory he was forced to abandon once he realized what difference runs between *material* and *psychical* reality. Like Columbus searching for a passage to India and encountering instead a new continent, Freud was looking for material, datable events but stumbled on sexual fantasies. But how to account for the fantasies themselves? Physicalist to the end, though recognizing psychical reality, Freud still searched for a material basis, if not

1 This paper was presented at the London meeting of July 2019 celebrating the 100th anniversary of the *International Journal of Psychoanalysis*.

in the individual history, then in the prehistory of the species. The irony is that his search for this bedrock led him to formulate a phylogenetic *fantasy* of his own—that of the primal horde. The presence and effectiveness of fantasies in psychic life was thus accounted for through an even wilder fantasy!

In spite of these inconsistencies, Freud's discovery of psychical reality was a true conquest whose importance did not escape a number of his followers. The psychoanalytic experience itself corroborates the central role of fantasies of a sexual nature—sexual in the expanded sense given by Freud to the German substantive *Sexual*. Actually, it is not a matter of mere expansion; we cannot simply put side by side the psychoanalytic Sexual and sexuality in general. What is at stake in psychopathology is not human sexual behavior itself but its unconscious underpinnings—that is, the Sexual as inextricably linked with, and marked by, repression.

The Sexual and the Psychoanalyst's Paradox

A paradox emerges here. Asserting the centrality of the Sexual and its repression does not entail that the Sexual is the interpretative key to everything a patient brings to the session. Psychoanalysis would appear to have a monomaniac's obsession if the Sexual were constantly the focus of our clinical endeavor. In fact, the analyst's natural avoidance of the Sexual is predicted by the theory of repression; and, mind you, the theory's own drifting away from the Sexual, as witnessed in many psychoanalytic schools today, is also predicted by the translational model of repression (to which we'll turn shortly). Theory, indeed, is itself a result of the central mechanism of repression/translation of the Sexual. The psyche's own well-differentiated structure, along with its theories, has its raison d'être in the resistance it opposes to the flow of the sexual drives. This may seem a vertiginous view of our discipline, but in what follows I hope to spare us the dizziness that might come with it.

While not everything is sexual, it matters to consider that the Sexual is present in everything human. The Sexual's place and role sink deep into the conception of how humans get on with their lives. Hence, tough psychoanalysis is *not* a theory *of* sexuality; it is a praxis concerned with the human psyche as it is determined, motivated, disturbed, impinged on, and elated by the Sexual.

For clarity's sake, let me propose a few terminological conventions:

- "Sexuality" refers to a set of observable human sexual behaviors; it is what sexologists study.

- "The Sexual" is the term I use, after Laplanche,[2] to designate the Freudian domain of sexuality, not sexuality in general or genital sexuality, but infantile sexuality or "the infantile."

- The term "infantile" in "infantile sexuality" does not so much refer to the epoch of its burgeoning as to the *state* of "infancy" it is in, the *in-fans* being, literally, a subject lost for words—not simply for not yet being able to talk, but also for lacking the very "code," as it were, for interpreting and integrating the Sexual.

The distinctions in these definitions parallel the path trod by Freud from the empirical domain to psychoanalytic theory and praxis. Approaching the Sexual at the empirical level, Freud collected stories of sexual abuse from his neurotic patients. This culminated in the theory of seduction of 1896, which he secretly repudiated one year later, putting his best hopes in the study of dreams, thanks to which he would discover psychical reality. It is commonly held that psychoanalysis was truly born out of this dramatic leap. Yet, even as Freud met psychical reality in dreams and fantasy life, his

---

2 *Freud and the Sexual: Essays 2000–2006*, trans. John Fletcher, Jonathan House, and Nicholas Ray (New York: International Psychoanalytic Books, 2011).

clinical accounts show that he remained passionately in search of material reality—that is, of actual traumatic events. Obviously, actual sexual abuses do happen and do matter. The problem, however, is that empirical facts may dazzle the psychoanalyst and blur the conceptual status of what he or she is after. Indeed, sexual abuse does not directly *explain* pathology; it is a traumatic process *itself in need of an explanation*—a metapsychological one. This is what the abandoned theory of seduction had attempted but failed to achieve. We are now in a position to say that this failure had to do with the lack, at the time, of the concept of psychical reality. In a way, Freud was already in possession of the general idea of it in 1895—though not under the name "psychical reality"— in his "Project for a Scientific Psychology." The seeds of psychical reality are present in what Freud then conceived of as the memory traces of the traumatic experience that are eventually reactivated by a second event (*après-coup*), thus giving way to overt pathology.[3] The main difference is that at the time the model implied a case of material sexual abuse was necessary.

Psychical Reality

The notion of "psychical reality" was introduced under that name in *The Interpretation of Dreams*, and it was a game changer. It inaugurated the truly conceptual stage of psychoanalysis. A testimony to the importance that psychic reality as a concept had for Freud is the fact that after having clearly identified it in the first edition of the dream book, he felt the need to add an even stronger formulation of it in the 1919 edition: "If we look at unconscious wishes reduced to their most fundamental and truest shape, we shall have to conclude, no doubt, that psychical reality is a particular form of existence not to be confused with material reality."[4]

---

3 "Project for a Scientific Psychology," *SE* 1:352-357.

4 *The Interpretation of Dreams, SE* 5:620.

The question is now this: What do we make of the decisive difference between material and psychical reality? For Laplanche and Pontalis, "psychical reality" designates "whatever in the subject's psyche presents a consistency and resistance comparable to those displayed by material reality; fundamentally, what is involved here is unconscious desire and its associated fantasies. . . . Neurosis, and *a fortiori* psychosis, are characterised by the predominance of psychical reality in the life of the subject."[5] Freud himself wrote that "in the world of the neuroses it is psychical reality which is the decisive kind."[6] The predominance of psychical reality is best illustrated by President Schreber's own testimony quoted in Freud: "Illusions of holding communication with God or with departed souls can properly only arise in the minds of persons who . . . already have a firm belief in God and in the immortality of the soul. *This was not by any means so, however, in my case.*"[7] Schreber thus makes a clear distinction between psychical reality and mere belief or illusion. He is all the more certain of his special relationship to God since *he does not believe* in God. This means that his experience rests not on some personal preference but on psychic reality. As for belief, illusion, opinion, or personal bent, they can all be gathered under the heading of "subjectivity." These subjective elements are, of course, themselves influenced by psychical reality, but unlike it, they can evolve under the influence of material reality and the opinions and beliefs of others—opinions and beliefs to which psychical reality remains quite impervious.

Distinguishing between subjectivity and psychical reality is crucial for the conception of the Sexual. But let me stress again that the "reality" in "psychical reality" must not be conflated with

---

5　Jean Laplanche and Jean-Bertrand Pontalis, *The Language of Psycho-Analysis*, trans. Donald Nicholson-Smith (London: Hogarth Press, 1973), 363.

6　*Introductory Lectures on Psycho-Analysis*, pt. 3, *SE* 16:368.

7　Daniel Paul Schreber, quoted in "Psycho-Analytic Notes on an Autobiographical Account of a Case of Paranoia (*Dementia Paranoides*)," *SE* 7:24n2.

material reality and therefore does not rest on the materiality of events. The only material substrate required is a living, excitable body, a "body-psyche" with the translational mechanisms thanks to which it shares the same domain of meaning and communication as other body-psyches. The excitable body is both the locus for experiencing the impact of the Sexual and a major source of imaginative forms that enter the child's response to that impact.

Translation and the Reality of the Message

Communication and meaning require at least two body-psyches. However, since psychical reality must not be mistaken for subjectivity, the communication between body-psyches cannot be truly called inter*subjective*. Yet it is the case that two *subjects*—that is, two centers of action—are involved in communication. Hence, I propose to call their relationship "inter*subjectal*." This "intersubjectality" implies a relative autonomy of the two subjects. Given the operational barriers that define their respective inner workings and ensure their identity, a process of translation or transduction is needed.[8] Subjects are essentially creators of meaning, so they each need to interpret what emanates from the other. Sharing the same communicational milieu makes this possible, but it does not follow that communication between them is transparent. A relative opacity results from the fact that the cognizance of outer reality—captured through perception and communication—cannot directly enter the inner space of the subject; its integration is limited by the subject's own translational capacity. This leads us back to the idea of Freudian conceptual clusters. Indeed, in the translational model expounded in Freud's famous letter to Fliess, translation is inseparable from repression, the latter being defined as a partial failure of the translational process.[9] It must be noted, however, that

8 Regarding transduction, see the discussion following chapter 1.

9 Freud to Wilhelm Fliess, December 6, 1896, in *The Complete Letters of Sigmund Freud to Wilhelm Fliess*, trans. and ed. Jeffrey Moussaieff Masson (Cambridge, MA:

failure of translation happens specifically in relation the Sexual. Other things may temporarily escape the infant's grasp, but the process of attachment, attunement, and maturation will one day clarify them. Not so with the Sexual. Here's why.

Untranslatable Sexual Contaminants

For Freud, the only drive subjected to repression is the Sexual—not the drive itself, actually, but its representatives, representation and affect, with representation undergoing true repression while affect is displaced.[10] Let us now consider Freud's operational definition of a drive "as the psychical representative of the stimuli originating from within the organism and reaching the mind [and] as a measure of the demand made upon the mind for work in consequence of its connection with the body."[11] Notice that in this definition, the drive is a "psychical representative" of the stimuli, not the stimuli themselves. Hence the drive itself is already a translation of what goes on at the bodily level. But why is the Sexual the only repressible drive? Translation again provides the answer, for while translating a self-preservative instinct into the appropriate psychical work is for the newborn a question of learning, the Sexual is the one domain where such learning is neither crucial for survival nor fully achievable by the infant.

 The newborn child is immersed in what Laplanche calls the fundamental anthropological situation,[12] created by the irreducible discrepancy between the adult world—replete with sexual meanings most of which are nonconscious for the adults themselves—and the world of the *in-fans*, who not only lacks the use of language in general but, even as he or she learns to speak, also lacks the adequate set

Belknap Press of Harvard University Press, 1985).

10 See the articles "Repression" and "The Unconscious," in Papers on Metapsychology, *SE* 14; [143-215].

11 "Instincts and Their Vicissitudes," *SE* 14:122.

12 In *Freud and the Sexual*, p. 107-120.

of representations for mastering the sexual dimension that travels as a stowaway within the acts of ordinary care. The infant, in this view, does not possess inborn fantasies or an infantile sexuality; these will result from the very process of attempting to translate the sexual elements of communications and failing at it, which is, as we saw, one of Freud's definitions of repression. For all its limitations, this translational process is inborn and definitional: we are essentially sense-making beings, always trying to predict what comes next. This predictive function, however, is compromised when it comes to what regards the Sexual. Indeed, for lack of any "code" regarding the Sexual, the child's interaction with the adult in this domain is clouded with enigmas.

The general theory of seduction (GTS) does not deny the too-frequent occurrence of sexual molestation of children, but it posits that, across all human experience, there exists an irreducible primal seduction. In support of this claim, all the GTS needs to consider is the "noise" in the adult-to-child communication, a noise reflecting the sexual discrepancy described above, resulting in the child's partially failed translation. The failure, however, does not preclude the child from *being excited by*—and *registering*—the "noise," the enigmatic sexual "contaminant" that travels within the otherwise attuned adult-to-child messages and implants the sexual core of psychic reality. In the previously mentioned letter of 1896, Freud calls these registrations "memory traces"; they result, he says, from the "signs of perception" that undergo consecutive attempts at translation. Each partially failed attempt leaves behind elements that cannot be brought up to date and integrated in the most advanced translations. These untranslatable residues constitute, Freud says, the repressed. Following Laplanche,[13] and in total congruence with the views Freud discussed earlier, I assert that the repressed *is* the Sexual. A Sexual is thus implanted in the infant's

---

13 *New Foundations for Psychoanalysis*, trans. Jonathan House (New York: The Unconscious in Translation, 2016).

psyche as an internal foreign body, which then affects the excitable body-psyche of the child from within.

The Sexual in the Structuring of the Psyche and in Psychopathology

A partially failed translation is also partially . . . successful! What then of this success? When a translated element makes sense to the child, it is integrated in the fabric of the ego. Yet one can easily agree with Freud that there are degrees or strata in the ego, some layers being readily accessible to consciousness while others retain part of the original enigma. Translation/repression is therefore the very mechanism by which the psyche progressively differentiates into unconscious and preconscious-conscious domains. This structuring is in constant flux, with a permanent renewal of memory by translation and retranslation, in a *nachträglich (après-coup)* manner. *Après-coup* retranscription and reinterpretation are continuous since the source of the excitatory Sexual is now an internal drive— that is, the index of the otherness within, an otherness that, by being incompatible with the structure of the coherent ego, never ceases to exert a pressure on the inborn mechanisms of sense making. This is because the sense-making function in the psyche is never at ease with what it cannot understand. Now, not only does the repressed press back from within; it is also frequently reactivated in the subject by the seductive enigma present in each new encounter with otherness. Thus, it is worth noticing that, conceived of within the framework of the general theory of seduction, the drives pertain to the intersubjectal relationship and are not reducible to a solipsistic point of view.

Successful translations borrow their representations from the tender, inhibited-as-to-the-aim forms of interaction between adult and child, and as already mentioned, they constitute the fabric of the ego. They therefore represent, from the economic point of view, the durably invested (i.e., cathected) armature of the ego. I am talking here of normal narcissism with its regulatory effect on the flow of exchanges between inside and outside, self and other, and between psychical and material reality. This armature makes the ego capable of containing excitation within certain limits. On this side of the equation, then, the Sexual is embedded, contained, and possibly concealed in enduring translations. It may become more apparent, however, when the narcissistic structure is not well secured or undergoes traumatic blows, which may reveal its roots in the sexual drives. A burst of megalomania, for instance, may resemble a direct expression of the drives.

To the question "What is the place of sexual drives in psychoanalysis?" my answer is then that it is central in structural, intersubjectal, and psychopathological terms. I hope to have shown that, opening our lens a bit wider, we find no contradiction between the internal structuring process and the intersubjectal origins of sexually compromised messages. Also, it goes without saying that the structuring will be disturbed by a number of accidents resulting from life's turbulence. At every major turn in the life of the individual—that is, whenever the subject is confronted anew with otherness—the fundamental anthropological situation is met again, challenging previous translations and requiring the construction of new meanings, a task sometimes conducive to warped responses. These can be temporary or durable, with various degrees of suffering in their wake, depending on how strong and stable the libidinal resources of the ego are.

Again, therefore, the Sexual is *not* an interpretive key of psychopathological formations. Rather, psychopathology itself is made of the ensemble of the subject's unsatisfactory responses to the challenges of the Sexual. In other words, the Sexual is the question to which psychopathology is the nonevolutive, arrested, and problematic set of answers. These answers, accumulated during a lifetime of internal struggle, need to be dismantled—that is, *analyzed*—to help the analysand come up with more satisfactory solutions.

In the analytic room, then, the Sexual comes cloaked under layers of translations and retranslations, displacements and sublimations, fixated in character traits and symptoms. To the question "Where is the Sexual in the session?" the answer is "Everywhere," if only we care to listen for it in terms of psychic reality rather than being befuddled by the lack of overt references to *sexuality*. The Sexual presents itself in the compulsive nature of pathology, with its repetitive life patterns. It is the energy that threatens or bewilders the patient's ego just as much as it animates and shakes up the analytic situation. As for resistance to the Sexual, it may stall and deaden the analytic process, but it is unavoidable. The Sexual is thus the disturbance that both motivates the patient to consult and resists our attempts at shedding light on it. This is because the Sexual is another name for the infantile—that which leaves us *all* are lost for words. But what cannot be verbalized—that is, expressed in shareable symbolic forms—tends to be enacted. And we must be reminded that *transference* is the most subtle, protracted, and central form of enactment happening during analysis.

So in the session, the Sexual is the essential ingredient of the transference, whatever form—positive or negative, erotic or aggressive—it may take. The Sexual, however, does not necessarily present itself in an openly erotic transference (though it often does) or under aggressive guises (though it does this also). The Sexual is behind the drive-like quality of events that take place in the course of analysis, its presence betrayed by its unbinding effects and the resistance they provoke. Behold the patient's efforts at preserving the bindings that be. Consider the reiteration of customary impasses. Take note of the reproduction in the session of the infantile puzzlement that comes with the reopening of the fundamental anthropological situation in the analytic room. In other words, think of the Sexual when facing the compulsion to repeat.

But wait! Was not repetition famously evinced by Freud under the nonsexual and even anti-sexual heading of the death drive? There is an answer to that objection, but because of our time and space limits, it must wait for another occasion.

Conversation

AS: This paper was given as part of the celebration of the hundredth anniversary of the *International Journal of Psychoanalysis*. The orienting questions of the celebration, which are also given in a slightly different form at the beginning of the essay, were: "What place do we give to 'the drives' and in particular the sexual drive? Where is the drive in the session, and what is its role?" Can you tell us a bit about how you understand the need today for a theorizing of the drive, and the sexual drive in particular? I ask because while I have found that the Laplanchean approach to the drives is incredibly enriching, I have observed that many analysts, especially those of younger generations, find the concept of the drive outdated or even anachronistic.

DS: As you know, the question of the drives is central in Freud's model of the mind, and therefore it is central for those who follow him; it is also one of the stumbling stones for those who dismiss Freud altogether, especially so if by "drive" one actually means, as one should, the *sexual* drive. There are analysts who believe that there is such a gap between psychoanalytic practice and psychoanalytic theory that it does not matter much whether or not you take some theoretical element into account. Now, this is a more complex matter than it seems. I do agree that there is a gap and that our theories, as Freud often wrote, are made to be changed. Yet this does not mean that every theoretical statement has the same importance. Obviously the notion of drive is essential in the theory of motivation. But in my view, the important word in "sexual drive" is the word "sexual."

That's because with the term "sexual," you have a powerful *motivational* factor (a motive being, literally, something that puts in motion), a factor so pervasive in human culture that one would expect it to be taken for granted. But while one finds sexual motivations everywhere (in love stories, of course, but also behind financial scandals, in wars, slavery, and political oppression . . . to name just a few examples), I am always surprised at how people, including many analysts, resist inscribing them within a formal theory of motivation. One reason for this, I surmise, is their very pervasiveness. Everyone breathes air, but a theory that seeks to explain that behavior would feel unnecessary because air is a vital need. The difference when it comes to the Sexual is that psychoanalysis has problematized the question of the Sexual. That is, it has shown that the Sexual is more complicated than its apparent universality suggests—it goes beyond the vital, beyond the biological, beyond the motivational aspect of sexuality. So while sexual themes may be everywhere, the problematized Sexual is another story as it always comes in as a disturbance in the eyes of the ego.

The *foundational* problem we have with the Sexual pertains, to begin with, to the odd timing of its appearance in our lives. Laplanche called it the fundamental anthropological situation, in which *acquired* (infantile) sexuality comes well before innate, biological sexual maturity. This problematization is something not taken into account in the celebration (or condemnation) of sexual pleasure, of sexual attractiveness, and so forth. The problematic Sexual in question is the *infantile Sexual*, a constant reminder of an insuperable gradient within our psyche in that, as we discussed in our previous conversation, the infantile Sexual does not mature and therefore there is always something infantile in us.

Another aspect of this issue is that it is easy to conflate the Freudian take on the Sexual and *sexuality* in general. Take for instance the belief, once widely shared, that "sexual freedom" would prevent neuroses and other forms of mental suffering. In fact, when I say that the adjective "sexual" is the most important term in "sexual drives," it is because of its origins in the other, and therefore the internal otherness it becomes; it therefore implies the decentering of the subject, the displacement of the ego, its "deposition," in the sense of the deposing of a king.

I would add that in the end it is a question of information. What I mean is that there is not much information in invoking a nutrition instinct or other instincts of self-preservation (we know that these are, by definition, vital) to explain eating, drinking etc.; nor, for that matter, is there information in invoking the sexual instinct to explain reproductive behavior. That is not what the sexual drive is about. So to take a trivial example, if you say that a sexual drive is at work behind a certain choice of career, you are producing new information, which is not always welcome, because we like to think that we humans dwell in higher spheres. But here the problems begin, because you must give evidence in support of your claim. Such evidence is not difficult to provide, but then someone raises another objection. Freud, as we know, has widely extended the meaning of "sexual" and the domains in which the Sexual has an impact. An obvious misreading of this is to say that for him the Sexual is the only thing that matters, that everything is sexual to him. Another, opposite misreading is to say that in Freud the Sexual has been spread so thin that it means nothing specific anymore, in the sense that if everything is sexual, then nothing is. These are "misreadings" because Freud was always very clear that *not* everything is sexual (for if it were, there would be no information to be gained in considering the Sexual: if everything is sexual, the Sexual loses its salience). Freud's idea is rather that the Sexual has a part in everything human. The difference is paramount. The assertion that there is a sexual dimension to everything *does* carry a lot of information about the human condition—and disturbing information in that it both deprives the ego of its pretense of being the master in its own house and, perhaps more importantly, *dramatizes* the sexual dimension of human existence.

AS: This distinction between the Sexual and sexuality is very important, and you come back to it often in your writings. Might we think of the difference between sexuality and the Sexual as the difference, among other things, between what is inert and what is not inert? Sexual identity, for instance, can be understood in an overly static way --e.g., when someone proclaims, "I am a straight man." Even a seemingly more roomy, because less conventional, claim, like, "I am gay," when proclaimed by a trans woman, may in some cases be identity-bound and, thus, turning away from the Sexual. The term "queer," it seems to me, can be used to both claim a sexual otherness and resist a fixity of identification—I say "can be used" because that's not by any means guaranteed, since queerness can also become fixed (e.g., I am thinking of a patient of mine who is perplexed about his erotic transference to me given that he is a queer man and I, as far as he can tell, am a queer woman). But there are also uses of the term "queer" that, I think, work to maintain that kernel of the Sexual's itineracy, that have the quality of ever-becoming.

DS: You introduce a clarification that I endorse because it highlights the importance of "becoming" over "being." I am reluctant to use the verb "to be" in situations where it designates, as you mention, a fixed state, a state of inertia. The question of identity is a crucial one, both in our clinical practice and at the social and political level. This also applies to the professional identity of psychoanalysts. I always cringe at the expression "I am a psychoanalyst" because psychoanalysis is not something in our nature. On the contrary, there is nothing natural about it. Obviously, in our daily parlance, it is easier to state, "X is a psychoanalyst," but I believe the legitimate expression is "X practices psychoanalysis." This may seem a detail, but we sometimes get the impression that with the notion of "being" a psychoanalyst, some people end up thinking that whatever they do in their consulting rooms *is* psychoanalysis because they "are" psychoanalysts. Certainly, there is a sense of belonging to a psychoanalytic community that provides a professional identity, but I think of myself as a person who *does* something called psychoanalysis. And doing psychoanalysis does not come easy—it requires a permanent struggle against the spontaneous attitude; it is an uphill battle to maintain the special kind of listening that really departs from one's ordinary stance. Far from a fixed identity, it is a position that must be conquered anew every day.

I believe the same holds true, mutatis mutandis, for what regards sexual identity. I think that we can readily accept the multiplicity of sexual preferences and orientations, but this does not require that we fixate them in a solid sexual identity. It is quite understandable that, for political reasons, sexual minorities needed to regroup and establish a sense of belonging to a community that upholds their right to be different. It is ironic, however, to see that the struggle to assert difference resulted in a compartmentalization into various "brands" as suggested by the ever-growing acronym LGBTQ+. It is understandable that every orientation seeks to be represented under the banner, but it also leaves a sense that every letter represents a fixed identity. So I follow you in thinking that the term "queer," as an overarching appellation, is preferable in that it both signifies difference and leaves open the future for "becoming." The ideal would be for society as a whole to endorse the psychoanalytic notion that human sexuality is queer by definition, irrespective of the actual sexual orientation of individuals, precisely because of the "odd timing" I mentioned above that results in the Sexual having always already infiltrated sexuality itself. But this would require overcoming of major and perhaps unavoidable resistance.

AS: I really appreciate your call on us, not just as a society but perhaps also as a psychoanalytic community, to come more to terms with the fact that human sexuality is, as you say, queer by definition. I use the term "queer" here not in the sense of gay or trans or polyamorous in particular (as that would fix sexuality in one particular aim and/or goal) but in the sense of polymorphousness, as you already emphasized.[14] For example, the notion of psychic bisexuality has been welcomed by many analysts as indexing Freud's most expansive understanding of gender (even as Freud does not use the word "gender"). For such analysts, psychic bisexuality is something to be inhabited in the realm of psychic reality or fantasy. This, in fact, becomes an argument leveraged against some trans people: it's argued that they transition medically because they don't accept their psychic bisexuality. If they did, the argument continues, they would be able to tolerate being, say, a feminine man or a masculine woman without a need for hormono-surgical interventions. I think that the position you argue for here suggests that queerness has to be taken seriously *in whichever way the subject inhabits it.*

DS: This topic requires a discussion of the difference between sexuality and gender. In my understanding, Freud's writings on bisexuality did not address gender not for lack of the word but because he was talking about bisexuality as a biological, constitutional reality. To my knowledge, Freud never used the expression "psychic bisexuality"; he spoke only of bisexuality, always meaning a constitutional given. The two (bisexuality and the issue of gender) somehow partially overlap, but in my view they address two very different dimensions. Also consider that queerness does not abolish difference; quite to the contrary, it *requires* difference in order to be, well, queer. So the question is how to think *simultaneously* in terms of queerness and of sexual (constitutional, anatomical) and gender (cultural) difference. Gender assignment is not simply the conscious observation: It's a girl! It's a boy! It is a highly complex message, carrying in its trail a number of unconscious determinants.

---

14 AS: See Teresa de Lauretis, "The Queerness of the Drive," *Journal of Homosexuality* 64, no. 14 (February 2017): 1913–1929, for a discussion of the queerness of the drive from a queer theory perspective.

AS: You start this paper by recounting Freud's move away from the seduction hypothesis (that "all neurotics were once victims of infantile perverse seduction") and how this led to his discovery of the notion of sexual fantasy. You note that even as Freud recognized the importance of psychical reality, he remained physicalist in locating sexual fantasies in the prehistory of the species[15] (e.g. by arguing that the Oedipus complex is biologically preloaded into the psyche in the way that a software program is preloaded into a computer). In making this point, you are referring to an idea that Laplanche returned to often, about how Freud mistakenly looked to phylogenesis to explain where these fantasies came from. Can you say a little about this and about what the implications of this were for Laplanche? It can look like a bit of theoretical hairsplitting, but once it becomes clear why Laplanche took issue with it, it also becomes obvious that this move on Freud's part has significant implications.

DS: Interestingly, Laplanche and Freud share the same motivation, which is to make psychoanalysis rest on the most secure scientific grounds. Freud believed he could achieve this by invoking his version of phylogenetic (i.e., biological) transmission. Laplanche thought that this was not good science, for if such transmission exists, we should be able to find other examples of the phylogenetic transmission of complex mental scenes or find the genes responsible for them. At this level, it was merely a matter of aligning psychoanalysis with an acceptable evolutionary view.

But the problem that Laplanche saw in Freud's "phylogenetic fantasy," as Stephen Jay Gould called it, was a deeper one. In Laplanche's view, by invoking the transmission of memories of primeval events, Freud was repeating the same mistake he had made when he believed that every hysteric patient had actually

---

15 See p. 124 above.

been sexually abused, except that he now situated the "facts" not in the individual's past but in that of the human species. This was a return of the first theory of seduction under a new guise because it still sought a basis in strictly material facts.

Now, as you know, Laplanche had a complex position on that theory and its abandonment by Freud. On the one hand, he acknowledged Freud's scientific probity, his being "Popperian" *ante litteram*, in rejecting his theory on the basis of its not being refutable. On the other hand, Laplanche reproached Freud for two things: First, for having thrown away too much, namely the primacy of the other, with the result that infantile sexuality ended up being seen as inborn rather than implanted from the outside. Second, for, in so doing, flattening the *après-coup* time structure into a linear time structure. Indeed, in spite of its limitations, the first theory of seduction implied that it takes at least two events to obtain a pathogenic effect of the Sexual in the subject's psyche, with the two events operating according to a complex time structure termed *Nachträglichkeit*, or *après-coup*, in which a resonance and a retroactivity intervenes between the events. With the theory of inborn infantile sexuality and of phylogenetic transmission, Freud apparently abandons *après-coup* in favor of a linear form of causality. In his new version of infantile seduction, the caretaker involuntarily excites the child through their ordinary care, and seduction is therefore "accidental," a minor anecdote. But when we look at his rendition of the Wolf Man case, more than a decade later, Freud seems to hold to the *après-coup* structure at the same time as he seems to hold to the materiality of seduction. This is where Laplanche stepped in, picking up the seduction theory but this time in a generalized form that relied neither on phylogenesis nor on the necessity of factual abusive seduction. One could say that Laplanche brought the theory up to date by resorting to a genuinely psychoanalytic model of adult-child communication.

AS: This is a quite considerable revision. Can you also help us see how the notion of the primal horde constitutes Freud's own fantasy, another idea that is mentioned in this essay?

DS: Freud himself said, in his 1921 work *Group Psychology and the Analysis of the Ego*, that the story of the primal horde was a "just so story," and he developed a very interesting view to deal with this circumstance, which we should highlight here because it answers your question in an unexpected way. In that same work, after having somehow disqualified the myth of a primal horde and of the primal father as a myth, he proposes that the true hero in myths is actually the epic poet who forges them — it is the narrator. I think that this is a most interesting view since it does away with the phylogenetic fantasy yet reinstates something that can be transmitted *culturally* through poetry: mythmaking, or mythopoiesis. The author of the myth is the actual hero because it is not the actions narrated in the myth but the myth itself that possesses the symbolic efficacy, without any need for it to be grounded in actual prehistoric "events." So the primal horde was indeed Freud's fantasy in more than one sense. It was his personal belief (borrowed, it is true, from Charles Darwin), but it was also an effective, powerful myth of his creation, one in which the hero (be it the primal father or the parricidal sons) was also himself.

AS: This very significant rerouting away from phylogenesis can be surprisingly derailing to some analytic thinking. One does not realize how much one relies on the biologism of phylogenetic fantasy until that rug is pulled out from underneath psychonalytic theory. For example, when I discuss gender in general, and trans issues in particular, with colleagues, I often find that analysts who would not necessarily have thought of themselves as Freudian will refer to castration anxiety (or manifest their own castration panic when, in hearing about a trans woman, for instance, they become excessively preoccupied with her genitals). One of the implications of moving away from phylogenesis is that we can no longer assume that there are unconscious fantasies that all people share. Or that, to the extent that we as analysts share them, this shared fantasizing is not ontological (i.e., it is not something "true" about human nature) but that for us (analysts) too, it comes out of translational processes (i.e., it is a product of our own self-making, of our autopoiesis, a term you've used elsewhere). For example, concepts like the Oedipus complex made available to children *by adults* may be used as tools with which to translate enigma. Could you talk to us a bit about what the implications are of this metapsychological shift? In other words, why does it matter in our clinical work if phylogenesis is not presumed to equip us with universal fantasies but, instead, such fantasies arise from our own fantasizing activity?

DS: You raise many interesting questions and subquestions. To clarify the issues, we should, for instance, distinguish between biology and *biologism*, which is parallel to the distinction between science and *scientism*. The question here is about what is legitimate—that is, epistemologically sound. The phylogenetic fantasy, as I said, is questionable on the grounds of scientific validity as well as within psychoanalytic logic itself. But you are right to signal that the general and often nonconscious background to (or rug underneath) the theory (of universal inborn fantasies, for instance) is that of biologism. The matter is a delicate one and requires a clear understanding of what we are talking about. For as we know, the "we are made this way" argument is sometimes legitimate: there are, after all, biological determinants such as genes, hormones, and so forth, and psychoanalysts have no reason to discard the role these play in a given personal configuration. On the other hand, it would be all too easy to misuse the autopoietic function by asserting that it means "It's all of your choosing," an idea that fuels "conversion therapy" and oppressive stances.

The metapsychological shift you mention first requires acknowledging both the subject's active role in translation and fantasy building in response to the enigmas posed by the other and the limits to this activity imposed by the embodied nature of the psyche and the cultural matrix in which one dwells. The embodied nature certainly limits the "degrees of freedom" – as they say in statistics – in the translational work, and the symbolic forms the cultural matrix provides strongly influence the psyche's evolution. Such a shift means accepting that the result of all these factors is not the product of linear causality but is, instead, open to a variety of combinations and, moreover, that these combinations are not final but open to becoming. The analyst is therefore freed from the obligation to discover the "personal equation" that would explain away a patient once and for all. We are reminded that psychoanalysis is not a normative science, nor is it there to retro-predict what the subject has become. It is, rather, devoted to opening up the future.

AS: In discussing Freud's discovery of sexual fantasy after the abandonment of his seduction hypothesis, you write: "Obviously, actual sexual abuses do happen and do matter. The problem, however, is that empirical facts may dazzle the psychoanalyst and blur the conceptual status of what he or she is after. Indeed, sexual abuse does not directly *explain* pathology; it is a traumatic process *itself in need of an explanation*—a metapsychological one."[16] In this passage you are saying several things, and I want to slow us down, as your writing can be really compact. It seems that you are saying that in cases where sexual abuse is a known event (as opposed to a nonspecific memory or a sexual fantasy), the fact of the abuse can command our attention such that we (analysts) proceed as if we understand something, when in fact we may not. What is the thing we may think we understand, and what do you think is still missing?

---

16 See p. 126 above.

DS: In the passage you quote, I am indeed saying many things at once. The first is that we must not satisfy ourselves with what seem to be unobjectionable facts, because our legitimate domain of study and work is psychic reality; hence, we are essentially concerned with psychic events. This is often misunderstood as meaning that we neglect material facts, which is not the point, nor is it true. The point is to keep in mind that whatever we hear from our patient emanates from their memory and its entanglement with their present psychical experience. This always entails a measure of distortion (Freud's *Entstellung*), not because the patient purposefully distorts things, but because we never have access to the unconscious thing itself, and in turn, the unconscious reality necessarily distorts the representation we can come up with. Still, we deal with psychic reality, which, it must be recalled, does not boil down to subjective choices and preferences or to personal whims. Quite on the contrary. Psychic reality is a different form of reality from material reality but just as sturdy and compelling. This means that while the material facts reported to us cannot be ignored, they cannot be dealt with as they are in a court of justice, for instance. We analysts are not called on to establish the material truthfulness or the causal role of those facts, especially if we keep present in our minds the constant reshuffling of *après-coup*. Causality in our field is a highly complex matter. But at any rate, as Aulagnier once wrote, one question analysts should *not* ask themselves is whether the patient is telling the truth.

AS: Every new encounter with otherness, you write, exerts "a pressure on the inborn mechanism of sense making."[17] The structuring of the psyche, you write later, can and will be "disturbed by a number of accidents resulting from life's turbulence."[18] We are always in the presence of one or another person's sexual unconscious, but we are not always in turmoil as a result. What

17 See p. 131 above.
18 See p. 132 above.

146

makes some of these contacts more likely to inflame the foreign body within us? Why would some turbulences bewilder the ego or cause a turmoil that presses for new translations whereas others don't?

DS: The pressure to translate is always present. My view is that what we really experience as an *encounter* (rather than just a casual meeting) is one where the other's presentation and "message" resonate with areas of our psyche where meaning is not readily available and unconscious derivatives show up instead with their "compromised meanings" — that is, their ambiguities — thus inflaming, as you say, the body-psyche.

AS: The presence of the Sexual, you write, is "betrayed by its unbinding effects and the resistance they provoke."[19] Can you give us an example of how you have seen this play out in your consulting room?

DS: The idea here is that the *Sexual* should not necessarily be sought in examples that speak overtly of *sexuality*. We often see clinical vignettes suggesting that something is sexual because it contains overt references to sexual behavior or sexual fantasies. What I try to convey instead is that the repressed *Sexual* can manifest itself in various ways, overtly sexual and not, and that its distinctive feature is the unbinding effects it would have were it not for the resistance it elicits. So, another way of saying the same thing is to say that the Sexual's impact is betrayed by the visible signs of a struggle in the analysand's mind. An even simpler formulation could be that the presence of the Sexual is betrayed by resistance. But this would amount to stating a law ("If resistance, then Sexual") that could seem to require an act of faith; fortunately, the analytic experience of transference tells us that it doesn't. The Sexual does manifest its disruptive effect in moments of intense transferential turmoil when it seems that the whole enterprise of treatment is at

---

19 See p. 134 above.

risk of falling apart at the same time as we get a sense that we are dealing with what truly matters. These are moments when maximal resistance (exhibited in the patient's intense transference feelings, their loss of interest in the process) corresponds with the maximal momentum of the repressed Sexual (aiming at obtaining actual possession and control of the transferential object).

A fuller answer would need to address in more detail the link between the repressed Sexual and the drive for power (*Bemächtigungstrieb*), something that I am trying to formulate in a forthcoming paper. For now, suffice it to say that Laplanche's "sexual death drive" seems to me to refer to this link. My idea is that the pregenital perverse Sexual is inseparable from the drive for unrestrained power and control over another human being reduced to the status of a part-object. We are in fact in the midst of a conceptual cluster including the repressed, the Sexual, the pregenital, the sexual death drive, the drive for power, cruelty, part-objects, and so forth.

The Feminine, the Analyst, and the Child Theorist[1*]

When looked at from an extra-analytic—anthropological, sociological, or historical—point of view, for instance through the work of Françoise Héritier and many others,[2] the word "feminine" narrates the story of a protracted and as yet unfinished struggle between asymmetrical forces within human society. The primal division of labor that rests at the source of many forms of domination, exploitation, and abuse was from the start a male/female division of labor, creating a relationship that is not just asymmetrical but also hierarchical, in which women occupy the lower end. For Héritier, this struggle has always been, in the end, the struggle for the control of the female body and its capacity of reproduction. It would be simplistic to consider this element of the equation alone, but certainly this has been a constant and covert factor in the story until relatively recently, when effective methods of contraception and the struggle around the control of fertility brought the issue into plain sight. This is a new story, only about six decades old; no wonder then that it has challenged the dominant ideology by

---

1 *Originally delivered as a keynote lecture to the 51st International Psychoanalytical Association Congress (London, July 2019). I wish to thank Avgi Saketopoulou for her judicious comments and suggestions on many aspects of this paper. Thank you also to Jane V. Kite for helping with the linguistic revision.

2 Héritier, *Masculin-Féminin*, 2 vols. (Paris: Odile Jacob, 1996–2002). Owing to time and space limits, I have had to leave out many significant contributions.

introducing rapid and unsettling changes regarding the place and role of men and women, the nature of gender identity, and the multiple forms of sexuality, questioning the apparently simple partition of yesteryears.

Consider for instance what Freud could write in 1908: "If we could divest ourselves of our corporeal existence, and could view the things of this earth with a fresh eye as purely thinking beings, from another planet for instance, nothing perhaps would strike our attention more forcibly than the fact of the existence of two sexes among human beings, who, though so much alike in other respects, yet mark the difference between them with such obvious external signs."[3]

If Freud could resume his bodily existence today, he would be surprised to find external signs not so much directed at marking the difference between the sexes as at blurring them. Even for his time, Freud was perhaps painting a too-simple picture, for though the external signs were different, he well knew that males and females can be more or less "masculine," more or less "feminine," incarnating and experiencing various mixes of the two qualities and giving them, consciously or unconsciously, different meanings and values. Freud was, of course, in many ways ahead of his time. By postulating, with his then friend Wilhelm Fliess, a basic bisexual human constitution, Freud had disturbed the *doxa* of his time; and psychoanalysis was probably the most revolutionary story in town when he also introduced the infantile sexual at the core of the unconscious, with the sexual drives expressing the "demonic" in the human soul. Yet regarding women, he ended up formulating a set of normative views aligned with the most conservative ideology! I will not go into much detail here, as these are well-known facts. Suffice it to mention that his views on feminine sexuality culminated in 1933 in, for us looking back, a rather embarrassing theory.

---

3   "On the Sexual Theories of Children," *SE* 9:211–12.

A sad irony is at work here. In the first pages of his lecture entitled "Femininity," Freud states: "Psychoanalysis does not try to describe what the woman is—that will be a task it could scarcely perform—but sets about enquiring how she comes into being, how a woman develops out of a child with a bisexual disposition."[4] This has all the appearances of a forerunner of Simone de Beauvoir's famous quote: "*On ne naît pas femme: on le devient*" ("One is not born, but rather becomes a woman").[5] Alas! The rest of the Freud's lecture is cause for major disappointment. The woman that finally comes into being in it is but a lesser version of a male human being. As a child, she "discover[s] that she is castrated [and this] is a turning point in a girl's growth."[6] For many years, I thought that Freud meant: "The girl *gets the wrong impression* that she is castrated." But a closer rereading of Freud's papers on the question shows that he was rather literal and that in 1933, he conceived of women as *actually castrated*. For him, when a woman came to analysis, she may have just been acting out the unrelenting wish "to get the longed for penis." He believed this to such an extent that he thought a woman's expecting from analysis "a capacity, for instance, to carry on an intellectual profession—may often be recognized as a sublimated modification of this repressed wish."[7] Even as she turns her libidinal longings to her father, the little girl is seeking only the penis that her mother has refused her and that she now expects from him. Here again one could think that Freud is simply *reporting* the infantile sexual theories uncovered during the analysis of his female patients without endorsing them. In fact, he was uncritically *importing* them into the official psychoanalytic theory (more on this later).

---

4   "Femininity," in *New Introductory Lectures on Psycho-Analysis*, SE 22:116.

5   Simone de Beauvoir, *Le deuxième sexe* (Paris: Gallimard, 1946), 2:13. The English version of this famous sentence is from the introduction by Deirdre Bair to the English translation by H.M. Parshley, New York: Knopf, 1952, Vintage Edition, 1989, p. VII.

6   *SE* 22:126.

7   *SE* 22:125.

In the normative path charted by Freud, "the feminine situation is only established if the wish for a penis is replaced by one for a baby, if, that is, a baby takes the place of a penis in accordance with an ancient symbolic equivalence."[8] In this process, parts of the woman's sexual anatomy must be relinquished, Freud says. The clitoris, for instance, being in his view but an atrophied penis equivalent, "with the change to femininity should wholly or in part hand over its sensitivity, and its importance, to the vagina."[9] As Karen Horney points out, Freud does not say why the woman could not invest her libido first in one part, then in the whole of her sexual apparatus, with no need to abandon one part for the other, or why the little girl's clitoral masturbation should be seen as a masculine sexual activity.[10] By advocating the abandonment of the clitoris in favor of the vagina alone, Freud was himself performing a theoretical castration, a symbolic excision of women in the name of a supposedly authentic femininity. Seeing women as castrated was therefore more of a *prescription* than a *description*.

*

In looking back at these Freudian views, my intent is not historical. The question of the feminine in psychoanalysis remains a potential stumbling block today. While we may not share Freud's views on the matter, we can still commit mistakes similar to his, for instance in proposing newer versions, well meaning as they may be, of what femininity "really" is. Freud's misconceptions were largely ideological, reflecting, under a scientific guise, the prejudices of his time. But things were assuredly not as simple as that, and there is more than one way of critically revisiting the question of the

---

8   *SE* 22:128.

9   *SE* 22:118.

10 "The Flight from Womanhood: The Masculinity-Complex in Women, as Viewed by Men and by Women," *International Journal of Psychoanalysis* 7 (1926): 324–39.

feminine *within* the Freudian opus. Jacques André, for example, made a major contribution in this regard, locating the feminine at the very origins of sexuality.[11]

This study looks at the problem from a different angle. If we consider that Freud had invented a revolutionary method of investigation, one that overthrew many traditional views of the human condition, the problem is how to explain his straying regarding the feminine. Jean Laplanche insisted that a thinker like Freud does not err lightly, that there must be reasons for his errors intrinsic to the theory-building process itself.[12] My goal, therefore, is to examine where, in what way, and according to which internal logic Freud, the theoretician, has gone astray, seemingly forgetful of his method and of his courageous battles against traditional thinking. In the spirit of Laplanche, I hope to show that it all started with the abandonment of the seduction theory.

A Common Denominator

Horney's important paper of 1926 ("The Flight from Womanhood") contains a table comparing, in two columns, the boy's infantile sexual theories and the official psychoanalytic view of feminine development. The resemblances are so striking that she remarked, "The present analytical picture of feminine development (whether that picture be correct or not) differs in no case by a hair's breadth from the typical ideas which the boy has of the girl."[13] Her demonstration of the almost perfect overlap between the boy's typical idea of the girl and the prevailing psychoanalytic views of feminine development is very useful in examining one major aspect of Freud's misconceptions. But one need not totally part ways with

---

11 *Aux origines féminines de la sexualité*, Bibliothèque de psychanalyse (Paris: Presses Universitaires de France, 1995).

12 *New Foundations for Psychoanalysis,* trans. Jonathan House, New York: The Unconscious in Translation, 2016.

13 Horney, "The Flight from Womanhood," 327.

Freud, as Horney did, to criticize his views. Her comparison of the infantile theories with the prevailing psychoanalytic theory gets deeper than she may herself have thought at the time into the theoretical problems hampering Freud. What psychoanalysis uncovers is the infantile theories that patients carry in their heads, but these must not be mistaken for the psychoanalytic theory that can be constructed out of the analytic experience. One fact is clear, and that is that Freud *did* conflate the infantile theories gathered from his patients, especially Little Hans, with psychoanalytic theory itself. The question is: How did this happen?

One hint at the answer is the fact that for Freud, off the mark as they were, infantile theories contained a grain of truth. This idea was strongly reinforced in him after he traded the seduction theory of neurosis for the phylogenetic theory of inborn primal fantasies. The trade was a dramatic one, as Laplanche has shown,[14] for while Freud was right to revise his seduction theory *as the etiological theory of neurosis*, he threw out much more than he needed to at the time—namely, the primacy of the other, the idea of complex psychic temporality (*après-coup*), and the translational model of psychic functioning. These are pragmatic notions, all closely knit together.

The primacy of the other means that infantile sexuality is not inborn but implanted through the adult's unwitting seduction of the infant. This is an unavoidable, generalized form of seduction occurring through the emission of messages that are "infected" by the adult's nonconscious sexual impulses and fantasies concerning the child. Children cannot make sense of that dimension of the adult's communication but are nevertheless impacted by the enigmatic character of the messages and enticed to translate it as best as they can. Freud had privately communicated to Fliess the hypothesis (today largely confirmed) that the psyche is continually transcribing and translating the memory traces of perceptions and

---

14 *New Foundations for Psychoanalysis.*

that what we clinically call "repression" is nothing but a failure of translation.[15] From this model Laplanche extracted the idea that the failure of translation, or primal repression, is an ongoing process engendering at once the ego (on the side of what is translated) and the repressed unconscious (on the side of the untranslated residues). Given that translation is a continuous process, it also accounts for the *après-coup* structure of psychic time and the nonlinear construction of the psyche; meaning has a retroactive effect, and it is subject to fresh, renewed efforts at translation. The past is constantly reconstructed rather than operating in a chronological line of causality.[16] By the way, this is what makes analysis possible, as the analytic moment of undoing the extant translations opens the road toward new, more encompassing *après-coup* translations (or symbolizations).

The child's translation does not imply that the resulting meanings are accurate renditions. Infantile sexual theories are egregious examples of how, in spite of their best efforts, children can translate only up to a point. The problem here is that Freud, relying on the theory of phylogenetic transmission, thought that the infantile theories were a reflection, if only imperfect, of actual archaic events. This explains in part why he so eagerly integrated Little Hans's infantile theories into the official psychoanalytic theory. Hence the infantile theory of castration ended up being looked on not as a theory elaborated by a child with limited translational capacity but as containing some historical truth carried over by genetic transmission from the archaic beginnings of humanity. *Thus, in abandoning the seduction theory, Freud in large part reinstated linear time in place of the* après-coup *structure.* This crucial theoretical

---

15 Freud to Wilhelm Fliess, December 6, 1896, in *The Complete Letters of Sigmund Freud to Wilhelm Fliess*, trans. and ed. Jeffrey Moussaieff Masson (Cambridge, MA: Belknap Press of Harvard University Press, 1985).

16 Dominique Scarfone, *The Unpast: The Actual Unconscious* (New York: Unconscious in Translation, 2015).

turn is reflected in Freud's own change of vocabulary. While in 1908 he called the infantile theories "false sexual theories" and "mistaken beliefs,"[17] some ten years later they had become "primal fantasies" — that is, a "phylogenetic endowment" capable of taking over when the child's theorizing was insufficient. In these primal fantasies, he claimed, "the individual reaches beyond his own experience into primeval experience."[18] Even if we give no credence to the theory of phylogenetic transmission of fantasies, *linearity* is still threatening; we are still at risk of committing the mistake of importing into psychoanalysis what is gathered through the direct observation of children. The temptation here is to interpret a given behavior of children as a "natural" occurrence to be mapped within a normative, and linear, developmental path.

The common denominator of Freud's strayings and those we are still at risk of today is forgetting that the child is a natural translator. As mentioned earlier, from birth on, a constant pressure is exerted on the child's psyche to make sense of what impinges on it from the environment. Then again, the mytho-symbolic forms that it uses to construct theories about itself and the world are provided by . . . the very same surroundings. Hence, as Horney—inspired by the philosophy of Georg Simmel—keenly remarked, it isn't surprising to find that the little girl's theories about castration converge with those of little boys; they were both raised in a patriarchal society. Horney invoked the idea of *interaction* between social and psychic factors but seemed at loss as to how this actually worked[19]. As for the translational model of the psyche, it has no need for interaction; rather, it describes a process in which nothing enters the mind without first being metabolized according to the translational capacity of the individual. Since the social environment provides

---

17 *SE* 9:215.

18 "The Paths of the Formation of Symptoms," in *Introductory Lectures on Psycho-Analysis*, pt. 3, *SE* 16:371.

19 Horney, *Op. cit.*, p. 325-326 and 338.

both the raw material to be translated (the enigmatic message) and the culturally determined symbolic tools used in translation, it follows that the direct observation of children cannot give us a picture of a "natural course" in the child's psychic development, because there is no such thing as a "natural course." The only truly "natural" thing is the child's constant effort at making sense of—translating—the messages emitted by the people that matter. Children's sexual theories and fantasies are the product of this effort. This does not preclude an apparent universality, passing for a "natural" or "inborn" state of affairs; indeed, the cultural determinants are quite similar for all members of a given culture,[20] and the bodily experiences of children are also similar.

Among the decisive messages that children must translate for themselves are those performing gender assignment. This assignment precedes by far the actual discovery of one's own sexual anatomy and/or that of others. This prompted Laplanche to formulate a proposition regarding sex, gender, and the unconscious. "The sexual," he writes, "is the unconscious residue of the symbolization-repression of gender by sex."[21] Of importance here is that gender assignment is a message, whereas sex (sexual anatomy) is the object of perception. For children who are at the receiving end of gender assignment and must interpret its enigmatic "contaminants" to make their own version thereof, perceiving anatomical differences—a perception not itself devoid of cultural influences—offers an important key. But gender assignment involves much more than the male/female dichotomy. Gender and sex never fully overlap. Translation (also

---

20 Except in cases of peculiar, closed subcultures and family systems, such as sects, for instance.

21 "Gender, Sex and the *Sexual*," in *Freud and the Sexual: Essays 2000–2006*, trans. John Fletcher, Jonathan House, and Nicholas Ray (New York: International Psychoanalytic Books, 2011), 159.

called by Laplanche "symbolization-repression"[22]) cannot possibly encompass all the determinants that, in fact, are unconscious for the adults themselves, comprised of their nonconscious wishes, fantasies, and identifications, passed on to children under the apparently "simple" notion of boy or girl. What the unavoidably incomplete translation will leave behind (i.e., repress) is the residual, unconscious "Sexual," the part no child can make sense of, for there is no code available.[23] Laplanche calls this residue the source-object of the drives, meaning that it will be exerting a constant pressure on translation/repression. The male/female lexicon, however, is an important tool in the translational efforts of the child, strongly influencing the infantile sexual theories, such as those formulated by Little Hans. Thus, it was the translational efforts of the child that became what Freud ended up mistaking for inborn fantasies.

What matters at this point is that infantile theories, fantasies, and complexes, with the castration complex at their center, are formulated *in response* to the enigmas that travel as stowaways within such apparently simple assertions as "You are a girl (or a boy)." They are therefore not "primal" in the phylogenetic or inborn sense and strongly influenced by the sociocultural matrix in which children are raised.

So What Can Be Said
Psychoanalytically about the Feminine?

As Françoise Héritier asserted, it is impossible not to refer to the male/female duality. Sexual theories, infantile or adult, necessarily refer to the sexed-as-perceived body—more precisely, to the *difference* the perceived sex connotes. Even terms that do not mention the duality (e.g., cisgender, transgender, queer, etc.) end

---

22 *Op. cit.,* 167.

23 Given this absence of a code, I prefer to speak of transduction rather than translation.

up alluding, if only indirectly, to the male/female dichotomy. By their very existence, the prefixes "cis-" and "trans-," for instance, point to the positioning of gender as related to sex—that is, they point to difference.[24] Similarly, the active claiming of deviation reflected in the term "genderqueer" suggests a departure from an implicit or virtual gender norm. It matters, though, to remark that in human sexuality the deviation is always already present and that no sexual straight line from which to deviate exists to begin with.[25] Nevertheless, this sort of thinking requires a systematic effort that may be difficult to carry over to everyday parlance. Since Copernicus we may have known that the sun is not really "setting," yet rather than referring to astronomical science in our daily lives, we still see a "sunset," and nothing can prevent this naïve perception. Likewise, the term "feminine" will always be in some layered relationship with the female sex, and a number of metaphors will ensue accordingly.

With metaphors, however, we risk too eagerly and uncritically importing questionable tropes such as "feminine receptivity" into our psychoanalytic language.[26] We can be too easily brought to naturalize and ontologize femininity by selecting one or more parts of the female body. We were, after all, all born to a woman—that is, expelled from her "hospitable" womb, which has possibly engraved an indelible though unspeakable memory trace in our psyches. Whatever the case, we must keep in mind the *après-coup* structure of time that results from the constant translational process, as this accounts for the construction—and the updating—of infantile

---

24 It could be said that what cannot be erased is the "/" in "male/female"—i.e., the marker of difference itself.

25 See Dominque Scarfone, "The Three Essays and the Meaning of the Sexual in Psychoanalysis," *Psychoanalytic Quarterly* 83, no. 2 (2014): 327–44.

26 John Steiner," Overcoming Obstacles in Analysis: Is it Possible to Relinquish Omnipotence and Accept Receptive Femininity?," *Psychoanalytic Quarterly* 82, no. 1 (2018): 1–20; Rosemary H. Balsam, "Response to John Steiner's 'Overcoming Obstacles in Analysis: Is It Possible to Relinquish Omnipotence and Accept Receptive Femininity?,' " *Psychoanalytic Quarterly* 87, no. 1 (2018): 21–31.

sexual theories. This means that just when we think we are referring to a natural disposition in ourselves, by formulating it in words, we are borrowing from the cultural elements that contributed to our capacity to formulate it. It follows that psychoanalysis has no way of *defining* without at the same time *prescribing* what the feminine is. Even a definition based on the most intimate personal experience of the analyst or his patient would be arbitrary rather than based on any solid metapsychological foundation.

Psychoanalysis is, I believe, an exemplar of what could be called an "ethepistemic" method, meaning that its ethics and its epistemology are two faces of the same coin.[27] The ethical stance we adopt determines the sort of psychical facts that we and our patients are able to elicit. One major ethical principle of psychoanalytic practice was formulated by Laplanche as the analyst's active refusal to know. Refusal, that is, to know what is the best route for the analysand to follow, or the best decision, the best object choice, etc. — essentially the refusal to know where the analysis should go except in a general way.[28] This is not neutrality for neutrality's sake. Rather, it reflects the fact that analyzing is mainly a *negative task* (to *analyze* is after all to *unravel*, to *unweave*), and we should therefore beware of making synthetic — and hence normative — assertions, especially when it comes to social values and their impact on individual choices. Freud seemed to concur with the view that synthesis is not our responsibility when, in a letter to Oskar Pfister, he wrote: "In the technique of psycho-analysis there is no need of any special synthetic work; the individual does that for himself

---

27 See Dominique Scarfone, preface to *The Ethical Seduction of the Analytic Situation: The Feminine-Maternal Origins of Responsibility for the Other*, by Viviane Chetrit-Vatine (London: Karnac Books, 2012); Dominque Scarfone, "On 'That Is Not Psychoanalysis': Ethics as the Main Tool for Psychoanalytic Knowledge and Discussion," *Psychoanalytic Dialogues* 27, no. 4 (2017): 392–400.

28 Jean Laplanche, "Transference: Its Provocation by the Analyst," trans. Luke Thurston, in *Essays on Otherness*, ed. John Fletcher (London: Routledge, 1999).

better than we can."[29] It's a pity he did not heed his own advice when it came to femininity.

If I am right that the ethics of the psychoanalyst determines to a certain extent what sort of facts (thoughts, theories, fantasies, affective complexes) are found in the course of analysis, it follows that the analyst cannot possibly entertain any idea—normative or not—of where the analysand should be heading in terms of gender identity, sexual orientation, or other connected issues. As analysts we simply cannot and should not claim to know what the feminine (or the masculine) is or should be like. Our role is to foster elaborative processes, with the aim of uncluttering the psyche of its rigid psycho-ideologies. As the analysis unfolds, our patients should become capable of making up their own minds about their femininity, masculinity, or queerness.

And Yet . . .

And yet, as I said earlier, citing Héritier, the male/female dichotomy holds a grip on our thinking such that, when it comes to speaking of the gendered position of the two analytic partners, we should forgive ourselves and our patients for conjuring up metaphors that pertain to a dual sexual endowment. I suggest, however, that there *are* effective ways of circumventing the ideological pitfalls regarding femininity.

For one thing, if we remind ourselves that the analytic task is essentially that of undoing the theories, ideologies, and so forth— in short, the *syntheses* that our analysands bring to the session—that means that we should always leave it to the patients themselves to reformulate the questions we have dealt with analytically. Can we do so unfailingly? Probably not. As Freud learned, suggestion, when

29 Freud to Oskar Pfister, October 9, 1918, in *Psycho-Analysis and Faith: The Letters of Sigmund Freud and Oskar Pfister*, ed. Heinrich Meng and Ernest L. Freud, trans. Eric Mosbacher, International Psycho-Analytical Library 59 (London: Hogarth Press, 1963), 62.

chased out through the front door, comes back around through the window. But this is a minor problem if the general atmosphere of the analysis and the elaboration of transference have given the analysand a sense of liberty, a capacity to think by themselves and to eventually contest and deviate from the ambient suggestions. It is, moreover, the analyst's responsibility to continually check for the unconscious collusion between patient and themselves, remembering Freud's precept that neither a patient's "yes" nor a patient's "no" is of any epistemological value.[30] What we aim at are interventions that open up new vistas for the analysand and elicit new material to analyze.

Another way of avoiding the ideological pitfalls is to elaborate conceptual tools that *sublimate* our spontaneously gendered metaphors. Freud gestured in that direction when he warned against conflating femininity with passivity and spoke instead of activity with a passive aim.[31] A better solution still is one proposed by Jean-François Lyotard, who suggested replacing "passivity" with "passibility."[32] The French term *passibilité* is just as uncommon as "passibility" is in English, but they share the same meaning: "The quality of being passible; capacity for suffering or sensation."[33] A good example of passibility is in the workings of the transference. Here, passibility captures the analyst's capacity for being affected or for bearing sensations that may be difficult to tolerate. But this has nothing specifically feminine in it. It is a nongendered, inherently analytic disposition. It demands of the analyst that which, after Hamlet, we could call a "readiness" to make oneself available to the analysand,[34]—that is, to offer a space

---

30 "Constructions in Analysis," *SE* 23:257.

31 *SE* 22:112–35.

32 *L'inhumain: Causeries sur le temps* (Paris: Galilée, 1988).

33 *Oxford English Dictionary Online*, s.v. "passibility," http://www.oed.com/view/Entry/138492.

34 See Dominque Scarfone, "De la disponibilité au transfert: Le leçon d'Hamlet,"

to both the filled-in and hollowed-out forms of transference.[35] The space in question may well be fantasized by the analysand, or the analyst, as a maternal womb. No one should take offense at such a gendered representation, inasmuch as it remains a matter for further analysis. Resisting possibility, on the other hand, may in turn reflect a resistance in the analyst to some self-representation they see as "feminine." Such was apparently the case with Freud when his patient Hilda Doolittle developed a maternal transference. She reported that at one point Freud told her: "I must tell you . . . , I do *not* like to be the mother in the transference — it always surprises and shocks me a little. I feel so very masculine."[36]

Then again, sexual dualism in our thinking is insuperable, as we have seen. As the struggle for control of the female body and its reproductive capacity reminds us, anatomy and physiology do matter. My daily practice with female patients shows me time and again how many of the traumas, frustrations, and vexations in their family, workplace, and love relationships point to the position of inferiority into which they, as women, would be relegated if they abandoned the fight to assert, day after day, their equality and dignity. Their struggle ultimately concerns the control of their bodies, around which infantile theories are easily reactivated and mesh all too well with the gross or subtle ideological surroundings. As their interlocutor, I would fail my patients if I were to ignore how these outer and inner representations coalesce and weigh on their condition, a condition that concerns the citizen in me. My role in the analytic session, however, is not to intervene in their outer social struggle (as analysts we cannot claim to possess the tools for that purpose). Only by implementing the analytic deconstruction of the infantile theories at work in the analysand's psyche, which, as we saw, collude with sexist ideologies, can analysis foster — in

---

Revue française de psychosomatique 53 (2018): 6–19.

35 See Laplanche, "Transference."

36 H.D., *Tribute to Freud* (New York: New Directions, 1956), 144.

female *and* male patients—their capacity to become aware of their feminine and masculine identifications with all of their complex implications. In this process, referring to the sexual binary is not a problem, inasmuch as these opposites are not frozen ideologically gendered representations but entrants in a living dialectics, elaborating their contradictions even as no final synthesis is in sight.

Conversation

AS: This essay was written to be delivered as a keynote lecture at the fifty-first International Psychoanalytic Association (IPA) Congress in London in 2019. The topic of that conference was the feminine, which came as a surprise to some analysts. For some, a preoccupation with gender is itself nonanalytic, inferior to considerations of, say, transference, dreams, or free association. That low regard for the topic was reflected in the composition of that year's conference attendees: analysts from certain psychoanalytic schools of thought were not as visible or vocal as they usually are at the IPA meetings. At the same time, analysts who do see gender as a topic that does and should concern psychoanalysis felt that the topic itself had a tinge of anachronism as it could be seen as inviting a reification of gender, as if there is some originary feminine that could be subject to singular theorization.

Your paper takes on the challenge of theorizing the feminine but takes an unexpected turn—showing us that gender in general and the feminine in particular are absolutely psychoanalytically relevant categories, though perhaps not in the way that it is oftentimes imagined by analysts. Further, you manage to show us how we should expect "the male/female dichotomy [to hold] a grip on our thinking" and that "we should forgive ourselves . . . for conjuring up metaphors that pertain to a dual sexual endowment" while also suggesting that "there *are* effective ways of circumventing the ideological pitfalls regarding femininity."[37] These are terrific examples of how you combine the rigorous and the expansive in your thinking. Could you say a bit about your process in working on this essay and what it was like to find your way around Freudian psychoanalysis's entrenched difficulties in thinking about gender?

DS: The experience of writing a paper is quite particular, as I imagine is also your experience, in that we start with a certain idea, but as we put words together, we discover at once unexpected

---

37 See p. 161 above.

obstacles and unexpected new directions in our thinking. So I did not know in advance where I was heading when I started working on this keynote lecture, and I can see only from the *après-coup* perspective what was guiding me. To be sure, my most reliable basis for the ideas in the paper was—and still is—what in shorthand we may call "the translational model" in psychoanalysis. It is a way of looking at the life of the psyche as *determined* when it comes to its functioning (i.e., it cannot help trying to make sense of its surroundings even while the semantic tools it uses are not infinite) and yet *open ended* when it comes to the products of such functioning (i.e., producing potentially infinite meaningful combinations, degrees of intensity, etc.).

In retrospect, it is obvious that Laplanche's views helped me on many levels. For one thing, I was reminded of the fact that human beings are essentially self-defining, self-theorizing beings, hence that in our analytic practice we are always dealing with theories and first and foremost with the theories our patients carry with them and bring to their sessions. This is often misunderstood as meaning that analysis according to Laplanche is an intellectual endeavor, a confrontation of theories. So I wish to indicate here what the word "theory" entails. The best reference I can think of is the dialogue between Karl Popper and Konrad Lorenz, where at one point they discuss the meaning of "theory." They recall that the Greek word *theōria* has to do with a procession and more generally a passage, and they end up stating something that is truly definitional and, to me, fundamental: they say that in a sense, "the eye is a theory of light."[38] The eye is indeed a physical passage for the part of the electromagnetic spectrum we call light, and it is also an organ by which that part of the spectrum is "interpreted"—that is, put to some important use by the *transduction* the retina operates and thanks to which light impulses are translated into nerve impulses

---

38 Karl R. Popper and Konrad Lorenz, *L'avenir est ouvert*, Champs (Paris: Flammarion, 2013, my translation).

informing the brain of what was captured by the eye. Thus, the theory in question is *embodied* at the same time as it implies the basic *translational function* to which I referred earlier. I therefore insist that the theories that patients bring to analysis are of the embodied kind, especially since they are *infantile theories* whose building blocks are derived from the infant's bodily experience — that is, their excitable body — more so than from abstract language.

This brings us to the distinction between the infantile theories that everybody formulates and carries in their mind and the abstract psychoanalytic Theory we are continuously working with and working on (I capitalized *T* for clarity's sake). Our Theory needs to account for the infantile theories we uncover in our work, but we should make sure not to uncritically elevate the latter to the status of the general Theory. This distinction is the first thing that helped me formulate a critique of Freud's ideas on the feminine, in which he clearly conflates Little Hans's infantile theories (such as the theory of castration and the theory phallic monism) with psychoanalytic Theory. I was impressed by the fact that very early Karen Horney had seen this theoretical confusion and that her well-documented protest had no effect whatsoever on Freud.

The other thing that had a major influence on me is what I would call "Laplanche's theorem," which states: *"The sexual is the unconscious residue of the symbolization-repression of gender by sex."*[39] It is, in my view, one of the most useful applications of his general theory of seduction to the advancement of psychoanalytic thinking about sex and gender. With these two thought instruments, I was quite naturally brought to taking the stance you referred to in your question but not before finding a correspondence between this and material in the social and anthropological fields about the status of women throughout human history.

---

39 Jean Laplanche, "Gender, Sex and the *Sexual*", in *Freud and the Sexual: Essays 2000–2006*, trans. John Fletcher, Jonathan House, and Nicholas Ray (New York: International Psychoanalytic Books, 2011, p. 167, italics in the original).

AS: From the first page of this keynote lecture, you identify the "feminine" as issuing from what "was from the start a male/female division of labor."[40] This situating of the problem of gender, of which the feminine is ostensibly at one end of the spectrum, in the domain of work might come as a surprise to those who don't know that you have a long history as a reader of Marx. Would you tell us a bit about your background in this area? We see you use some of that background here in discussing gender, and I am also curious about how you see your contact with Marxist theory as having influenced your psychoanalytic theorizing overall.

DS: Let me make clear that I am not a Marxist scholar. I read Marx in my youth and was a left-wing activist for a few years during my medical studies and my psychiatry residency. In the face of all the blatant historical failures of applied Marxism, I stopped subscribing to the communist ideals many decades ago, but I still find that Marx's analysis of capitalism was valid and useful to the working class at large in understanding how the capitalist system works.

Now, as you know, Marx and Engels considered class struggle the main motor of history so that for them the division of labor that mattered was that between the laboring classes and the ruling classes, in the different forms these took at different epochs. Closer to us, Horkheimer and Adorno, in their *Dialectic of Enlightenment*, held the view that the fundamental division was between manual and intellectual labor.[41] Both these divisions are certainly very important for understanding human societies throughout history, but they also leave out the male/female division of labor as if it went without saying, a natural datum. Thanks to the work of feminist researchers, such as the anthropologist Françoise Héritier, whom

---

40 See p. 149 above.

41 Max Horkheimer and Theodor W. Adorno, *Dialectic of Enlightenment: Philosophical Fragments*, ed. Gunzelin Schmid Noerr, trans. Edmund Jephcott (Stanford, CA: Stanford University Press, 2002).

I cite in my article, I am now convinced of the fundamental role played not only by the male/female division of labor but also by the struggle for the control of the female body, which is inseparable from the division in question.

For me as an analyst who believes that we are not working with natural categories, it was of the utmost importance to see if and how my critique of the Freudian views about the feminine converged with the feminist views on the division of labor. It became quite clear to me (though this may not be original at all) that the dominant ideology can, consciously or unconsciously, select—in the Darwinian sense—the infantile sexual theories that help perpetuate its dominance. This makes it crucially important that psychoanalysis, which presented itself historically as in the service of truth and opposed to oppressive ideologies, does not concur in the conflation of infantile theories and an enlightened psychoanalytic Theory.

AS: I have in fact never heard it put that way: that dominant ideology finds its foothold in and makes use of infantile sexual theories to buttress its hegemony. I am familiar with the first idea, that dominant ideology exerts an effect that may then become internalized. And the second idea—namely, that infantile sexual theories have a bearing on how we understand the world—is also in wide circulation. But the way you link them here stands out to me because it brings together the social and the psychic in an original way. In other words, this is not the usual formulation we encounter in which "the outside gets introjected and becomes installed in the psychic domain." Instead, you give us a way of being able to see *how* the outside compels us: because it is, from the get-go, syndicating with the materials of the inside (the infantile sexual theories), which are themselves, as you show, always already infiltrated by the outside (since they borrow on the mytho-symbolic to become psychically represented). I hope you will excuse me for breaking this down even more—I do so because I think that for analysts who already think about gender expansively, it could be easy to miss that what you are bringing that's unique is this very particular connection, this novel link you make between the psychic and the social.

You mark for us how in theorizing the feminine through a number of assumptive (and, perhaps, indefensible) premises— for example, that femininity needs to involve the vaginal taking priority over the clitoral—Freud performs "a symbolic excision of women," prescribing rather than describing what makes someone "feminine."[42] Feminist theory, queer theory, and relational feminist theorizing in psychoanalysis (I am thinking of Ken Corbett, Muriel Dimen, Dianne Elise, Virginia Goldner, and Adrienne Harris to name a few) have all taken up this point to challenge assumptions deeply embedded in analytic thinking about femininity—and, by extension, what is masculine. But you are unique in placing this in the metapsychological framework of Jean Laplanche to ask: Why is Freud making this mistake? You are asking: How can we understand Freud's conflating of the infantile sexual theories of his patients with a developmental line? You explain that this error draws from the fact that what the analyst "discovers" through the child's translating activity, is then taken to be an elemental structure. And that Laplanche's translational theory permits us to see why "an apparent universality [passes] for a 'natural' or 'inborn' state of affairs."[43]

What about forms of gender that deviate from the strict binary? How might we understand those when the translational tools at hand are mostly male/female?

DS: I wish I could refer our readers to Laplanche's second book of the series Problématiques, whose title translates as "Castration-

---

42 See p. 152 above.

43 See p. 157 above.

Symbolizations," which is not yet available in English. There we can find luminous pages on the topic you are raising. Laplanche starts by crediting Freud with a more complex view on the question than we usually recall. For instance, there is the use by Freud of two words: *Unterschied* (difference) and *Verschiedenheit* (diversity). I will not engage here in the complexity of the matter but will only bring up some of Laplanche's important remarks. For one thing, difference can be reduced to a bipolar difference by convention—1/0 (in computer language), black/white, and so forth. For what regards the male/female difference, one must notice that there are elements that indeed, most of the time, point to a dichotomy, but it can be looked at as a strict difference only if we concentrate on one element, such as penis/vagina. Laplanche, though, points out that this is, in a way, circumstantial and that nothing in principle would impede the existence of three or more *sexes*.[44] However, let us concede that with the exception of "true hermaphroditism" (ovotesticular disorder) with its anatomical ambiguities, most of the time there is a penis/vagina polarity. Except that this is true only for scientific anatomical knowledge but far from being the case for the *imaginary* anatomy that we carry in our psyche. Nor is this imaginary anatomy a deliberate or random choice—it is determined by psychic reality. As Laplanche posits, if this were a choice, then reading books of anatomy would cure hysterical conversion symptoms (which rest on an imaginary anatomy).

Going back to your question, we see that the situation is inextricably complex: Anatomical difference can be more or less reduced to a binary code (though there are undecidable cases) by scientific discourse. But if what matters in people's lives is indeed the imaginary anatomy, then *diversity* introduces itself in the very tools that the psyche uses to translate the message of gender.

---

44 *Problématiques*, vol. 2, *Castration-Symbolisations* (Paris: Presses Universitaires de France, 1980), 51.

Let's go back to what I dubbed "Laplanche's theorem": "*The sexual is the unconscious residue of the symbolization of gender by sex.*" In it we see that gender is what needs translation (i.e., symbolization-repression). This means that Laplanche takes gender as the overt message ("It's a girl!" or "It's a boy!") that the child receives but needs to translate. Remember that translation in this situation carries two simultaneous consequences: symbolization *and* repression, in that the repressed is nothing but what could not be symbolized. The Sexual then *is* the repressed—that is, the unconscious residue of the child's effort at symbolization. Now let's leave this aside for a moment and concentrate on gender and sex.

We already said that gender is, at first, of the order of the message: gender is first *attributed* to the individual by the parental (or societal) gaze and judgment. But this is only the beginning of the story. Throughout childhood and adolescence, the individual has to keep translating and retranslating for himself the message of gender to *assume* their gender identity.[45] This, according to Laplanche, is done with the means of sex, which Laplanche states is dual. But here things get even more complicated because Laplanche states the duality of sex is due, on the one hand, to the laws of sexual reproduction (and hence to physiological difference of the sex organs) but "*also by virtue of its human symbolization, which sets and freezes the duality as presence/absence, phallic/castrated.*"[46]

---

45 DS: The ambiguity of the verb "to assume" is highly significant in this context: to assume may mean "to take on oneself, to take charge of" but also "to make a hypothesis, to presume." This opens up an interesting problem that I cannot explore here.

AS: Interestingly, the philosopher and queer theorist Gayle Salamon has also used the verb "assume" in this polysemic way in her book, titled "Assuming a Body: Transgender and Rhetorics of Materiality." For her, rather than something that is given, the body is psychic, something we assume through complex processes, which is very compatible with what you are outlining here. The ways the body can be inhabited, she argues, cannot be taken for granted a priori, and in that sense Salamon, is also taking aim at biologism, all the while not denying biology. The distinction between biologism and biology proves especially consequential in thinking transness.

46 *Freud and the Sexual*, 167; italics in the original.

The "freezing" into a duality by human symbolization implies that the very tools with which symbolization is effectuated are not natural but socially and culturally determined. This may seem a pessimistic view in that the reigning ideology is that of the "phallic logic," but in fact it is good news: it means that the means of translation can be modified through cultural and political intervention or struggle. Why is this possible? Because besides the logic of difference, there is the logic of diversity. The binary phallic logic of difference goes like this: if not male, then female. But the logic of diversity goes like this: if not male, then female at the physiological level but not necessarily so at the level of the assumed gender. And this is possible because the tools of translation are themselves not natural, not determined by scientifically established anatomy, but influenced by the imaginary anatomy—that is, by the relatively extended freedom to translate.

This to me is what renders it theoretically legitimate to insert the open-ended possibilities of social debate into our metapsychology. Unlike anatomy, metapsychology, when taking transduction/ translation as the basic function, allows for quite a large degree of diversity in the end products of translation, which include identifications, gender assumption, and so forth.

At this point, however, I need to bring back the Sexual, the repressed, which is always operating in the wings. The assumption of a given gender can hardly be considered free of unconscious influences on the part of the parents. For instance, the parents may exclaim, "It's a boy!" while one of them may be unconsciously thinking: "I know it's a boy, but all the same, it's not a boy." And "It's not a boy" may mean "It's a girl" or "It's a boy, but I wish it would have a feminine character" . . . and a great variety of combinations are possible. What I am saying is that in practice the very action of translation by the subject can give the impression of a free choice of one's gender, while in fact the subject is unknowingly obeying the untold desire of the other (the parents). And of course, other influences will also manifest that will use these unconscious determinants as levers to guide apparently free individual choices. So translation is the tool for the construction of oneself, but it does not operate in a sterile field. As you know, *implantation* cannot be devoid of *intromission*, and what "intromission" means here is that the other impinges on the subject's most intimate process: that of translating or interpreting the message of the other. This, by the way, is why I always considered Piera Aulagnier's "violence of interpretation"[47] a necessary complement to Laplanche's theory of seduction, which is actually called for by his brief study of intromission.

An ethical issue is at stake here in terms of how society—that is, families, therapists, medical doctors, and so forth—respond to a request for changing one's gender identity, especially if it involves altering (sometimes irreversibly) the sexual anatomy.

While it would be cruel to deny an individual their autonomy in the choice of gender identity or sexual reassignment, all the same I am concerned when I hear stories of three-year-old children who, soon after they state that they belong to the other sex or gender, are quickly confirmed in this by their parents and health professionals for fear of denying them their "true" nature. Let me be clear: it may be the case that a consensus of this kind is arrived at while respecting the autonomy of the subject; after all, who says that a subject's choice is freer when assuming a nonqueer identity? A specific gravitas, however, is added to the situation by the supplementary tools provided by the medical profession. These new opportunities do not escape the double nature of the *pharmakon*: they can be tools for more freedom or tools for implementing yet another ideology if the autonomy of the subject is not what guides the assumption

---

47 Piera Aulagnier, *The Violence of Interpretation: From Pictogram to Statement*, trans. Alan Sheridan (London, Routledge, 2001).

of their gender. So there is a work of disentanglement between, for instance, the child's sexual/gendered self-theory and the benevolent pressure from a parent's need to fulfill their own self-image as "free minds." The question is: Do we do all it takes to free the child from a surplus of pressure—pressure in excess of the unavoidable emission of enigmatic messages? What matters most to me is to assist the individual in making as free a choice as possible, and this implies helping them to have a relative freedom from certain unconscious determinants—that is, as much as possible, it should be assured that these determinants are not in the nature of intromission. In other words, a demand for reassignment, when it involves hormonal or surgical intervention, should—to the extent this is possible—accompany the child's working through their self-theory, which, after all and given all I said earlier, may well be one more infantile theory.

Since I first formulated these worries, however, I read a paper by you and Ann Pellegrini that answered them brilliantly. I discussed them here all the same, for the reader's benefit, and for the same reason, let me quote from your paper, which includes a clinical case of a gender-variant child and his relationship with his mother, about which you write:

> What is at stake here is not a question of locus (did it start in him or in her [that is, did the child's gender originate from within the child himself or from the mother's intergenerational intrusion] because the infantile Sexual is always stimulated and arises in us by the intervention of the other (Laplanche 1987; 2011). It is, rather, to treat [the child's] gender in its full complexity: as a form of translation that fits well enough *for him*—is congruent enough with his own sense of being, and, as such, needs to be nurtured and supported—*and also* as a way of being that

has accommodated an interlock of subject-object dynamics that his [parent's] history seems to have required.[48]

And:

> To hold the paradoxical tension between the work my patient's gender may be doing for the [parent] and what felt like a goodness of fit between [the patient's] gender and his being—and to work with this therapeutically—would involve a complex way of holding the complementarity of these dynamics so that neither is negated and, simultaneously, neither has to stand in for the other. The clinical task would be extremely complex: to help my patient recognize the parental pressures that tasks him to perform both otherness and compliant normativity *but doing so without implying that his gender is not his own.* (26; italics in the original)

Your approach truly answers the issues I formulated, and it is extraordinary that you had put it in words well before I formulated the questions in my mind.

AS: Thank you Dominique. What was important to us in writing this paper was to describe precisely this particular tangle between the pressure of intergenerational transmission and gendered experience. And to highlight that what comes from the realm of the intergenerational can be uptaken by the self-theorizing child for their own translational usage, yielding translations that are still one's own. That seemed important to us because, oftentimes, the

---

48 Avgi Saketopoulou and Ann Pellegrini. "A Feminine Boy: Normative Investments and Reparative Fantasy at the Intersections of Gender, Race, and Religion". IPA Tiresias Essay Prize. A developed version of this essay is published in Saketopoulou, A. & Pellegrini, A. (2023) Gender without identity. NY: Unconscious in Translation Press

circulation of parental trauma in the relationship between caretaker and infant is taken by analysts to mean that the child's gender is forced out of its "proper" (aka normative or cis) course. What we wanted to show is how, in the course of coping with the strain of being exposed to parental trauma, a child innovates, and that that innovation inflects the complexity of one's gender. Innovation, to put it more clearly, is not derailment from a "proper" course, but how something comes to feel one's own.

But there are also some other things you said that I'd like to follow up on. You write, "The question is: Do we do all it takes to free the child from a surplus of pressure—pressure in excess of the unavoidable emission of enigmatic messages? What matters most to me is to assist the individual in making as free a choice as possible, and this implies helping them to have a relative freedom from certain unconscious determinants—that is, as much as possible, it should be assured that these determinants are not in the nature of intromission." The "surplus of pressure" that concerns you is over and above the expectable surfeit that involves the enigmatic; it is more about intromission (i.e., the interdiction to the child *against* translating enigma freely, therefore forcing meanings into a child). Can you help us think about what this process of "freeing" the child from surplus pressures can look like? I am asking because the verb "free" can be tricky, especially since all translations are constrained, and thus delimited, by the mytho-symbolic tools on which they have to rely in order for new meanings to be churned. This takes us back to Aulagnier and her notion of primary violence, which you alluded to already. Can you flesh that out for us a bit more?

DS: You do well to remind us that the word "free" can be misleading. Of course, there is no total freedom; it's more a matter of the child's operating their own construction with the elements they find in their environment, which are finite in number. Even in the most favorable situation, the parents' conscious and, still more so, unconscious wishes and desires do influence the child's constructions. What matters is what I would call an "optimal degree of freedom," an openness to becoming that reflects the general atmosphere in the family where the child is reared. We can experience freedom when we are able to operate within certain limits that still allow for a sense that we are creating something that is ours. Aulagnier is indeed an important reference here since she calls our attention to the unavoidable "primary violence" at work in rearing a child inside any given cultural environment, while warning against the avoidable "secondary violence" that deprives the child of any real possibility of choosing.[49]

AS: If, as you write, femininity requires that certain characteristics are prescriptively amputated in women, how might we think of their excision in men? If femininity, as you show us, is an infantile sexual theory that psychoanalysts have, following Freud, taken as ontology, then it would follow that it would not, or should not, appear only in women. So what are the implications of your thinking in considering femininity in men?

DS: It follows indeed that normative rules amputate men of certain potentialities and that this carries an enormous cost for them. The very common rule "Boys don't cry" is an easy example, and if one needs to show that this is totally tied to a given ideology, one needs only to open the *Iliad* and see the fierce Achaean or Trojan warriors weeping intensely at the loss of a comrade, friend, lover, or motherland. The freezing into binary categories entails a loss for everyone. I think here, for instance, of the many deaths and injuries that were caused by what Christophe Dejours called "the defensive ideologies" of male workers in industries such as construction, where until quite recently those who followed safety rules were

---

49 Aulagnier, *Violence of Interpretation. op. cit.*

called "sissies."[50] And we, as analysts, know of a continent of suffering that rests on the same kind of ways of thinking in more private situations.

Here again it is a question of how cultural determinants and infantile theories may clash or concur—that is, be selected by an ideology that in turn reconfirms them in each individual. The difficulty and the limits we encounter here are, obviously, that after having denounced the normative stance of others, psychoanalysts cannot prescribe new norms . . . So while as citizens we have a right to our own preferences, in our practice as analysts, we must struggle to remain agnostic.

AS: Following Laplanche, you make an important distinction regarding processes of identification as they are usually understood in regard to gender development (i.e., the boy identifies with his father to be spared the terror of castration and the girl with her mother to preserve her mother's love). It is the process of being *identified by* the other, you write, that is more important here. This is parallel to what trans studies calls "gender assignment," though, as far as I know, trans studies do not consider the impact of unconscious factors. In your thinking, to be identified *by* an other involves the category of the message—a message that, as we've seen again and again, is always parasitized by the adult's *sexual* unconscious. What is the role of identification *within* this process? With gender assignment (i.e., identification by) being the most central operation does identification *within* this process lose importance or disappear?

DS: As I may have hinted in my long response above, *identification with* (secondary identification) seems to me to be one of the forms taken by the transductional efforts of the child. It appears to me as the "taking form" that occurs when the child unavoidably follows the model of the loved object, but with enough freedom for them

---

50 *Travail: usure mentale.* (Paris: Éditions du Centurion, 1980, my translation).

not to become a clone. There is a metabolization of the message of the other, about gender or anything else, and a reshuffling of the cards of primary identification. It is a process that I believe is never completely terminated and that has at least two peaks: one during childhood and the second during adolescence. The reshuffling of adolescence is probably the one that seals, more or less, the fate of identification.

AS: Are you saying, then, that for you the role of "identification with" has to do with the adult's own psychic complexion offering features that can be selected by the child (not with conscious intention, of course) for their translational efforts?

DS: Identification is a tricky process because it at once instantiates a memory and an erasure. "Identifying oneself with" means forgoing the active link to the object and, all the same, not entirely letting go of the object, because a trait of the object has become a trait of the self. Secondary identification, then, does correspond to a process of translation but only to a certain extent in that the trait of the object is now possessed by the subject as if it has been *borrowed*, not *transformed* as in translation proper. Obviously, being inserted among the other traits of personality, the "borrowed" trait takes on different meanings, but it could always be traced back to its source in the lost object, as is the case for certain Greek marble columns that can be recognized in Roman Catholic churches in southern Italy. The columns were certainly not "digested" or "translated," but they have been inserted in a new context and therefore tell a different story, though the original story was never truly erased.

AS: Can you say a bit more about the emphasis you place on the distinction between anatomical difference and the perception of anatomical difference? The key word here seems to be "difference." Could you talk about why "perception" should concern us?

DS: It is now widely accepted, I believe, that, as Freud thought, perception has nothing passive in it but consists in an active sampling of the surroundings through a periodic emission of "sensors."[51] Today, the theory of perception holds not only that we actively sample but also that this sampling is the perceiver's way of testing their *predictions* about the environment.[52] This means that there is indeed no perception that is not always already oriented by the mind's effort to predict what there is to perceive. We have thus one more reason to believe that the mytho-symbolic tools provided by the environment (parental, familial, or societal) influence perception of the anatomical differences. So as we saw above, when we speak, following Laplanche, of the symbolization-repression of gender by sex, it must be stressed that the "sex" in question is not simply the natural anatomical difference but also and perhaps more importantly the "frozen" dichotomy brought about by the culture that informs perception to a large extent.

AS: If I understand you correctly you are, then, saying that our "perception" of sexual difference is not a rendering of a truth, but rather it is itself infiltrated by the social, that it is always already organized through a social lens. I am asking for clarification not to be repetitive but because you are showing us how the social and the psychic cannot be separated and because I have in mind here analysts who might argue that to think about the social is not psychoanalytic, since the social inscribes itself on the psychic *après-coup*.

DS: You understood me well, and let me add that the *après-coup* inscription is not an argument against thinking about the social in psychoanalysis—quite to the contrary! The social does inscribe itself in the psychic in a process of *après-coup*, but it does so *no more and no less* than everything else psychic. Freud wrote somewhere that every representation was once a perception. What we are calling

---

51 Sigmund Freud, "Negation," *SE* 19:227–39.

52 See Andy Clark, *Surfing Uncertainty: Prediction, Action and the Embodied Mind* (Oxford: Oxford University Press, 2016); Mark Solms, *The Hidden Spring: A Journey at the Source of Consciousness* (London, Profile Books, 2021).

attention to is that there is no pure perception, that perception is to a certain extent culturally determined inasmuch as what we refer to is in fact the judgment we exert on what our senses capture—that is, the *account* we give ourselves about what we perceive. Such an account is indisputably a social fact no matter how private it may seem.

AS: Thank you. That is so crisply and helpfully put!

I also want to turn to another part of your paper if I may. You foreground the ethical dimension of the analyst's refraining from synthesizing. And you use the term "ethepistemic" to mark how psychoanalytic ethics and our epistemology are closely knit together. To some degree, you note, it's impossible for the analyst to not make any synthesis: even the act of asking about one thing as opposed to another when, for example, a patient shares a memory has a synthetic undertone.

But your point is larger than that; our role is to guard against becoming overly invested in any one outcome, unavoidable as that may be. Critical to this, it seems to me, would be to be mindful of when we, as analysts, become too invested in this path or another for a patient. Sometimes, however, we don't know that we are invested until after the fact; actually, in real time our "investment" may not feel (to us) like an investment in anything other than the patient's "well-being." I see this frequently, for example, when I discuss trans issues with colleagues. One often-arising question is: Why would you let a patient move forward with, say, genital-altering surgery. What about their fertility? Their sexual excitability? And so forth. These types of concerns, as you can imagine, become extremely layered and difficult in discussing trans children and adolescents. Of course, these matters (fertility, excitement) are important considerations, and they are not treated lightly. But the larger point I am trying to make is that concerns for the patient's fertility or sexual arousal are not seen as "investments in outcome" on the analyst's part; they are understood by the analysts who raise them as part of the "do no harm" rule.

The Hippocratic maxim, "ὠφελέειν ἢ μη βλάπτειν" in ancient Greek, has come under some pressure in recent years as it has been charged with being paternalistic because it assumes that it is the doctor (or analyst or other health expert) who decides what's harmful and what's not.[53] I have recently been reading the work of Eleni Askitopoulou and Antonis Vgontzas on this matter. They note that the spirit of the maxim was to foreground that the doctor's responsibility is to their patient and not to the social contract or to upholding established societal values.[54]

You and I discussed "Do no harm" a bit in our conversation on chapter 1, but I return to it in this context as I am so curious to hear your thoughts on this topic from a theoretical perspective because the position you propose (and with which, I should say, I agree) has considerable implications.

DS: I always understood "First do no harm" as a call for one of the major virtues of ancient Greece: prudence, the opposite of hubris. It is a reminder that the doctor does not know all the answers; hence, basic prudence demands that whatever we attempt, we must at least make sure that the cure is not worse than the illness. I see no paternalism whatsoever in this and find it quite reassuring to know that doctors, analysts, and so forth abide by this maxim.

As for the neologism "ethepistemic," it came to me when I wanted to stress the fact that the analyst's ethical stance is not

---

53 See, e.g., Andrea Long Chu, "My New Vagina Won't Make Me Happy: And It Shouldn't Have To," *New York Times*, November 24, 2018, https://www.nytimes.com/2018/11/24/opinion/sunday/vaginoplasty-transgender-medicine.html; Julian Gill-Peterson, *Histories of the Transgender Child* (Minneapolis: University of Minnesota, 2018).

54 E. Askitopoulou and A. Vgontzas, *Ωφελέειν ἢ μη βλάπτειν: Διαχρονικές αξίες ηθικής και δεοντολογίας στο έργο του Ιπποκράτη* [First do no harm: The diachronic value of ethics and deontology in the work of Hippocrates] (Athens: Ελληνικό Ανοιχτό Πανεπιστήμιο, 2021).

something *added* to their "know-how" but is a precondition for accessing material that would not show up otherwise. It is the ethics of truly listening in a nonoriented way, of being available to hearing the unexpected rather than, say, what their theory or their personal preference would predict.

With regard to the trans issues you mention, to the extent that I understand the situation correctly, the questions you bring up are complicated by the fact that the person who consults you sometimes puts you in a specific role as the one who can attest to a third party that nothing opposes the transitioning, for instance. This seems to me to pose an additional challenge to the "ethepistemic" stance, in that your listening may indeed be hijacked, so to speak, by practical problems such as addressing the expectations of the patient in terms of critical decisions. As you know, I had some apprehensions regarding this aspect of these situations because as soon as we feel that there is someone waiting at the door of our office, our listening is overburdened. But then, as Laplanche has pointed out in a less well-known paper of his, the same kind of problem exists in child analysis—when parents expect results that normalize the child— that is, make the child well-adjusted to the family's status quo.[55] The same goes for training institutes who still practice "training analysis," to which—contrary to the full open-endedness we advocate for analytic treatment—a goal (training) is adjoined, which may seriously interfere with the analysand's freedom to express deviant traits, for example, *and* with the analyst's capacity to keep on analyzing rather than worrying about the training aspect. The problem facing the analyst during the session is how to ignore all these distractions so as to help the patient access their own desire, irrespective of the expectations of others—their analyst, their partners, their family, the analyst's training institute, and so

---

55 Jean Laplanche, "The Training Analysis: A Psychoanalysis 'on Command,'" in *Between Seduction and Inspiration: Man,* trans. Jeffrey Mehlman (New York: Unconscious in Translation, 2015), 97–106.

forth. This obviously requires some courage, and situations often arise when passing compromises, with regard to the expectations I mentioned, may be unavoidable lest we see the analysis stall or come to an abrupt end.

AS: In discussing the space that the analyst offers for filled-in and hollowed-out transferences, you write that the "space in question may well be fantasized by the analysand, or the analyst, as a maternal womb, but this is only a fantasy. Still, no one should take offence at such a gendered representation, inasmuch as it remains a matter for further analysis."[56] If we unpack what you are saying here, assuming I don't misread you, you are pointing out that while the receptive space the analyst creates for the patient is not gendered per se, it may become gendered—it may be gender*ized*, if you will—through fantasy. Such genderizing, you indicate, is not necessarily a problem—you've already told us that, in fact, the duality of sex may be unavoidable—as long as it remains possible to examine the ascription of "femininity" to the receptive space of the analysis *as a fantasy*. I find this formulation helpful because while many analysts would agree today that conflating receptivity with the feminine may be problematic, you are giving us a way to think analytically about this—that such conflation would be an infantile sexual theory itself. I am wondering if you have any thoughts about why such genderizing may occur? Why would gender, as opposed to any other translational tool, so readily lend itself to describing the analytic situation?

DS: My spontaneous answer is that whether we talk of difference or of diversity, of two genders or sexes or of more, at some point the individual opts for a certain "bricolage," a certain combination of elements. The image of the analyst as offering a maternal womb is, in my experience, quite frequent and easily explained since, as I say in the paper, the fact is that everyone came out of a womb! That this function can be fantasized by the patient regardless of the analyst's

---

56 See p. 163 above.

sex or gender speaks of the function's translational nature and therefore its relative freedom from the contingencies of anatomy. This brings us back to Laplanche's discussion of difference and diversity. He explains that diversity has to do with the fact that there is not one single element that differentiates individuals: there are dual elements, such as penis and vagina/uterus, but there are also other attributes such as breasts, pilosity, and so forth, and one could add height, plumpness, voice pitch, and whatnot. It is a common experience in analysis that a man can be the object of a maternal transference. The plasticity of fantasy building, to which we can add the intervention of linguistic signifiers that play with the perceived reality, can give rise to multiple forms.

As analysts, I believe, to allow our patients the freedom to fantasize is to not introduce any requirement for concordance with *our* perceived reality, which is as personal as theirs.

AS: The more we talk the clearer it becomes why your proposition that psychoanalytic Theory or theories are inevitably the products of infantile sexual theories is important. We have approached this idea from various angles and keep returning to the matter of the analyst's perceived reality—that reality that you help us see is not mere prejudice or opinion but a fundamental way of being in the world. Many have critiqued psychoanalytic theories that may be too conservative or even harmful in this or that way or that may be little more than an analyst's own preconceived notions, but you are giving us a way to understand why and how we, as analysts, become not only convinced but also *psychically invested* in certain theoretical presuppositions. Because you reformulate them as more than ideas (ideas may more easily be swapped out for better ones if one becomes convinced that other ideas are superior) and frame them, instead, as invested translations, your work can also help us understand the resistance we encounter in revising our analytic lexicons and tool kit for working with new populations and in wider cultural contexts.

DS: I would not say that psychoanalytic Theory or theories are the *product* of infantile theories. What I tried to show in the paper is that infantile theories can *infiltrate* the psychoanalytic Theory, just as they can be selected by – and therefore infiltrate the prevailing world views in a given culture. What I say is that I believe that we, individuals, are our *memory*—and I mean memory, not *memories*, which as we know are more labile. In the same line of thinking, we *are* our deeply embedded and strongly invested self-theories. Obviously, we also entertain *opinions* about ourselves, and these too can more easily change than our memory, in that they are influenced by opinions that others have of us and by changing circumstances. So I concur with you in seeing in our personal investment in our theories an important source of the resistance to changing them. Now, this resistance could, in principle, also apply to psychoanalytic Theory as a whole (or to psychoanalytic theories) in that the infiltrated infantile theories probably take part in the resistance to change. One more reason for following Laplanche's example, which consists in forcing the very Theory to continuously explain itself *to itself.*

AS: This distinction you draw, between theories not as products of, but as infiltrated by, sexual theories seems very meaningful to me. I think that the fact that these infiltrations can then have a share in the resistance to change is also something we see in the resistance that we have, as analysts and as a field, to evolving ideas: our existing theories are not just ideas we have about things, they would be (and in my opinion often are), to use your phrase, "strongly invested self-theories."

One of your paper's other important takeaways is that in speaking about gender, clinically and perhaps otherwise, "referring to the sexual binary is not a problem, inasmuch as these opposites are not frozen ideologically gendered representations but entrants in a living dialectics."[57] This can help reconcile us, as analysts, with the notion that however expansively gender is lived by any one person and however idiomatically and autonomously translations vis-à-vis gender may be made, the organizing conceptual framework of sexual *dualism* is here to stay. I find that sobering because it offers an opportunity for us to relax our grip when it comes to how we oftentimes come back to terms like "male" and "female"; as long as we do not reify them, we may keep using them. But even as I raise this with you, I feel some anxiety: not reifying these and considering them as "entrants in a living dialectics" is, I think, easier said than done. Do you have any advice on how we can keep this tension taut?

DS: My answer is tentative since I do not pretend to have a recipe here. I think of how we go about using our psychoanalytic vocabulary. It is very tempting to try and fixate our terminology once and for all, but this would be a mistake, a hopeless effort to control the evolution of language, which parallels (and feeds on) the evolution of society, of knowledge, and of thinking. I believe in the inescapable ambiguity of the human condition, so I find it contradictory to advocate diversity while trying to control how people use language. I say: let the ambiguity prevail in everyday parlance, and bet on the fact that language will find its way. Every known effort at orienting speech, especially during the twentieth century, resulted in disaster.

The language of psychoanalysis has an inherent ambiguity, and we know that Freud resorted as much as possible to everyday vocabulary. The translational model that I advocate also speaks for the necessity of leaving space open for new translations.

AS: Relational psychoanalysts have made some of your points about gender before: I am thinking of Muriel Dimen's formulation that gender is "less a determinative category than a force field" of

---

57 See p. 164 above.

dualisms, Adrienne Harris's dubbing gender a "necessary fiction," Jessica Benjamin's calling it a "real appearance," and Virginia Goldner's aptly calling it a "false truth."[58] You join these analytic thinkers, and many others since, in treating gender as something that is not ontologically fixed and derives not from anatomy but from the relationship one develops *to* one's excitable body. But by building on Laplanche's ideas, you are elaborating a different analytic as to how gender inhabits the types of contradictions used to describe it above, presenting it is a translation based on infantile sexual theories. I have been preoccupied with trying to formulate what the difference is between your work here and work that has already been done on gender in psychoanalytic thinking, which will be important for readers who are more familiar with the North American theorizing on gender and work less with ideas from Freudian or French metapsychology and your thinking in particular.

I have arrived at the following, and I am curious if you'd agree. It seems to me that, in arguing for the centrality of infantile sexual theories as translational tools in the crafting of gender, you accomplish two things that are new.

First, you give us a way to keep in mind that there is an irreducible arc between gender and the infantile Sexual and that the disruption of the infantile Sexual always subtends the seeming coherencies of even normatively assembled gender (i.e., cis genders). That seems like a meaningful contribution because psychoanalytic gender theory that has expanded our thinking on gender by leaning on insights from feminist thinking and queer theory has problematically cleaved the Sexual from gender. It has done so in

---

58 Dimen, "Deconstructing Difference: Gender, Splitting, and Transitional Space." *Psychoanalytic Dialogues* 1, no. 3 (1991): 335–52; Harris, "Gender as Contradiction," *Psychoanalytic Dialogues* 1, no. 2 (1991): 197–224; Benjamin, "Father and Daughter: Identification with Difference — a Contribution to Gender Heterodoxy," *Psychoanalytic Dialogues* 1, no. 3 (1998): 277–99; and Goldner, "Toward a Critical Relational Theory of Gender," *Psychoanalytic Dialogues* 1, no. 3 (1991): 249–72.

the effort to delink gender from biological sexual difference and to claim space for gendered experience that is not rooted in biology. But this has had the inadvertent, and problematic, effect of treating gender as virtually desexualized. Because you are working with a Laplanchean theory that does not reduce the sexual body to biology, you are not constrained this way; that is, you don't have to leave out the Sexual to accomplish a more enriched understanding of gender diversity. Within Laplanche's metapsychology it is possible to have one's cake and eat it too—to delink in our theories the experience of gender (i.e., gender identity) from the biological without also delinking it from the sexual, excitable body.

Second, you are doing with gender something that Laplanche also understood as the analytic task—you are not giving us new concepts; what you are doing is liquidating the links *between* concepts, stitching them together anew. Perhaps that's a different way to describe "blinking concepts," concepts that when examined "wave at you," as you discussed in our conversation on chapter 1.[59] For example, you are saying that there is a relationship between the sexual body and gender but that it is not one of biological determinism, that male and female are, and will continue to be, conceptual staples but that they may rally together differently refracted through the infantile Sexual rather than biology.

OK, I've said a lot here, but I hope you see my excitement about your thinking and about what it can enable in further research; I am really curious about any thoughts you have about this.

DS: You are much more knowledgeable than I am about North American theories of gender and thus in a better position to appreciate what may be new or different in what I say. I am in total agreement with your conclusions, except that I would remark that infantile sexual theories are *not*, from the get go, *translational tools*. They are themselves the products of translation, but obviously,

---

59 See p. 44 above.

once they are in place they influence newer translations.

I have already said a few words in praise of ambiguity, so I will not repeat myself except to say that what you mentioned about "liquidating the links *between* concepts" is a very important observation. It reminds us, first, that unbinding is at work in our theoretical practice and, second, that it takes the form of a potentially productive work of deconstruction and not of destruction. This work, I believe, feeds on the inescapable ambiguity of our human condition and therefore also of a vocabulary that tries to account for it and that I praised earlier.

AS: I can sense you are also drawing a distinction between the two here – between infantile sexual theories being translational tools versus them influencing new translations. If that is correct, could you please explain to us briefly what you see the difference between something being a translational tool versus influencing newer translations? Is your point to emphasize that there are still some degrees of freedom involved, however rigid the theories are?"

DS: There is not as clear a distinction as my use of words suggests, but I think you've exactly formulated the idea lurking behind my remark. There is indeed more freedom when an infantile theory works as just one among many, influencing other ideas and being influenced by them, therefore taking part in an evolutive process, than when an infantile theory is THE translating tool, rigidly interpreting what goes on in oneself and in the surroundings.

Actuality of Seduction[1]*

I

Jean Laplanche's immense contribution to psychoanalysis unfolds along three axes: firstly, a method for reading Freud critically; secondly, an essential work of translation of Freud's writings; finally, the general theory of seduction. We do not have to choose any these three contributions over the others, as the solidarity between them is quite obvious. But having been invited to talk about the general theory of seduction, I will say at the outset that the third component is to me but a product of the first—that is to say, a consequence of Laplanche's fundamental activity: putting Freud back to work. Were I forced to choose only one of these three Laplanches—Freud's reader, his translator, and the author of the general theory of seduction—I would choose the first since I would be sure that through him I would eventually meet the other two.

The method developed by Laplanche is important in that it forces the Freudian theory to explain itself, as it were, to self-theorize. Laplanche derived it from the very method invented by Freud, a sign that the knife that Laplanche has often said must be stabbed into the Freudian text is not deadly. First of all, the method bears witness to Laplanche's admiration of and confidence in the

---

1   *This is a somewhat expanded version of a paper originally published in French as "Actualité de la séduction" in *Annuel de l'APF* 1 (2015): 147–58. Translated by the author.

Freudian oeuvre that he wished to put back to work. I will not repeat here all that Laplanche has said about Freud's strayings— which he did not mean to simply refute but to take as clues and guides on paths where more thinking is required.

Dare I say how much Laplanche's approach to Freud's texts is what attracted and seduced me from the beginning? I know of few authors who have shown so much transparency in their theorizing and who have been able to find their way with such clarity through the dense forest of Freudian thought. To such an extent that to read Laplanche is not merely to pick the dogmatic fruits of his reflection. Rather, at every moment, Laplanche tells us the what and the how, so that we learn first to read Freud with Laplanche but finally to read Freud, and Laplanche, by ourselves.

This is perhaps why, despite the important dissemination of his work and his great theoretical authority, Laplanche did not create his own "school"—that is, he did not seek to reform psychoanalysis or to initiate a new psychoanalytic movement. Instead, he worked on the foundations, on the underpinnings, as he put it, which is where one could argue the fate of a discipline is really played out.

II

With regard to the general theory of seduction (GTS), I said that it appears to me as but a particular moment of Laplanche's substantive activity, which is critically reading Freud, but I think it is important to put this theory into perspective. It is not, in my opinion, just one more psychoanalytic theory; it is not a mere Laplanchean battlement on the walls of the psychoanalytic fortress. By this I mean that Laplanche did not first develop a method of reading and then try to apply it to this or that part of Freud's work. What happened is that as a consequence of the critical reading of the whole Freudian work, taking up the theory of seduction imposed itself as necessary. Having identified in Freud's abandonment of his *neurotica* the greatest cataclysm in Freudian theorization, Laplanche was led to propose a renewed theory of seduction so as to give firmer foundations to psychoanalysis.

The theory of seduction is indeed the locus at which converge — or from which emanate — most of the central questions in psychoanalysis: the origin of the unconscious and of the ego (including narcissism), the theory of repression and of the drives, the theory of analytic treatment and of transference, the theory of trauma and of *après-coup* . . . From a meta-anthropological point of view, these can all be put under a single heading: *the primacy of the other in psychoanalysis*.

Obviously, whereas I call the GTS a particular moment in Laplanche's reading of Freud, the "moment" extends over a long period, a period whose strongest markers are *Life and Death in Psychoanalysis* and *New Foundations for Psychoanalysis*.[2] There is, of course, much to be said about all the work Laplanche did leading to these two important milestones in his theorization. But I must content myself with going straight to the point since I am not attempting an exegesis of Laplanche, but rather I want to pay him the best tribute he could have wished for: to do to him what he did to Freud — that is, put Laplanche back to work.

III

The elaboration of the General theory of seduction begins in *Life and Death in Psychoanalysis*, the writing of which started in 1968, where one can already see him denouncing the insufficiency of

---

2 Jean Laplanche, *Life and Death in Psychoanalysis*, trans. Jeffrey Mehlman (Baltimore: Johns Hopkins University Press, 1976); Jean Laplanche, *New Foundations for Psychoanalysis*, trans. Jonathan House (New York: The Unconscious in Translation, 2016.).

anaclisis, or leaning-on.[3] This theory, which Laplanche and Jean Bertrand-Pontalis had extracted from Freudian texts, was a major theoretical tenet, one whose criticism would open the way to the new foundations.

Remember that the theory of anaclisis draws a line of demarcation between self-preservation and sexuality, with concomitant sexual excitation as a linchpin[4]. In this view, the Sexual was to somehow emerge from self-preservation; caricaturing this idea a little, one might say, "as if by mere friction", so that the intervention of the other seems only an instrument, a kind of photographic developer merely revealing the Sexual that was already there. This same view can be found in Freud's second model of seduction where he describes the involuntary seduction of the child by its adult caretaker, a seduction that one could call "mechanical."

In proposing that seduction is the truth of anaclisis, Laplanche not only generalized the facts of seduction but also relieved seduction of its mechanical physiology. While not necessarily denying concomitant libidinal excitation, one must consider it just one of the possible intervening factors in the generalized view of seduction. The GTS indeed falls under the heading of compromised messages. The message in itself is quite ordinary: "I take care of you." Yet the incidental, inadvertent excitation of the child's body through ordinary care inserts in the message the "compromised" sexual element. Note that in so doing, self-preservation (implied in *anaclisis*) is not evacuated. The carrier messages in question can be, as I have indicated, messages of care and attachment— that is, relatively well adapted to the needs of the child. These messages belong, if not exclusively to self-preservation, at least to preservation at large—they pertain to the vital order. The difference,

---

3   See Dominique Scarfone, *Laplanche: An Introduction*, trans. Dorothée Bonnigal-Katz (New York: Unconscious in Translation, 2015).

4   S. Freud (1905), *Three Essays on the Sexual Theory*,

however, is that under the aegis of generalized seduction, one can no longer conceive of human self-preservation as a mere fact of nature; the child who is in a state of helplessness is always already immersed, so to speak, in the caring stance of an adult endowed with an unconscious Sexual.[5] The "compromised" element—"contaminated," as it were, by the unconscious Sexual—travels as a stowaway within otherwise ordinary, well-attuned messages. There is still a divide between self-preservation and the Sexual, but the novelty here is that the dividing line does not run between two aspects of the individual infant's endowment but is instead experienced as a noise in the communication channels between adult and child.

It could be said that seduction thus redesigned absorbs the old anaclisis and recontextualizes it as an epiphenomenon. The contradiction that ran between the vital and the sexual dimensions has thus been displaced and is now at work within the relationship, or the exchange, between adult and child.

IV

As I was just quickly treading the path from anaclisis to generalized seduction, an alarm rang in my head: I realized that, for an uninformed reader, I would seem to be describing an empirically observed situation and that the GTS could even end up sounding like a developmental sequence such as: a child, lacking an unconscious and with as yet undifferentiated psychic agencies, is confronted with the compromised message of the adult other, and from there the child is forced to do a work of translation/repression that initiates a psychic differentiation, and so forth.

This is indeed what the theory seems to say, but for all we

---

5   Or a sexual unconscious, if one prefers.

know, Laplanche did not start from the observation of babies any more than Freud had when he wrote his *Three Essays*. Of course, the fundamental anthropological situation invoked by the general theory of seduction[6] eminently concerns the adult-child relationship, but one should remember that this early relationship involving seduction, whatever its degree of truth, is not observed from the outside but derived from another scene of seduction: the analytic session, where the analyst-theoretician is party to the process and not a simple observer. The adult-child scene is hence a scene *constructed* out of what the analytic experience can teach us. It surely describes an actual relationship and inserts itself within the general view of parent-child attachment processes, but it inserts something that the theory of attachment does not concern itself with: the sexual dimension. The theory is here operating according to another of its own major tenets: the *après-coup* temporal dimension. The sexual factor is evinced from the analytic experience on the couch and is intercalated, though the GTS, into the theory of the origins of the unconscious, which informs in turn the very practice whence it originated.

I must therefore insist on the following: the general theory of seduction would be but a hypothesis, just one more theory, if we didn't realize that it emanates not from the observation of exchanges between mother and child but from the actual experience occurring in analytic sessions—that is, from the situation in which the analytical instrument invented by Freud fully operates. The analytic session is our essential "terrain" in that it concentrates and raises to higher levels the intensity of what happens in the interhuman relationship, thus revealing, much in the manner of a particle accelerator, what has previously gone unnoticed, and once

---

6 Jean Laplanche, "Starting from the Fundamental Anthropological Situation," in *Freud and the Sexual: Essays 2000–2006*, trans. John Fletcher, Jonathan House, and Nicholas Ray (New York: International Psychoanalytic Books, 2011), 99–113.

revealed, it can be traced back to the fundamental anthropological situation of the origins. Hence, the analytic session is not a mere place of observation and description of psychic development; it is itself instrumental. It establishes and amplifies the relationship to the other, a relationship that concerns humans of all ages. What happens in the session is induced by the Freudian method and the refusals of the analyst,[7] which contribute to raising the intensity of the encounter and at the same time establishing the perimeter required for the analytic process to happen. The resulting process highlights the sexual factors, in the broad sense, that would normally go unnoticed, combined and shrouded as they are within ordinary exchanges. As the Freudian method goes, the analytic perimeter proceeds from the exclusion of the vital order, of the adaptive elements, or as Laplanche sometimes says, of the utilitarian "railway schedule."

The Sexual in analysis is hence not observed in a naturalistic fashion but extracted by an appropriate analytic method from the relational ore. The fundamental anthropological situation is therefore not the observational basis in which one detects the primal seduction. Mind you, the incidental behavioral aspects of involuntary seduction *can* be observed and described, actually in very simple terms. For instance: the breasts that suckle the baby, which are eminently sexual organs; the parents playing at "eating up" the baby, much to its excitement; the closed door of the parent's room and the enigmatic noises of what goes on behind it; and the "double entendre" sexual jokes that even older children cannot "get." These are but few examples of the empirical aspects of the general process of seduction, facts of seduction that come embedded in ordinary, ongoing parent-child—or even child-to-child—communication. Yet strictly speaking, the FAS is a situation

---

7   Laplanche, *New Foundations for Psychoanalysis.*

reconstructed thanks to a to-and-fro between the disjoint elements captured in the analytic room, thanks to the Freudian method and the consideration of the communication processes between adults and children. This epistemological detail, it seems to me, is of some importance.

V

The establishment of the analytic situation, repeated with each new session, is what makes it possible to highlight precisely the aspects of communication that point to something beyond the adaptive "good understanding" between the infant and the adult caretaker. On the other hand, the "misunderstandings" that happen during the session allow us to extrapolate the characteristics of the original seduction to other occurrences of the fundamental anthropological situation—that is, to any asymmetrical interhuman encounter, of which the adult-infant situation is the paradigm.

When indeed the analysand's discourse, at first more or less well formed, comes up against an unexpected resistance—when the analysand is at loss for words—then we know we are approaching the unconscious Thing, the enigmatic remains, the nonmetabolized parts of the message of the other. This transitory lack of words. this *aphasia*, we could call it *infantia*, which is its exact Latin equivalent. This reference to *infantia* is called for as it reminds us that, in Latin, the *infans* is defined as the one who cannot speak. Confronted with this *in-fantia* in the course of analysis, we are justified to wonder in what place other than the session we could find it best illustrated. At that point, the adult-child relationship comes up quite naturally, and we therefore deem it is legitimate to generalize and theorize, from within the analytic situation, what goes on in the newborn immersed in an adult world replete with preexistent sexual fantasies and hence with Sexual-carrying messages.

Obviously, then, we do not start from the naturalistic situation of the child and then discover the Sexual secretly transferred through the ordinary messages of attachment. We start from the Sexual highlighted by the exclusions specific to the analytic method and situation, from which we infer what happens in the adult-child relationship. Yet nothing prevents us from gathering, from the analysand's associations and memories, indexes of the Sexual that sneak among adult-child communications. Aren't, indeed, the scenes drawn by our analysands from their childhood memories indirect proof that the "reality of the message" and its enigmatic stowaway have been at work from early on?

Whether in the analytic situation or in the adult-child situation, in any situation that is a variant of the fundamental anthropological situation, it is always an *infans* who is summoned by the enigmatic nature the other's message and who must translate, create meaning, symbolize.[8] The difficulty of metabolizing the enigmatic part of the message constitutes the aphasia/*infantia* from which all the more or less successful psychic formations stem. The less successful ones will be the most fragile, the most likely to expose the subject again to the trauma of the encounter with the unconscious Thing, a Thing that is sexual in the psychoanalytic sense. However, I must point out that the disorder this Thing causes results not from its sexual nature in the trivial sense but from its status of *infantile Sexual*, which Laplanche, in his late writings, began to call by the German term *Sexual*.

VI

Let me emphasize that the *infans* I speak of is not "the child in the

---

8 Such construction of meaning from the "noise" in the communication is therefore more akin to transduction than to translation, but for simplicity's sake I shall keep referring to it as translation.

adult." There are *fans* (speaking) and *in-fans* (speechless) parts in both children and adults. We must perhaps resign ourselves to letting the ambiguity in this matter persist, since when we think of the child as speechless, we think of this with a vision of the future in which one who does not speak today will one day start doing so. This is a perspective that also applies, mutatis mutandis, to the analysand in the course of the session since we hope too that the person who does not yet possess the words that symbolize and allow for a psychic work of mourning will one day, thanks to the very work of analysis, come to possess them. Yet in precise theorizing, I find it necessary to posit that *infans* or *infantia* do not designate an age of life but the experience of being speechless *at any age*, a state that exposes adults and children all the more easily to trauma since the spoken word is the best stimulus barrier there is. What speech does not take up, does not symbolize, does not historicize, remains in an "actual" state,[9] amounting to a nonmetabolized foreign body, reiterating from within the pressure that was exerted from without by the encounter with otherness. It is not difficult, then, to conceive that this nonmetabolized, infantile part is the source of the "contaminant" in the compromised message of the adult. Hence, at work here is a sort of transcendence of the actual, a term by which I designate the repeated transmission from one human being to another of a remnant that resists symbolization.[10] This "actual" in the transmission seems to me a constitutive part of the fundamental anthropological situation.

Here, however, another question arises:[11] Is this nonsymbolized

---

9 D. Scarfone (2015) *The Unpast. The Actual Unconscious*, New York: The Unconscious in Translation.

10 Dominique Scarfone, "Sexual and Actual," in *Infantile Sexuality and Attachment*, ed. Daniel Widlöcher, trans. Susan Fairfield (New York: Other Press, 2002), 97–110.

11 From this point down to the end of section VII, the present version is sometimes quite different from the corresponding sections in the original French article since, while translating it, I realized that my ideas in the original were not as clearly formulated as they should be.

Sexual, this contaminant of the message of the other, necessarily unconscious? If one posits as a condition for the emission of a compromised message that the whole set be unconscious in the systemic sense, then the theory of seduction is exposed to the danger of the infinite regress. If indeed the repressed unconscious of the adult is a condition for the tainting of the message to the child, we end up attributing the formation of a primal repression, and hence of the unconscious, to a preexisting systemic unconscious, explaining repression in the one by repression in the other. We could, of course, from a practical point of view, postulate that this is how it works in most cases, but for the sake of sound theorizing, we cannot hold this to be always the case.

Laplanche saw this problem and answered it by saying that he did not need to posit a repressed unconscious in the emitter. Adults endowed with "some unconscious" i.e. an unconscious in the descriptive sense, are all we need "to be able to show the formation of a repressed unconscious in the child"[12]. On the other hand, Laplanche seems to have also relied on the fact that the repressed in the adult is not a hypothesis—it is an empirical observation resulting from psychoanalytic practice. He therefore does not seek to establish the origin of the unconscious in the human race; he is content with describing its birth in each individual case.

It seems to me, however, that the problem could be solved in a more complete and coherent way by addressing the status of the seductive elements in terms other than "conscious" or "unconscious," even in their descriptive sense. Obviously these elements *can* be descriptively unconscious or even repressed. What I suggest is that *we do not need* to qualify them in those terms. What I mean is that when one speaks of the "unconscious Thing," the decisive part of the phrase is the word "Thing"; it is the "thingness" (a term on which Laplanche often insisted) that matters. Consider

---

12 Laplanche, "The wall and the Arcade" in *The Unfinished Copernican Revolution*, New York: The Unconscious in Translation, 2020, p. 383.

for instance the downright perverse form of seduction, in which repression shines, so to speak, by its absence. Are we going to say that the perverse seducer is utterly conscious of what they are doing? Isn't their own perverse sexual behavior subjected to the infantile sexual urges in them? Yet in this case, we speak neither of repressed unconscious nor of mere unconsciousness. What then is the case here?

As we know, in the case of perverse seduction, Laplanche invoked a mechanism, intromission, which is the violent variant of the implantation of the Sexual that occurs in "ordinary" seduction. But the violence of intromission need not be accounted for in terms of being conscious or unconscious; all we need to consider is the *nonsymbolized state* of the sexual Thing that travels, with various intensities, from the transmitter to the receiver. This indicates that the sexual Thing can be found either in an *attenuated* form, more or less "shrouded" in the soft form of seduction corresponding to implantation, or as an unvarnished and more *brutal* imposition of the Sexual in intromission, with all the possible degrees between the two. We usually consider this nonsymbolized Thing unconscious, which in a way is correct since it operates outside of the subject's capacity to truly account for *what* is going on and *why*. But we see that what matters is whether the *Thing* in question is amenable to symbolization—that is, whether it can be subjected to translation and subjectivization or whether it totally retains its otherness, thus alienating the subject.

VII

Based on the Laplanchean critique of anaclisis, we do not ask anymore if the message of the other belongs mainly to the vital order or, on the contrary, to the Sexual. Thanks to the refusals of the analyst in the course of the session, we are able to discern a sexual core that is always at stake. But in the previous section, I dared suggest not even asking if the sexual Thing is conscious or unconscious. At any rate I deem it necessary to tighten the meaning of the term "unconscious," which Freud himself found unsatisfactory. What matters is how both the emitter and the receiver of compromised messages are able to deal with the Sexual. In other words, what matters is the status of the sexual element—is it in an "actual" state, or is it subjected to transformation, attenuation, symbolization, sublimation? Of course, as I said earlier, in any communication that matters, there will always be something of "actual" because part or all of the excitation has not been fully absorbed and sublimated or symbolized in the emitter, so the sexual Thing is transmitted to the receiver in an incompletely assimilable form.

So we are leaving behind the model of anaclisis for good. Now, the current actual-versus-psychic balance concerns the Sexual on both sides: sexual (i.e., erotic) tenderness on the side of what in the old model used to be called "self-preservation," sexual passion on the side of what Laplanche designates by the German word *Sexual*. Sexual tenderness is by definition symbolized, while the infantile Sexual is necessarily "actual."

It seems to me that Laplanche himself goes in this direction, though not using the exact same terms. In a 2003 article titled "The Sexual Crime," he refers to Sándor Ferenczi's famous paper "Confusion of Tongues Between Adults and the Child" and examines sexual abuse—incestuous or otherwise—looking not for the perpetrator of an act that is forbidden by the laws of kinship but for "someone who is prey to his own infantile sexuality."[13] "Prey to"—that is to say, incapable of symbolizing what agitates them in the actuality of their drives and thus pushes for enactment. Two

---

13 Laplanche, "Sexual Crime," in *Freud and the Sexual: Essays 2000–2006*, trans. John Fletcher, Jonathan House, and Nicholas Ray (New York: International Psychoanalytic Books, 2011), 156.

paragraphs before, Laplanche points out that, going from abuse in general to incest and the Oedipus complex, there is not "simply a way of escaping the problem by reducing it to the better known paths of the Oedipus complex. It is also a *real* movement of mastery and symbolization" (155). Mastery and symbolization happening in culture as in psychoanalytic theory but perhaps also in the situation of abuse itself, where the "passion" of the adult pervert is partially circumscribed by the alibi of love for the child, a symbolization better implemented still when the passion becomes subject to an oedipal inhibition by transferring itself to the domain of fantasy and its psychoneurotic derivatives.

I once suggested that Ferenczi's text contained a chiasm. Since what is at work in the adult perpetrator is the infantile Sexual, there is indeed a crossover: the infantile in the adult is what puts the traumatized child in a state of *infantia*.[14]

At the end of the text quoted above, Laplanche concludes with what he calls "two major imperatives" in the study of sexual crime:

"to look for the *infantile* in analytical investigations;

to look for the *message*, the residue of message and communication, which are always present, even in what are apparently the crudest of acts."[15]

As we can see, the message here is not only the vehicle of the Sexual as a stowaway, as it is according to the traditional definition of the "compromised message." Here the message is itself to be sought *in the act*—that is, in the enactment provoked by the Sexual; and in this act it is the infantile that must be sought by analytical investigation. Now, if the infantile Sexual is to be sought in the midst of what is already clearly sexual—in the Freudian sense—this means that there is no need to posit in the perverse seductive adult

---

14 Scarfone, "Sexual and Actual."

15 "Sexual Crime," 157–58.

something unconscious, be it repressed or simply nonconscious. What we are dealing with is something "actual," to which the adult is prey during their enactment. The word "actual" is here intended in many senses: As in "actual neurosis," it is not symbolized and not inserted in a psychical network of meanings. "Actual" also means that it is of the order of the act. And finally it operates in the "now time." It is therefore an enactment that, by not being symbolized, requires that we look for the *message* that is buried in the act, in what appears to be the reverse of the situation of "ordinary" seduction, where we look for the *act* buried within the message. But the reversal is apparent only since, in both cases, what matters is the balance between what is "actual" and what is symbolized: the two elements trade their respective roles of container and content depending on whether we are in the realm of primal seduction (in which the symbolized message contains the actual Sexual) or in the realm of perverse seduction (in which the perverse act contains a remainder, the index of a message).

VIII

It should be noted that in situations other than those of flagrant abuse, what is symbolized in the one—with the symbols always shrouding an "actual" kernel—may be more or less "actual" for the other, depending on the degree of asymmetry in the communication. Lacan indicated long ago that transference occurs wherever there is a "subject supposedly knowing"[16]; this supposedly knowing subject emerges when there is a demand, when the terms of the relation are uneven. This is commonly what happens with the demand addressed to the analyst, and their refusals only increase the asymmetry, the inequality of the exchange. Inasmuch as the

---

16 Lacan, Jacques. *The Seminar. Book XI. The Four Fundamental Concepts of Psychoanalysis*, 1964. Trans. Alan Sheridan. London: Hogarth Press and Institute of Psycho-Analysis, 1977. p. 232.

analyst remains the guardian of the enigma—that is, refuses to know—the analysand is presented with a gap in symbolization, a sexual enigma. This is, by the way, how a new production of the Sexual occurs, with no need for anaclisis.

The Freudian method introduces in the session an asymmetry that provokes the transferential productions, those about which words go missing—this is the analysand's aphasia or *infantia* when they are dealing what is "actual" in the message for lack of symbolization. Transference is therefore a form of action whose symbolization can be initiated by words—be they the analysand's or the analyst's—or even by acts usually inhibited as to the goal. Words that begin to epithelialize, as it were, the actual sexual Thing and to make it assimilable. Thereupon, the patient's ego does not need to keep rearing up against the so-called foreign Thing. Less guarded against the pressure of what is still in need of translation, the ego can come to tolerate that, as Laplanche puts it, "[t]here where there was id, there will be always and already the other."[17]

---

17 Jean Laplanche, "The Unfinished Copernican Revolution," trans. Luke Thurston, in *The Unfinished Copernican Revolution*, New York: The Unconscious in Translation, 2020, p. 40..

Conversation

AS: This is such a beautiful and crisp paper, which I think will act as a particle accelerator for our discussion. You are taking us deep into the weeds of how Laplanche's interventions draw on Freud, and in a very Laplanchean move, you put Laplanche to work, as he did with Freud. We continue to see here that the Laplanche we are reading with you is *your* Laplanche, a faithfully unfaithful one, to use the phrase by which he himself described his reading of Freud. We could say that the "knife" that Laplanche applied to Freud gets passed around, and that in taking it in your hands to use it on Laplanche, testing his theory, you are also handing it to us. That knife, the incitement to put theory to work, is part of what Laplanche's theory bequeaths to us, and this is something we learn further not from Laplanche (who uses it on Freud) but from the fact that you, use it on him.

But a knife is never *just* a knife, and we can't deny the aggression in the signifier. While Laplanche insisted that he simply "put" Freud to work, it seems to me that the deeper we go into Laplanche, the harder it is to defend the idea that his interrogating of Freud's thinking via the Freudian method lands him in purely Freudian territory. Or rather, since Freud is of so many minds, to say that Laplanche is working to fortify the Freudian edifice means little without also defining *which* Freud Laplanche puts to work—certainly not the Freud of ego psychology or the Freud read by Kohut, or so it seems to me. We are, then, in the terrain of Laplanche's expanding on Freud, not just building new foundations. You write, for example, that Laplanche's method "forces the Freudian theory to explain itself . . . to self-theorize"[18]—but would this self-theorizing process not cause even the Freudian concepts he is working with spin out of their orbitals? Does it not cause the concepts to "blink," to return to your delightful phrase from our discussion of the first

---

18 See p. 191 above.

chapter of this book?[19] And if that's the case, how is Laplanchean metapsychology not a method that starts from (a certain reading of) Freud but develops its own distinct conceptual density?

DS: It would be hard indeed to claim that Laplanche always lands in Freudian territory, if by this we mean Freud's theories. Still, we must take Freud's own word that theory is what can be changed because it stands at the top of the edifice, not at the foundations. So what we have here is Laplanche's claim that he is providing new foundations to psychoanalysis, which can easily be misunderstood as meaning that the new foundations in question consist in the formulation of a new theory called the general theory of seduction (GTS). This would put these new foundations in direct contradiction with Freud's view of where the theory stands. The GTS is proposed by Laplanche as the new foundations, but this is because it is not just one new theory—it is rather a novel scaffolding for the whole Freudian construct. Most of what was built by Freud is preserved but following a new internal logic. The GTS has displaced the old viewpoint by acknowledging the primacy of the other and the radically decentered status of the subject. If we care to put it to use, we realize that it is inseparable from the translational model of the psyche and the *après-coup* time structure, and we'll soon find that the doctrine made up by these three elements reorganizes the entire psychoanalytic domain.

We can also say that Laplanche stands in Freudian territory for another reason. His most original contribution is indeed applying Freud's analytic method to the critical examination of Freud's texts, a method that in turn can be applied to reading Laplanche and so on. This is the passing of the knife you described. The question of the method is therefore what keeps Laplanche faithfully unfaithful, as you reminded us, because there is no other choice: if you faithfully apply Freud's method on Freud's own manifest discourse, you

---

19 See p. 44 above.

will *necessarily* land on a territory that is new or renewed. But because of the faithfulness to the Freudian method, we can still call that territory Freudian. So for instance, while the GTS is clearly Laplanche's theoretical landing, it is critically rooted in Freudian grounds. It could be said to be Freudian in spite of Freud.

I would not, however, spend too much energy discussing this aspect, as I believe that labels (Freudian, Lacanian, Kleinian, Laplanchean, etc.) may at best be shorthand for stating in advance where a speaker or author stands but at worst political banners, claim to a sense of belonging to a certain community. I would like to think of myself as belonging to the community of psychoanalytic researchers who are anticommunitarians. I mean that in the end, it matters little if where we land is an official Freudian theory; what matters is to work with what Freud has bequeathed us: the psychoanalytic method. This is what brings me to say that if forced to choose one of the three main dimensions of Laplanche (the critical reader of Freud, the translator, and the author of the GTS), I would always choose the first, confident that the other two sides of his work depend on his methodical critique.

Taking up the method, examining its requirements anew, reasserting and demonstrating its relevance, I believe, is what could help analysts from different "schools" eventually convene around what they have in common and thoroughly discuss their differences. So yes, what matters is that concepts at some point begin to "blink," just as, during a session, some word a patient says in passing, without even noticing, starts calling the analyst by their name.

In the end, Laplanche's own theory requires a critical reading and, possibly, also transformation, so I'm pleased indeed if you find that my work does that. Let me be clear: I don't get up in the morning with the project of transforming Laplanche's theory; the idea is that if one works as faithfully as possible with Laplanche's "knife" in hand, new, and hopefully more solid, views will necessarily emerge. On the other hand, I follow William of Ockham's precept not to multiply concepts needlessly, so to avoid misusing Laplanche's "knife," I keep Ockham's "razor" in my other hand!

AS: The notion of exigency is an important one for Laplanche — and, I think, for many Laplanchean thinkers — but also a very hard one to understand, or at least it has been hard for me. We encounter it here when you write that "taking up the theory of seduction imposed itself as necessary."[20] Can you help us understand what you mean by something "impos[ing] itself as necessary"?

DS: The notion of exigency runs throughout Laplanche's critical reading of Freud. I would say that it is a natural extension of one major Freudian discovery: that there exists a "psychical reality," different from material reality yet as real and sturdy in the sense that it doesn't let itself be "bent" by subjective preferences.

AS: Sorry to interrupt you here, but before you continue, can you give us a very brief description of the difference between subjective and psychic reality? I want to be sure everyone is on the same page.

DS: I speak of "subjective preferences," which could also be called "psychological reality." This refers to the conscious or semiconscious set of thoughts, memories, opinions, and world views that, by definition, correspond to the subject's subjective take on reality — that is, that which accommodates best the (pre-)conscious person. It may contain a number of things that are shared with others (few or many others), such as political preference and ideology, but these are always things that can be studied psychologically or sociologically — for example, through questionnaires — and that are bound to change over time depending on the forces that drive the ambient culture. Let me give a personal example. Years ago, with our family growing, my wife and I decided that we needed

20 See p. 192 above.

a minivan to accommodate our three children and their eventual friends on our weekend trips. We set our minds on a certain brand and size of vehicle, but we discussed the color at length with our children and eventually reached a consensus: our minivan was to reflect what we thought was our very distinctive preference; it was going to be "forest green." So we went to the car dealer and discussed the model, its dimensions, the extra seats we needed, and so on. As for the color, the dealer did not wait for us to say anything. He simply stated: "And of course you want a dark green minivan." Or jaws dropped as we wondered how he could have known! At which point he said that the car industry's surveys had determined that the most preferred color in families with children the age of ours that year was green.

This is psychological reality: it can be studied and even allow for rather accurate predictions, and it could also be shown to activate "reward systems" in the brain or whatnot. My example may seem quite trivial, but it reflects something serious. Let me refer here to Hermann Broch's book *Die Massenwahntheorie*— "The Theory of Mass Madness"—of which there is no English translation. In this dazzling and puzzling unfinished work, Broch posits a "crepuscular" or "oniric" state of the human psyche that is nothing other than our ordinary state of mind, about which he has this to say: "It is inasmuch as, and only inasmuch as, they live day after day in an 'oniric state' that human beings can be apprehended by the theory and the laws of history. Within this object domain— that is, the dreamy existence of the crepuscular man—the laws of the theory of history finds an authentic scientific validity."[21] This to me is an impressive statement because it signals something dramatic about the nature of psychological reality, which is open

---

21 Hermann Broch, *Théorie de la folie des masses*, trans. Didier Renault and Pierre Rusch (Paris: Éditions de l'éclat, 2008), 107. Originally published as *Massenwahntheorie: Beiträge zu einer Psychologie der Politik* (Frankfurt am Main: Suhrkamp, 1979). My translation from the French edition.

to influence by opinion, fashion, ideologies. It speaks, I believe, of what in our jargon we call the ego, in contrast with the subject, the latter requiring a critical stance, a temporary flight from the ego's crepuscular zone.

As for *psychical reality*, it is not the subject itself, but it is what the subject must unendingly work to assume or come to terms with. It refers to formations of the unconscious that resist outer influence precisely because they do not operate under the control of consciousness. In that sense it is paradoxical because even though it escapes the subject's conscious control, its imperviousness to outer influences is a cornerstone of the subject's uniqueness and possible autonomy with regard to opinion, ideology, or groupthink in general. Psychical reality is, of course, the repressed unconscious, defined as such by Freud in the last few pages of *The Interpretation of Dreams*. Obviously, psychological reality is influenced by psychical reality, of which the former is but an outer shell, in contact with and under the influence of the outer world.

Because of psychical reality's imperviousness to outer influence, the search for it entails exigency, and exigency can take many forms, but Laplanche used the word to describe Freud's continuous effort not to let go of his object of research: the unconscious as a specific reality and not simply the nonconscious aspect of mental functioning. As is visible in some texts, such as *The Ego and Id*, Freud struggled with the term "unconscious" and was not totally satisfied with it. So when he realized that a large part of the ego was itself unconscious, he needed to come up with a "something else" opposite to the coherent ego, and which he called the id. This is but one example of Freud's responding to an exigency posed by his object of inquiry. The same goes with Freud's handling of the theory of drives. In his first theory, he would refer to the sexual drives as disruptive forces and thus incompatible with the ego. Then through the introduction of narcissism, he found the ego to be itself libidinally charged, so that the Sexual no longer appeared as foreign to the ego as before, and this led Freud to present the whole Sexual as Eros, the force that creates links. Yet Freud's exigency of accounting for the otherness of the unconscious forced him to introduce a force opposite to Eros, the death drive. This is how exigency moved Freud's work of theorization.

Notice that, in itself, this exigency does not entail any "final word." Laplanche, for instance, does not follow Freud in his conception of the id as a biological source of the drives, nor does he concur with Freud's conception of a death drive. Still, Laplanche acknowledges that, however erroneous in his view, these are products of Freud's unrelenting exigency to account for the "something else" at work in our minds and hence are worth examining anew. The logical consequence of heeding Freud's exigency, therefore, is not to accept the specific results but to consider they are worth spending more time on. Laplanche would say something like: "Freud went astray, but he did so for a reason (the exigency), so let's give it another look."

AS: In this essay, you walk us through the work that Laplanche did in tackling the concept of anaclisis—which he sees as a pseudoconcept, in that it wasn't fully fleshed out by Freud.[22] This work showed that key to the derivation of the Sexual is not mechanical coexcitation but the intervention of the other's always-compromised message. But you also caution us: while we tell the stories that form the basis of the theory of primal seduction and of the FAS in a linear fashion, we should do well not to forget that that those stories are themselves *derived scenes* insofar as they come to the analyst from within another scene, the analytic one. This introduces the time scramble of the *après-coup*, issuing the important reminder

---

22 Jean Laplanche, "Sexuality and Attachment," in *Freud and the Sexual: Essays 2000–2006*, trans. John Fletcher, Jonathan House, and Nicholas Ray (New York: International Psychoanalytic Books, 2011), 33.

that memory and experience are in nonlinear relation to the event of implantation and to primal seduction. Can you highlight for us what this understanding of nonlinear psychic temporality adds to the analyst's thinking?

DS: I clearly remember an International Psychoanalytic Association conference on *après-coup* organized in Paris by Haydée Faimberg in 1998. It gathered analysts from many countries, and many American colleagues attended. I was asked to moderate one of the discussion groups where French, British, and American analysts tried to reach an understanding about what *après-coup* was all about. I was therefore witness to the great cultural divide between continental Europe—France in particular—and the British and American analytic world. In retrospect, I think I realized an important distinctive trait of the American outlook on the subject when distinguished colleagues kept asking: "How can I use this concept in my work with my patients? What does it add to my armamentarium that I don't already possess?" These, in my view, would have been legitimate questions if they had referred to, say, sessions of variable length in the Lacanian sense or if *après-coup* led *directly* to a change in the way one formulates an interpretation (it certainly influences the way the analyst interprets, though not directly). Now, while I do believe that taking the *après-coup* time structure into account changes a lot of things, it is important to realize that this time structure is not a technical tool. I would compare it to the theory of evolution, which does not immediately translate into a technical device in a biology experiment. While the analytic method is Freud's major *invention*, the time structure of *après-coup* is one of his major *discoveries*, by which I mean that it is at work in our lives whether we are in analysis or not. It was a revolutionary discovery, yet Freud seemed to take it for granted. Hence, he never wrote a paper on *Nachträglichkeit*! Lacan can be credited as one of those who noticed its importance in Freud's theory.

In my view, *après-coup* redefines our psychoanalytic epistemology. It is a reminder that the link between present and past is not linear and that while we may feel that we are looking at the past (or, for that matter, the present), we are in fact dealing with a complex to-and-fro between these times. So much so, that an event B happening "after" an event A changes the situation to such an extent that A and B combined not only give another meaning to both of them but also create a novel impact *in the present*, an impact that changes the significance of both A and B taken separately.

The *après-coup* time structure is, by the way, a necessary (though not sufficient) condition for analytic work itself. What is it indeed that the analytic experience provides (through repetition, transference, and working through) if not the possibility of a new *après-coup*, reshaping the past and, by the same token, offering a turn of events that changes the outlook on the future? Yet *après-coup* is not something that analysts can actively implement. We do not "use" *après-coup*; we base our work on the belief that the past is not "accomplished" and that, as Faulkner wrote, "it is not even past." This is one more reason that I have proposed the notion of the unpast, if I am forgiven the neologism, and a reason to see analysis as a process that instantiates a true past, as Winnicott and M'Uzan formulated long ago.[23]

It is important, however, to notice that *après-coup* structures a trauma as much as it can offer a way toward symbolizing it. While two or more of the "blows" implied in *après-coup* are necessary for constituting a significant psychic event, the result can be either a closed, nonevolutive symbolization (think of little Emma in Freud's example) or an open, evolutive one, as happens in analysis.

---

23 D. W. Winnicott, "Fear of Breakdown," in *The Collected Works of D. W. Winnicott*, ed. Lesley Caldwell and Helen Taylor Robinson, vol. 6, *1960–1963* (NewYork: Oxford University Press, 2017), 523–31; Michel de M'Uzan, "Analytical Process and the Notion of the Past," *International Review of Psychoanalysis* 1 (1974): 461–66.

It is interesting to note that the ego itself is always intervening "after the fact." Though this is not exactly the full *après-coup* mechanism we are talking about, the ego is always late to the scene of psychic events as it can justify only afterward the subject's choices or actions, giving the best rational explanation it can find, like any PR agent. This raises the question of the subject's ethical responsibility. For to say that our ego is late to the scene doesn't imply that we are not responsible for our unconscious choices. We can go as far back as Freud's "Project" of 1895 to see that in his view, the ego's primary function is that of an inhibition. And we find the same idea in chapter 7 of the *Interpretation of Dreams* where the ego (*Ich*) is said to exert a relative control of the motor pathways; hence, it may not be the chooser, but it can inhibit the action at the last moment.

AS: One of the most complex matters in Laplanchean thought is the fact that the infantile Sexual, which inflects the way he understands the unconscious, never matures or develops—something we discussed in depth in our conversation after chapter 2. You expand on this here, clarifying that we think of the child as "speechless" in the developmental sense of the word—as the infant who has not *yet* acquired the facility of language. But when you speak of the *infans*, you mean it in a different sense—as the part of the unconscious that does not, and never will, have speech, as that part that will always remain unsymbolized. This links to the "actual," a term we have already touched on and that you explain in great detail in your magnificent text *The Unpast*, which I can't recommend highly enough to our readers. In this essay, you are, by necessity, more brief, but I am hoping you can help us see how the actual is different from enigma itself.

DS: The word "actual" refers to the time dimension of the unconscious, so it is not on the same category level as the enigma. Laplanche, by the way, does not speak of "enigma" but uses the adjective "enigmatic" and, even then, not systematically. What matters here is that, as discussed earlier, the message confronting the *infans* is enigmatic because the senders themselves are not aware of this opaque element, of this "noise" in their communications. The link with the actual is that what is implanted through such noise is not something that can be dated nor something that will erase itself with time or become integrated. The implant is what remains unsolved by the translational efforts of the child, so it is the repressed as it results from the failure of translation. It is therefore always actual in that it is not subjected to the passage of time and is always "actually" reiterating the subject's exposure to the enigma of otherness. Except that the otherness is now within.

AS: Thank you. This is very helpful.

I also want to see if we can think together about the problem of infinite regress that you raise. You write, "If one posits as a condition for the emission of a compromised message that the whole set be unconscious in the systemic sense, then the theory of seduction is exposed to the danger of infinite regress. If indeed the repressed unconscious of the adult is a condition for the tainting of the message to the child, we end up attributing the formation of a primal repression, and hence of the unconscious, to a preexisting systemic unconscious, explaining repression in the one by repression in the other." As you note, Laplanche does not posit "a repressed unconscious in the emitter; a simple, descriptive 'unconsciousness,'" suffices to "form the enigmatic side of message,"[24] and this is how Laplanche gets us out of the problem of infinite regress.

This is an excellent illustration of how easy it can be to become confused about, or to misread, Laplanche. One form of misreading would be to appropriate him into what we already know from other analytic theorists. We have a better chance of resisting such misreadings, it seems to me, if we understand how he is using his

---

24 See p. 201 above.

terms and especially the different meanings he furnishes to the terms "repression" and "unconscious." When he theorizes that the other's sexual unconscious intervenes with us, introducing a noise in the message, he is not referring to a repressed *represented* unconscious (e.g., unconscious fantasies) or to content that has become relegated to the domain of the unconscious because that content was unbearable (e.g., difficult memories or traumatic events). He is referring to *what has never been represented*, to the part of the adult's message that could not be translated in the first place. Therefore, the unconscious he has in mind is a different kind of unconscious than the one most analysts usually refer to: it is not something occluded from access but something that nevertheless exists somewhere else. Similarly, by the term "repression," he means something different than the everyday psychoanalytic use of the term: he uses it to mark what remains after translation, after the message has been rendered meaningful through translation— as opposed to repression marking something that is evicted into a submerged psychic chamber from which it will emit symptoms and parapraxes. You have been addressing all these points throughout the papers in this volume, and in this essay you speak to them again with a different inflection point by bringing in the Thing—to emphasize that it's the thingness, the Thing quality (we are, in other words, here in the domain where translation, even transduction, does not venture), that directs us to recognize that we are in the presence of the unconscious (in the Laplanchean sense of the term).

DS: I think that the essence of your remarks is correct but that the issue is not as clear-cut in Laplanche's thinking. For instance, Laplanche *does* point at an unconscious fantasy of the adult at the source of the compromised message. However, he also always insists on the "thing quality" or the "thingness" of the repressed you mentioned. For example, for him, Freud's "thing-presentation," which is characteristic of the unconscious, has nothing representational about it—that is, it is not the unconscious representation of a thing. Laplanche also uses the expression "designified signifiers." So, in my view, the unconscious fantasy he speaks of must also belong to the category of the unconscious "Thing," which may seem a contradiction in terms, but it's not. This, in my understanding, resonates with a similar problem in the Kleinian theory of unconscious "phantasy," where the different spelling is not a matter of linguistic preference, but rather it serves to insist that the phantasy in question *is* the internal object, *is* the psychical reality itself. But you will notice that if we follow that line of thinking, then what we have is a *phantasy* that is precisely not a *fantasy*—that is, it is not a representation. Now, if we consider that for Freud, conscious or unconscious, there was no difference in the nature of the fantasy itself, we see that we run into a theoretical impasse. Freud and Klein cannot both be right about this; and as we also see, there is an internal contradiction in Freud since he holds that the unconscious deals only with thing-presentations. The way out of this impasse, I suggest, is that of looking at the time dimension and of sticking with the "thingness" of the repressed, as you mentioned. From that perspective, the Kleinian unconscious *phantasy* and Freud's and Laplanche's unconscious *fantasy* are both thinglike *presentations* but not *representations*. And if we ask what gives them this "thingness," it is their not having been transcribed into the realm of meaning. Meaning would have required the adjoining of word-presentations, which entail insertion in the flow of chronological time.

AS: This reminds me how delighted I was recently to discover that some of my Greek colleagues have a distinction of that sort built into their psychoanalytic lexicon: the ασύνειδο (*asineido*, pronounced asineetho) speaks to the Thing quality of the unconscious, while the ασυνείδητο (*asineidito*, pronounced asinitheeto) has more to do with the quality of being unconscious for something represented (that is, something that has already been translated but is now out of sight, psychically-speaking). This different usage makes one wonder if we may not need different terms to mark that distinction in English as well—or at least variations on the term "unconscious", as in Greek. I know that no one wants to add more terms, but in this case, it seems confusing to not be able to succinctly capture these distinctions. You have been moving in the direction of preferring the term "actual," and we touched on that in my previous question. It seems to me that it might be a preferable term to "unconscious," which carries the possible confusions—between the system unconscious and the quality of being unconscious—that you highlight in your paper. Is there some reason not to more wholeheartedly embrace the "the actual" as a term for the kind of unconscious that Laplanche describes as arising out of primal repression?

DS: I envy our Greek colleagues, and I am, once more, impressed by how the travel between languages always helps us find original solutions to conceptual problems. As for using "the actual" for, let's say, the radical unconscious we are referring to, I would have no objections, of course, but I would not insist on its adoption either. If the term gains any traction, it will be because of its usefulness in addressing the problem we are discussing. But this is nothing new. Freud himself, as I mentioned, was not really happy with the term "unconscious," yet, even as he introduced the id, he never let go of the word "unconscious," because he thought "the property of being conscious or not is in the last resort our one beacon-light in the darkness of depth-psychology."[25] For my part, I think of it as practical shorthand in everyday analytic parlance (which sends us back to the question of ambiguity).

AS: You highlight that "it is always an *infans* who is summoned by the enigmatic nature of the other's message and who must translate, create meaning, symbolize. The difficulty of metabolizing the enigmatic part of the message constitutes the aphasia/*infantia*

---

25 *The Ego and the Id, SE* 19:18.

from which all the more or less successful psychic formations stem. The less successful ones will be the most fragile, the most likely to expose the subject again to the trauma of the encounter with the unconscious Thing."[26] Can you say a bit more about what you mean by "most fragile"? Or to put it differently, by what metric would you assess some symbolizations or translations as less successful?

DS: That is something we always know in the aftermath or, to put it a better way, in the *après-coup*. So there is no question of any metric. We merely realize, after the fact, the extent to which symbolizations, representations, identifications, libidinal positions, are sturdy or, on the contrary, how easily they collapsed, be it in the patient's past or in the course of analysis. But this is too simply put. The most fragile translations may reveal themselves quite resistant in that they are the last available "solution," and hence they are prone to the repetition compulsion and offer a great resistance. These are the ones that sometimes invite us to be more prudent and not insist on analyzing (i.e., dissolving) them.

AS: One of the major contributions of this paper, where I think you lead us in a rather different direction than much Freudian thinking, comes close to the end. You write that "the message here is not only the vehicle of the Sexual as a stowaway, as it is according to the traditional definition of the 'compromised message.' Here the message is itself to be sought *in the act*—that is, in the enactment provoked by the Sexual; and in this act it is the infantile that must be sought by analytical investigation."[27] Here you are going well beyond the notion of the noise that disturbs the message itself. Can you flesh out for us how you are using the word "act" in this context?

DS: Your question really pleases me because you are the first one to notice something that I had thought would provoke criticism

---

26 See p. 199 above.

27 See p. 204 above.

on the part of fellow analysts familiar with Laplanche. I believe that in the passage I quoted from "Sexual Crime," Laplanche gives us an opening toward a more granular conception of what is at stake in seduction, especially in what we refer to as abusive seduction, or intromission. Laplanche asks us to "look for the message, the residue of message and communication, which are always present, even in what are apparently the crudest of acts."[28] This strikes me as something different from looking for the "contaminant" in ordinary messages, as in the case of implantation. Laplanche seems to turn things inside out and to call for the reverse of the usual procedure: consider an action and look for the message in it, whereas we usually consider a message (say, a tender-loving-care message) and look for the covert action of the Sexual in it.

AS: So what would it mean to consider the action and look for the message in it? How does that differ from looking for the covert action of the infantile Sexual in the message?

DS: In a very interesting paper titled "Responsibility and Response," Laplanche draws from the Bible an example that strikes me as problematic of a nonverbal message. The example is that of the persecution of Job by God. The killing of Job's herd, then a series of fires and plagues, that is the message, says Laplanche.[29] And we could certainly agree with him if the killing and the plagues were perpetrated by a real person. But the example is problematic because it postulates God (or the devil) as the sender of the message. Now, ascribing the message to a divine or evil sender is a reaction that we observe all the time and that does pertain to the Laplanchean category of the message. It is a retrospective, imaginary attribution after an otherwise unexplainable event. To me, it is important to distinguish this general mechanism from the

---

28 "Sexual Crime," 165.

29 Jean Laplanche, "Responsibility and Response," in *Between Seduction and Inspiration: Man*, trans. Jeffrey Mehlman (New York: Unconscious in Translation, 2015).

genuine *après-coup*, to which I will get back later. The mechanism of retrospective attribution corresponds to the tendency that manifests itself on the occasion of any significant event—for instance, drought destroys our crops, and even in our times of scientific knowledge, we may wonder: "What have I done to deserve this?" As Ernst Cassirer notes in *Language and Myth*, in those moments we invoke a "momentary god"[30]—that is, we resort to mythos—while we also look for objective causes through logos.

If we turn to acts performed by someone real, my view on them is that there are acts—namely, destructive acts—that can perhaps be considered "objective messages" but that were not intended as messages by their authors. These acts can be the result of the accumulation of an unbearable tension within their author, resulting in an irrepressible discharge with no addressee in mind—actually, *mindless* acts. I think here, for example, of a fictional character: Fritz Lang's Hans Beckert in the movie *M*, as recalled by Michel de M'Uzan in his famous paper "Slaves of Quantity."[31] Near the end of the film, when Beckert tries to defend himself before the jury formed by the mob, the child murderer can only explain that he cannot control the impulse that takes hold of him from time to time. Obviously this raises a difficult question in terms of responsibility, to which I'll get later. But for now, I wish only to stress the fact that Beckert's kidnapping, abusing, and then murdering of a child does not seem to me to contain any message in the usual sense. It is pure discharge. And yet we could say that the social group that is revulsed by Beckert's behavior resonates to it as if it is a message—that is, by organizing a chase and then condemning Beckert.

Laplanche, in the paper I mentioned, speaks of this sort of situation in these terms: "He who screams for death in the trial of a child murderer (punish him!) or even he who screams on the subject

---

30 *Language and Myth*, trans. Suzanne K. Langer (New York: Dover Publications, 1946), 33.

31 *Psychoanalytic Quarterly* 72, no. 3 (2003): 711–25.

of Bosnia (Bomb it!) . . . is also he who, from childhood on, screams: 'It's not fair!' In brief, he who thirsts for justice—and that means each of us—is also the person yelling out against what attacks him from within, against the torturer inside himself." [32]

So it turns out that there *is* someone at the receiving end, *sensing a message* and resonating to it unconsciously because of "the torturer inside himself." This calls for seeing the notion of *après-coup* as central to the matter. It means that we can conceive of an action as pure discharge of the tension brought about by the infantile or unconscious Thing, which at the moment of its expression, may have no meaning and hence no "message" in it. However, in its aftermath we can do two things: (1) We can retrospectively attribute the act to a deliberate will, since we do not tolerate a complete lack of meaning for too long, and therefore after the fact we attach to the act any meaning we can formulate; but this is the trivial, easy part. (2) A more difficult but fundamental fact is that, in the *après-coup*, we can conjugate the action and the context (affective, social, political, racial, etc.) and *extract* a message from this ore. For instance, let us imagine Beckert consulting a therapist and linking his lack of impulse control to the violence he himself was subjected to in his family. We could say that there is an objective "message" at work in his murderous acts, an unspoken reference to the violence endured and a resulting rebellious challenge to the social order, even though his acts were not meant to communicate anything. The message has to be formed in the *après-coup* of the analysis of the whole situation, even its transgenerational dimension.

AS: So what you are saying is that the infantile secretes actions, so to speak, that only in their aftermath become meaningful. And that those meanings borrow from the social—just as translating leans on existing social templates to render the inchoate into something more tangible or understandable?

---

32 "Responsibility and Response," 142.

DS: Yes, but we must always heed the difference between spontaneously assigning meanings to actions —this is the easy part I was mentioning— and the effective *après-coup* mechanism which *extracts* the message from the action, which raises more dramatic issues.

AS: So the second part you described has to do with the complex balance between forces that are not entirely in our control but the effects of which we are nevertheless responsible for, right?

DS: Right. This is the question of responsibility I mentioned.

AS: So the action of the drive is not controlled by the ego exactly, right? In fact, we might say that the ego mobilizes its inhibitory operations precisely to prevent the action of the drive. Still, the action does belong to the subject (though perhaps not to our subjectivity)—we are responsible for that which we do not consciously intend or execute. This way of thinking raises very complex, possibly irresolvable questions about responsibility, agency, and ethics. And certainly about consent—a topic of great interest to me. In any case, maybe this is a reason Laplanche backed off from following his thinking about the demonic aspects of the drive as far as it could have taken him. And this is where, if I don't utterly misread you, you pick up to ask us to think of how to contend with these complexities.

DS: Yes, not only do you not misread me, but you point to something I had not clearly formulated in my mind. In "Sexual Crime," just after the short passage I quoted, Laplanche seems to posit that there is always some psychological mechanism at work even in the crudest act. So the message he asks us to look for is, in the end, always lurking, albeit minimally. I diverge from him here in that I do not think that we need the message to always be there, as this would send us back to the linear way of thinking and therefore to the danger of infinite regress we already talked about. I believe I am actually following Laplanche's method if I say that we *extract* a message from an, at best, inchoate ore,[33] through the mechanism of translation/repression that he himself puts at the center of the general theory of seduction and that is the operator, so to speak, of *après-coup*. The "something" that may have affected Beckert in Lang's movie may well have been contained in a message, say, from his putative violent father. But this does not imply that his own murderous act contains a message, though it carries over the "something" from his own experience.

So as you saw, this raises difficult questions in terms of complexity, agency, and ethics. Indeed, it implies following the logic of seduction, transduction/translation, and *après-coup* to its end. As I understand it, Laplanche's imperative to look for the message in the crudest of acts does not mean "Look well and you'll find it," nor does it mean "Interpret the act from your knowledgeable position." It means keep listening to the act itself, of course, but also to all the concomitant factors that the subject's associations can conjure, so that a process of transduction/repression becomes operative. But this is where things get even more interesting. Ordinarily, the subject works from a trivial message (of care, for instance) and translates it, producing meaning on the one hand and a repressed "Thing" on the other. Here we have a "something" from which we need to extract a message, as if we had the "Thing" to work with and bring to a state where it yields a message . . . to be translated. Hence, it's as if we are *installing* the very category of message. "*Saxa loquuntur,*" wrote Freud at some point[34], "Stones speak"—except they don't speak by themselves; we have to make them speak by offering them an addressee through our listening.

The ethical issue that is raised here is indeed that we are to be held responsible even for an act that was out of our control,

---

33 The idea of extraction, by the way, speaks in favor of my preference for calling this a transduction, for it is precisely not a translation.

34 S. Freud, (1896) "The Aetiology of Hysteria". *S.E.*, *(3)*,192

which is paradoxical of course. Laplanche addresses this issue in the paper I quoted above ("Responsibility and Response"), where he signals the difference between moral responsibility and material obligation. But it seems to me that he tries to stay away from the ethical or moral debate, replacing the question of "being responsible for" with that of "answering to"; on the way there, he dismisses Emmanuel Levinas, which is a pity because I believe Levinas helps us, among other things, to distinguish between responsibility and guilt.

To give one more brief example: In discussing Freud's "*Wo Es war, soll Ich werden,*" Laplanche proposes a "slightly prosaic and flattened out translation: "There where there was (some) id, (some) ego should be."[35] But this seems to downplay the very material obligation he has mentioned, let alone the moral responsibility. How, I ask, can "some id" become "some ego" if not by taking up frontally the cruelty of the internal tormentor, with all the work of mourning, symbolization, and sublimation that is required? But it would take us too far astray to discuss this now, so let me just say here that I am not totally convinced.

AS: Your bringing in Levinas in relation to the distinction between guilt and responsibility makes me think as well about Stephen Mitchell's important call for us to tend to the difference between guilt and guiltiness. He does not reserve for the category of "guilt" the complexity that you flesh out here vis-à-vis responsibility, but he does, via the notion of "guiltiness," help us think about a more superficial relationship to guilt, a type of "guilt-assumption," where the subject becomes more narcissistically preoccupied with their feelings of guilt, which can lead to a pressure to make a quick and thus shallow repair—a manic reparation. Ultimately, this corrective is about the subject protecting their sense of themselves (e.g., as a good person, as a person who wouldn't

---

35 "Responsibility and Response," 143.

harm anyone) rather than about seriously contending with the matter of responsibility.

At the heart of the question of responsibility is the question of the subject and the subject's agency that you so elegantly raised. It involves this very interesting tension that has to be kept taut—or rather, that one has to work to ensure remains taut, as it will easily relax or be evaded if we don't work at maintaining the tension. This tension has to do with the fact that we are still responsible for that which obtains from a nonpersonal part of the self, from something that springs from within us but that we did not intend and might not even stand behind.

There are tremendously interesting implications here, and the particular example that comes to mind for me has to do with Whiteness and with the many ways in which the concept of reparations owed to African Americans and Native Americans is being discussed today. If you'll permit me a personal association, perhaps we can think through the following example together from the perspective you are proposing: During a recent trip I took with my good friend Angela,[36] I accidentally dropped something heavy on my foot, which resulted in a broken metatarsal. The damage was minimal, but full immobilization and crutches were still required to help it heal and to prevent further damage. My friend helped me through the visit to the hospital. When I was back at my hotel room, she offered to run to a nearby store to purchase some supplies I would be needing. Without much thought, I rather naïvely offered Angela my credit card. Angela matter-of-factly said that she could not, as a Black woman, use someone else's credit card in a store. I instantly knew what she meant; in fact, in any other context, I would have been aware of this fact (that using my card would make her vulnerable), but in this case, overly preoccupied with my injury, it

---

36 I am using this vignette with my friend's permission, and I should also say that Angela is not her real name.

hadn't come to mind. I have given a lot of thought to the fact that I so casually suggested something to her (using another person's card) that for me, as a White woman, would have likely had very little implication but which for her, as a Black woman, could have become dangerous. I acknowledged this and apologized. Angela accepted my apology. The incident deepened our conversations about our racial difference. The point I want to raise in the context of this conversation with you is that I meant no harm and yet did something that could have put her in harm's way. If she had taken the card, used it, and gotten arrested or, it's terrifying to think, if something worse had happened, I would have been—and held myself—responsible for it to some degree.

My story relates to what you were saying in the following way: There was no intent or malicious motive in my act. And while we can look for ambivalence, aggression, and a host of other possible "explanations" (all of which, no doubt, would exist on the representational level), it seems to me that something coursed through me that was both mine and not only or entirely mine. That something, I would venture, has to do with my being White and with my Whiteness—which seeps into the act of my offering the card. This is akin to how, as Adorno writes in *The Jargon of Authenticity*, "History does intrude on every word [and, following you, we'd have to say that it also intrudes on every action] and withholds each word from the recovery of some alleged original meaning."[37] Whiteness is not my doing or a property of my character alone—it is a characteristic distributed among a group of people to whom in many ways I belong, it is a current produced in and circulating through me (since I was the one who suggested she use my card.) Though it is not something I consciously control in that moment, I am nevertheless responsible for the act it generated, even though it did not arise from me as a sovereign subject, or, to say it differently,

37 Theodor W. Adorno, *The Jargon of Authenticity* (Evanston, IL: Northwestern University Press, 1964), 8.

from my subjectivity. Assuming responsibility for it involves recognizing that my offering of the card invited trouble for my friend, and it also involves the readiness to hold myself accountable for that trouble. Both of these (the recognition and the readiness) occur in the *après-coup* of my action.

To put this another way, partly because I am myself trying to flesh out my ideas on this as we speak, my act cannot be dismissed as just White privilege, as my being "naïve," or as having to do with not appreciating the differential in our racialized positions, nor is it as useful, from the angle you are suggesting, to think only of what personal, subjective motives powered my gesture. I am reminded here of Laplanche's saying in his Kent Seminar that even when we think we are creating, "we are always being worked by foreign messages."[38] The matter of taking responsibility for the foreignness in us, in this case the way in which my Whiteness erupted for me as if foreign *to* me, is as strange as it sounds; and it is, as you point out, ethically pressing.

I am curious whether you see this example as touching on the distinction you are drawing in your expansion on Laplanche.

DS: Your example is extraordinary and multilayered. Ideally, we would examine each layer in detail, but this is not possible here. This example also poses one major difficulty with respect to what we were discussing above, in that it clearly is a case of an ordinary message carrying something that is heterogeneous to the manifest communicative intention. I dare suppose that your intended message to Angela was: "You are already helping me a lot, so I cannot possibly expect that, on top of helping me, you will also pay for the things I need, so take my card." Let's suppose that she had accepted and had been arrested and that she later recounted

---

38 Jean Laplanche, "The Kent Seminar," in *Jean Laplanche: Seduction, Translation, Drives; A Dossier*, ed. John Fletcher and Martin Stanton, trans. Martin Stanton (London: Psychoanalytic Forum, 1992), 33.

this event to her analyst. Regarding the event and your message in particular, Angela's theoretical analyst could assist her in discerning the "Thing" that traveled unconsciously within the well-meaning offer. In other words, this would be the common instance of an action that was not of pure discharge: it was a deliberate and thoughtful offer on your part.

But what you propose here is to look at the message from the point of view of the sender—that is, you. So let us concentrate on your act alone (offering your credit card), artificially isolating it from your intention. What do we see? We see that your action, whose intention resulted from a friendly attitude, from gratitude, contains many more dimensions than you could have thought of at the moment. Though this is not exactly what is at stake in the problem of looking for the message within "even in what are apparently the crudest of acts," it nevertheless engages the problem of responsibility. It was not your intention to get Angela arrested or worse, and you would not be *held guilty* of what might have happened to her. But none of this dispels your *objective responsibility*. And this point is obviously in agreement with Laplanche and Nietzsche about material obligation: Angela's arrest, if it had occurred, would have, at least in part, resulted from your offer (it goes without saying that this also means that she would have thoughtlessly accepted your offer to let her use your card, and this in turn would require us to analyze her relationship to you, but let us ignore this and other complexities).

Yet is this simply a "material" or "objective" link between your offer and the hypothetical disastrous consequence? Could we not say that in the *après-coup*, during an analytic session, your friend would also be able to discern in your action a message that, though it did not *emanate from* you, had nonetheless *traveled through* you, a message whose sources go back to the American situation at large, to the historical roots of slavery, segregation, racial prejudice, and so on? I may seem to overextend the area of responsibility, but I believe that psychoanalysis can claim a role in the attribution of collective responsibility, because what might have happened to Angela, had she accepted your offer, would not have been your fault, but it certainly would have been your responsibility and that of every American citizen who does not take a stand against racism in all its forms.

So we see that in the end we have a three-tiered event: your friendly message, which contained an action that itself contained a deeper message. This is possibly not something Laplanche would say or agree with, but I feel the need to connect the individual work of the psyche to the social and even political facts, which, after all, all dwell in the realm of meaning, a realm traversed by powerful, obscure, and conflictual energies.

AS: This is all very interesting, and thank you for engaging in this particular exchange. I do have a further thought on this and one more question.

First, my question: You spoke of this message that did not emanate from me but traveled through me and which has to do with the long pained history of anti-Black racism in the US. It is beginning to sound, though, as if we are speaking of a message with content—and as if, if that is the case, we are moving away from the notion of a compromised message (that can be translated but has no content per se). I know you don't think of it this way. Can you help me out? What am I missing or misunderstanding?

DS: I see your point, and your question will help me clarify things. It is a fact that any message has content, and the compromising forces also are "content," though unspeakable content, at least for the person at the receiving end. This is why, at the risk of repeating things I've already said, I stress the time dimension: Speakable content is by definition inserted in the flow of time. Unspeakable content is "actual"; it does not pass with time, and this suffices to make it a foreign body, an excitatory contaminant. For if it were subjected to the flow of time, its excitatory load would be spent and would finally pass. The appearance of the social energies we were talking about on the scene of your action are also content. But the forces in question also belong to the "now time" of what I call "the actual" in that they are *a constantly present origin* that no one can claim to possess or master, an unspeakable dark core in human history. They belong to a cultural process of its own kind that, like all cultural processes, develops "over and above humankind," as Freud says in *Civilization and Its Discontents*.[39] They will stay as a constant source of motion even as society as a whole works toward sublimation and symbolization—my way of saying that "the end of history" is nowhere near.

AS: Thank you. The temporal dimension is important here, and it always requires effort to keep it in mind.

All right, so here is my thought, borne of your response to me: I have heard you say often that as analysts we need to be mindful of the fact that we provoke the transference not through our actions but through a seduction. This provocation infuses the analytic relationship with a particular kind of responsibility on the analyst's part, a responsibility that specifically issues from the seductive dimensions (and I use "seductive" in the Laplanchean sense of the term, in the sense of seduction in the FAS) of the analyst's offer. Obviously, my relationship with Angela is not of the analytic order, as we are friends. But the way that you were thinking this through made me wonder about whether the offering of the card, if we exclude my conscious intent and set aside those motivations that pertain to the vital order (of gratitude, concern about burdening

---

39 Sigmund Freud, (1930) *Das Unbehagen in der Kultur*, in *Gesammelte Werke*, 14:456.; my translation. Strachey's translation reads: "a process of civilization which mankind undergoes," (*Civilization and its Discontents*. In SE, 21:139) but this does not fully render the idea Freud seems to have when he writes *"der über die Menschheit abläuft,"* literally: "that runs over/above mankind."

her, etc.), might not have also conducted something sexual in the enlarged sense of the term. Sexual how? A hypothesis emerging for me now is that there may have been a seduction involved in my offering her the card—insofar as my momentary lapse in remembering our racial difference invited her into Whiteness, as if in offering my card to her, I acted, and invited her to act as well, as if we were both White, as if we could both enjoy the privileges of Whiteness, as if I could singularly accomplish that in my White privilege—a flash flood, perhaps, of racial naïveté and racial privilege. This is all conjectural of course, but it does remind me of Claudia Rankine's play *The White Card*, which tracks the importance, but also the difficulty, of White people reckoning with their Whiteness.[40]

This hypothesis arises in my mind in the *après-coup* and pursuant to the discussions you and I are having about your paper. The more we talk about it the better I am understanding how central the concept of seduction is to thinking about action. I am not consciously aware of thinking of Whiteness as a gift to be shared, but perhaps this is another way in which something that is nonpersonal courses through me as a White subject, a certain hypervaluation of Whiteness, which I now will have to think about more deeply.

DS: I am delighted that my rough analysis of the event has provoked these ideas in your own thinking, to which I eagerly subscribe. They in turn provoked another idea in me. I wonder if, as every dream (except in traumatic neurosis) is a wish fulfillment (Freud) and as every demand is a demand for love (Lacan), we could say that every offer is, at least in part, a seduction. I am not competent in the field of anthropology, but this reminds me of the problem of the gift in Marcel Mauss's work, which appears to be a simple fact but entails complex social dynamics.

---

40 *The White Card: A Play* (Minneapolis: Graywolf Press, 2019).

AS: How could every offer *not* also be a seduction? Your idea seems entirely plausible to me! I am finding that as we are thinking this through, my mind is also going back to our earlier discussion about the aura, which—I just checked—you described as "the very active element in the form."[41] We explored, through Walter Benjamin's work, the notion that there may be an aura, in addition to the enigmatic itself, that can help us think about intergenerational phenomena. This, unlike the enigmatic element, is not only freighted with history but also carries specific memories, images, events—for example, of the race and the ethnos. Can we try to think this through a bit further? Where would the aura fit in our discussion of the category of action in relation to the actual?

DS: Your question raises complex issues. I will try to respond in the simplest way I can. I would start by saying that the aura we borrowed from Benjamin is not, in my mind, something *added* to the enigmatic. I would rather say that the aura is an *index* (in the Peircean sense) of the enigmatic; it obscurely signals that there is something else there. You are right, however, to point out that in addition to signaling the enigmatic core, the aura also points to the specific images and stories that are linked to the element in question—the element whose aura can be sensed in the *après-coup*—and which were simultaneously hidden and pointed at.

AS: In your paper, and in your response to me, you are thinking of the category of action as not necessarily indexing an inability to contain or symbolize in the sense of a subject who is unable to use symbols because their capacity for symbolization is underdeveloped or compromised. You are suggesting instead that there is something in the Sexual that favors action, that is more likely to manifest in the act because the Sexual is ontologically outside symbolization. Such acts, you write, operate in "now time."[42] To me

---

41 See p. 116 above.

42 See p. 205 and 232 above.

this is an astonishing theoretical move: it lifts "acting out" out of its degraded status as marking lack, pathology, or developmental arrest. And it also directs us, as analysts, to pay attention to action as a potentially rich domain of inquiry, though not so that we may discover "hidden meanings" but so that we may make note of something else entirely—how we are ourselves, in the analytic situation, addressed by the patient. Can you say more about this idea and help us appreciate its implications for clinical work?

DS: Freud's famous quotation of Goethe at the end of *Totem and Taboo*, "In the beginning was the Deed," and every instance in which Freud considers thinking itself as a form of action should already give us a hint that there is nothing wrong with action in itself. But action can be treated as a very general category; it therefore needs to be dissected. We could start by looking at action as a noble thing if we think, for instance, of the work that has been done in recent decades in philosophy of mind around consciousness as action. I also think of the place Hannah Arendt, in *The Human Condition* (1958), has given to *action*, in contrast to *labor* and *work*, putting action, so to speak, at the apex of human capabilities even as it can take on tragic dimensions. So for one thing, I believe we must start by sorting out the different levels of action; secondly, we should always remember that the "talking cure" does not do away with action. The analytic situation transfers to speech the energy that would normally be part speech and part action; thus, speech takes an even greater relevance than in ordinary life, and in some critical moments, it *is* a form of action. All this, in my view, suggests that action is not necessarily devoid of symbolic value and that there are utterances that may not be as symbolic as they seem but are raw actions. Hence, a phrase uttered during a session, no matter by whom, can in fact be an enactment, or an acting in, or whatever expression we use to declare it outside of the more symbolic form of communication. This is a reminder that we should not rely on general categories but really look into the concrete situation and consider all its dimensions. Action is everywhere. Perhaps in the end, the question is of an ethical nature: Is this action working in the direction of dealing with a subject, or is it instrumentalizing the other as a part-object?

AS: There is a nuancing in what you are saying of the (sometimes overly) sharp division between action and symbolization that I really appreciate. It brings the matter of ethics to the forefront. And it reminds me how you end this paper, by referencing how the transference is itself "a form of action whose symbolization can be initiated by words . . . or even by acts inhibited as to the goal." These words, you continue, "begin to epithelialize . . . the actual sexual Thing . . . to make it assimilable."[43] Is this the most we can hope for when it comes to the actual—a covering over that makes it usable to us?

DS: The cover, the epithelium, is indeed what we have to work with. I don't know, however, if it makes the unconscious Thing usable. What I mean is that the Thing is what always stays out of grasp, out of reach, and yet it is the necessary substrate that "grounds" the psychic domain. One could say that it corresponds to the raw energy of the psychic events that come into our experience. But we cannot experience the raw energy itself. There is, in other words, a necessary theoretical space for the unrepresentable Thing—necessary in that it gives substance to the representational world. Without it, representations would simply be the immaterial things they are, without any weight or consequence.

Transference, in that respect, is a way of giving form—in action, in dreams, and in words—to the Thing that is summoned by the analytic process. Saying this, I imagine objections such as: Why then bother with a "Thing" that is unrepresentable? The answer is that, just as it gives weight to representation, it is also what makes

43 See p. 206 above.

238

the analytic process consistent. We would not have a clue as to what puts the transference in motion if we did not refer to something that cannot be totally represented or whose energy cannot be totally passed on to representations.

One can see that this notion of a Thing belongs to a cluster of concepts such as libido, drive, quantum of affect, cathexis, and decathexis. None of these notions refer to something observable in itself, but we experience their impact daily in our work and in our life.

In practice, this also means that we are always dealing with surfaces, which may seem ironic when we think that Freud also called psychoanalysis "depth psychology." This notion of depth has been called into question by Lacan, probably because he based his work on signifiers, and there are no "deep" signifiers. But when rereading Freud carefully, we find many indications that our work has to do with surfaces; for example, the ego itself, as is well known, was defined by him as a "surface entity" and "the projection of surface,"[44] and in his technical papers, he advised analysts to always work with the psychical surface presented by the patient. Now, one immediately thinks that if there is a surface, there must be something *beneath* the surface; hence, we are indeed doing depth psychology. Except that in my view, beneath (or, for that matter, above) the surface, we can find only another surface so that "depth" is in fact another name for the complexity, the crisscross, the labyrinth, of psychic surfaces that we engage in, without possibility of establishing that one is truly deeper than the other—and we know how in practice the same patient can present an indefinite number of such surfaces over time. What is truly deep, if I may say so, is the unrepresentable, no matter whether we call it "the Thing," "the actual," or any other name in the same conceptual cluster.

---

44 *SE* 19:26.

AS: This conversation could go on forever—and probably should! But it does also feel that I should tie myself to the mast and stop asking you more questions.

Thank you for making yourself available, for your eagerness to think things through in real time, and for your willingness to make provisional formulations. Mostly, thank you for the deep pleasure of thinking with you!

Bibliography

Adorno, Theodor W. *The Jargon of Authenticity*. Evanston, IL: Northwestern University Press, 1964.

André, Jacques. *Aux origines féminines de la sexualité*. Bibliothèque de psychanalyse. Paris: Presses Universitaires de France, 1995.

Arendt, Hannah. *The Human Condition*. Chicago: University of Chicago Press, 1958.

Askitopoulou, Eleni and Antonios Vgontzas. Ωφελέειν ἢ μη βλάπτειν: Διαχρονικές αξίες ηθικής και δεοντολογίας στο έργο του Ιπποκράτη [First do no harm: The diachronic value of ethics and deontology in the work of Hippocrates]. Athens: Ελληνικό Ανοιχτό Πανεπιστήμιο, 2021.

Aulagnier, Piera. "Demande et identification." In *Un interprète en quête de sens*, 161–98. 1967. Reprint, Paris: Rivages, 1984. Page references are to the 1984 edition.

———. *The Violence of Interpretation: From Pictogram to Statement*. Translated by Alan Sheridan. London: Routledge, 2001.

Balsam, Rosemary H. "Response to John Steiner's 'Overcoming Obstacles in Analysis: Is It Possible to Relinquish Omnipotence and Accept Receptive Femininity?'" *Psychoanalytic Quarterly* 87, no. 1 (2018): 21–31.

Beauvoir, Simone de. *Le deuxième sexe*. 2 vols. Paris: Gallimard, 1949.

Benjamin, Jessica. "Father and Daughter: Identification with Difference—a Contribution to Gender Heterodoxy." *Psychoanalytic Dialogues* 1, no. 3 (1991): 277–99.

Benjamin, Walter. "The Work of Art in the Age of Mechanical

Reproduction." In *Illuminations: Essays and Reflections*. Edited by Hannah Arendt, 217–51. New York: Schocken Books, 1969.

Broch, Hermann. *Théorie de la folie des masses*. Translated by Didier Renault and Pierre Rusch. Paris: Éditions de l'éclat, 2008. Originally published as *Massenwahntheorie: Beiträge zu einer Psychologie der Politik* (Frankfurt am Main: Suhrkamp, 1979).

Bromberg, Philip M. (2008) "'Grown-Up' Words: An Interpersonal/Relational Perspective on Unconscious Fantasy." *Psychoanalytic Inquiry* 28, no. 2 (March 2008): 131–50.

Butler, Judith. *Gender Trouble: Feminism and the Subversion of Identity*. London: Routledge, 2006.

Cardinal, Marie. *The Words to Say It*. London: Women's Press, 2000.

Cassirer, Ernst. *Language and Myth*. Translated by Suzanne K. Langer. New York: Dover Publications, 1946.

Chu, Andrea Long. "My New Vagina Won't Make Me Happy: And It Shouldn't Have To." *New York Times*, November 24, 2018. https://www.nytimes.com/2018/11/24/opinion/sunday/vaginoplasty-transgender-medicine.html.

Clark, Andy. *Surfing Uncertainty: Prediction, Action and the Embodied Mind*. Oxford: Oxford University Press, 2016.

de Lauretis, Teresa. "The Queerness of the Drive." *Journal of Homosexuality* 64, no. 14 (February 2017): 1913–29.

Dejours, Christophe. *Travail: Usure mentale*. Paris: Éditions du Centurion, 1980.

Deleuze, Gilles. *Difference and Repetition*. Translated by Paul Patton. New York: Columbia University Press, 1994.

Deleuze, Gilles, and Félix Guattari. *A Thousand Plateaus: Capitalism and Schizophrenia*. Translated by Brian Massumi. Minneapolis: University of Minnesota Press, 1987.

Dimen, Muriel. "Deconstructing Difference: Gender, Splitting, and Transitional Space." *Psychoanalytic Dialogues* 1, no. 3 (1991): 335–52.

Ferenczi, S. "Confusion of the Tongues between the Adults and the Child— (the Language of Tenderness and Passion)." *International Journal of Psychoanalysis* 30 (1949): 225–30.

Fletcher, John. "Seduction and the Vicissitudes of Translation: The Work of Jean Laplanche." *Psychoanalytic Quarterly* 76, no. 4 (October 2007): 1241–91.

Foucault, Michel. *The History of Sexuality*. Translated by Robert Hurley. Vol. 1, *An Introduction*. New York: Vintage Books, 1990.

Freud, Sigmund. (1887-1904) *The Complete Letters of Sigmund Freud to Wilhelm Fliess*. Translated and edited by Jeffrey Moussaieff Masson. Cambridge, MA: Belknap Press of Harvard University Press, 1984.

———.(1895) "Project for a Scientific Psychology." In *SE* 1:295–397.

———. (1896) "The Aetiology of Hysteria". In SE 3:192.

———. (1905) "Fragment of an Analysis of a Case of Hysteria (Dora)." In SE 7: 3-122.

———. (1905) *Three Essays on the Theory of Sexuality*. In *SE* 7:123–246.

———. (1908) "On the Sexual Theories of Children." In *SE* 9:207–26.

———. (1911) "Formulations on the Two Principles of Mental Functioning." In *SE* 12:213–26.

———. (1911) "Psycho-Analytic Notes on an Autobiographical Account of a Case of Paranoia (*Dementia Paranoides*)." In *SE* 12:1–82.

———. (1912) "On the Universal Tendency to Debasement in the Sphere of Love (Contributions to the Psychology of Love II)." In *SE* 11:177–90.

———. (1914) On Narcissism: An Introduction, *SE* 14:73-102.

———. (1915) "Repression" and "The Unconscious", in Papers on Metapsychology, *SE* 14:143-215.

———. (1916-1917) "The Paths of the Formation of Symptoms." In *Introductory Lectures on Psycho-Analysis*, pt. 3. In *SE* 16:358–77.

———. (1916-1917) *Introductory Lectures on Psycho-Analysis*, pt. 3. *SE* 16, p.241-263.

———. (1916) "On Transience." In *SE* 14:303–7.

———. (1917) "Mourning and Melancholia." In *SE* 14:237–56.

———. (1918) Sigmund Freud to Oskar Pfister, October 9, 1918. In *Psycho-Analysis and Faith: The Letters of Sigmund Freud and Oskar Pfister*, edited by Heinrich Meng and Ernest L. Freud, translated by Eric Mosbacher, p. 61–63. International Psycho-Analytical Library 59. London: Hogarth Press, 1963.

———. (1920) "Beyond the Pleasure Principle." In *SE* 18:7–64.

———. (1921) *Group Psychology and the Analysis of the Ego*. In *SE* 18:65–144.

———. (1923) *The Ego and the Id*. In *SE* 19:1–66.

———. (1924) "The Economic Problem of Masochism." In *SE* 19:155–70.

———. (1925) "Negation." In *SE* 19:227–39.

———. (1930) *Civilization and Its Discontents*. In *SE* 21:57–146./
Das Unbehagen in der Kultur. In *Gesammelte Werke*, vol. 14,
edited by Anna Freud (London: Imago, 1948).

———. (1933) "Femininity." In *New Introductory Lectures on
Psycho-Analysis*. In *SE* 22:112–35.

———. (1937) "Constructions in Analysis." In *SE* 23:257–69.

Gill-Peterson, Julian. *Histories of the Transgender Child*.
Minneapolis: University of Minnesota, 2018.

Goldner, Virginia. "Toward a Critical Relational Theory of
Gender." *Psychoanalytic Dialogues* 1, no. 3 (January 1991):
249–72.

Gould, S. J. "Freud's Phylogenetic Fantasy: Only Great Thinkers
Are Allowed to Fail Greatly." *Natural History* 96, no. 12
(1987): 10–19.

H.D. *Tribute to Freud*. New York: New Directions, 1956. Kindle
Edition.

Harris, Adrienne. "Gender as Contradiction." *Psychoanalytic
Dialogues* 1, no. 2 (1991): 197–224.

Héritier, Françoise. *Masculin-Féminin*. 2 vols. Paris: Odile Jacob,
1996–2002.

Horkheimer, Max, and Theodor W. Adorno. *Dialectic of
Enlightenment: Philosophical Fragments*. Edited by Gunzelin
Schmid Noerr. Translated by Edmund Jephcott. Stanford,
CA: Stanford University Press, 2002.

Horney, Karen. "The Flight from Womanhood: The Masculinity-
Complex in Women, as Viewed by Men and by Women."
Internatinoal Journal of Psychoanalysis 7 (1926): 324–39.

House, Jonathan. "Après-Coup." Sauvayre, Pascal & Braucher,
David (Eds). *The Unconscious: Contemporary Refractions
in Psychoanalysis*, edited by Pascal Sauvayre and David

Braucher, 157–73. Psychoanalysis in a New Key. New York: Routledge, 2020.

Imbeault, Jean. "Petit et grand infantile." *Le fait de l'analyse* 8 (Spring 2000): 23–43.

Jablonka, Eva, and Marion J. Lamb. *Evolution in Four Dimensions: Genetic, Epigenetic, Behavioral, and Symbolic Variation in the History of Life*. Cambridge, MA: MIT Press, 2005.

Kahn, Laurence. *L'écoute de l'analyste: De l'acte à la forme*. Le fil rouge. Paris: Presses Universitaires de France, 2012.

King, Homay. *Lost in Translation: Orientalism, Cinema, and the Enigmatic Signifier*. Durham, NC: Duke University Press, 2010.

Laplanche, Jean. "The Derivation of Psychoanalytic Entities." Chap. VII In *The Unfinished Copernican Revolution. Selected Works, 1967–1992*. New York: The Unconscious in Translation, 2020.

———. "Freud and Philosophy." In *Freud and the Sexual: Essays 2000–2006*, edited by John Fletcher, translated by Jonathan House and Nicholas Ray, 267–74. New York: International Psychoanalytic Books, 2011.

———. *Freud and the sexual: Essays 2000–2006*. Edited by John Fletcher. Translated by Jonathan House and Nicholas Ray. New York: International Psychoanalytic Books, 2011.

———. "Gender, Sex and the *Sexual*." In *Freud and the Sexual: Essays 2000–2006*, edited by John Fletcher, translated by Jonathan House and Nicholas Ray, 159–201. New York: International Psychoanalytic Books, 2011.

———. *Hölderlin et la question du père*. Paris: Presses Universitaires de France, 1984.

———. "Interpreting (with) Freud." in: *The Unfinished Copernican*

Revolution, op. cit. p. 57-74. . ———. "The Kent Seminar."
Jean Laplanche: Seduction, Translation, Drives; A Dossier,
edited by John Fletcher and Martin Stanton, translated by
Martin Stanton, 21–40. London: Institute of Contemporary
Arts, 1992.

———. *Le fourvoiement biologisant de la sexualité chez Freud.* Paris:
Synthélabo, 1993. (Engl. Trasnl. The Temptation of Biology.
New York: The Unconscious in Translation. 2015.)

———. *Life and Death in Psychoanalysis.* Translated by Jeffrey
Mehlman. Baltimore: Johns Hopkins University Press,
1976. Originally published as *Vie et mort en psychanalyse*
(1970; repr., Paris: Flammarion, 1992).

———. "Masochism and the General Theory of Seduction."
Translated by Luke Thurston. In *Essays on Otherness*, edited
by John Fletcher (London: Routledge, 1999).

———. *New Foundations for Psychoanalysis*, trans. Jonathan House,
New York: The Unconscious in Translation, 2016.

———. *Nouveaux fondements pour la psychanalyse.* Paris: Presses
Universitaires de France, 1987.

———. *Problématiques, vol. 2, Castration, symbolisations.* Paris:
Presses Universitaires de France, 1980.

———. "Responsibility and Response." In *Between Seduction and
Inspiration: Man*, translated by Jeffrey Mehlman, 123–44.
New York: Unconscious in Translation, 2015.

———. "Sexual Crime." In *Freud and the Sexual: Essays 2000–2006*,
edited by John Fletcher, translated by Jonathan House
and Nicholas Ray, 139–58. New York: Unconscious in
Translation, 2011.

———. "Starting from the Fundamental Anthropological
Situation." In *Freud and the Sexual: Essays 2000–2006*,

edited by John Fletcher, translated by Jonathan House and Nicholas Ray, 99–113. New York: Unconscious in Translation, 2011.

———. "Time and the Other." Translated by Luke Thurston. In *Essays on otherness*, edited by John Fletcher, 234–59. London: Routledge, 1999.

———. "The Training Analysis: A Psychoanalysis 'on Command.' " In *Between Seduction and Inspiration: Man*, translated by Jeffrey Mehlman, 123–44. New York: Unconscious in Translation, 2015.

———. "Transference: Its Provocation by the Analyst." Translated by Luke Thurston. In *Essays on Otherness*, edited by John Fletcher, 214–33. London: Routledge, 1999.

———. "The Unfinished Copernican Revolution." Translated by Luke Thurston. In *Essays on Otherness*, edited by John Fletcher, 53–85. London: Routledge, 1999.

Laplanche, Jean, and Jean-Bertrand Pontalis. "Fantasy and the Origins of Sexuality." *International Journal of Psychoanalysis* 49 (1968): 1–18.

———. *The Language of Psycho-Analysis*. Translated by Donald Nicholson-Smith. London: Hogarth Press, 1973. Originally published as *Vocabulaire de la psychanalyse* (Paris: Presses Universitaires de France, 1967).

———. "Post-scriptum." In *Fantasme originaire, fantasmes des origines, origines du fantasme*. Paris: Hachette, 1985.

Luhmann, Niklas. *Introduction to Systems Theory*. Translated by Peter Gilgen. Cambridge: Polity Press, 2013.

Lyotard, Jean-François. *L'inhumain: Causeries sur le temps*. Paris, Galilée, 1988.

M'Uzan, Michel de." Affect et processus d'affectation." In *De l'art à la mort*. Collection Tel 84. Paris: Gallimard, 1977.

———. "Analytical Process and the Notion of the Past." *International Review of Psychoanalysis* 1 (1974): 461–66.

———. "Slaves of Quantity." *Psychoanalytic Quarterly* 72, no. 3 (2003): 711–25.

———. The same and the identical, *The Psychoanalytic Quarterly*, 76:4, (2007) 1205-1220.

Pontalis, Jean-Bertrand. *La force d'attraction*. Libraire du XXe siècle. Paris: Seuil, 1990.

Popper, Karl R. & Lorenz, Konrad. (2013) *L'avenir est ouvert*. Champs. Paris: Flammarion, 2013.

Rankine, Claudia. *The White Card: A Play*. Minneapolis: Graywolf Press, 2019.

Reis, Bruce E. (2020). *Creative Repetition and Intersubjectivity: Contemporary Freudian Explorations of Trauma, Memory, and Clinical Process*. London: Routledge, 2002.

Saketopoulou, Avgi, and Pellegrini, Ann "A Feminine Boy: Normative Investments and Reparative Fantasy at the Intersections of Gender, Race, and Religion." Tiresias Essay Prize.

Salamon, G. *Assuming a Body: Transgender and Rhetorics of Materiality*. New York: Columbia University Press (2010).

Scarfone, Dominique. "De la disponibilité au transfert: Le leçon d'Hamlet." *Revue française de psychosomatique* 53 (2018): 6–19.

———. "In the Hollow of Transference: The Analyst between Activity and Passivity." *Sitegeist* 4 (2010): 7–20.

———. "'It Was Not My Mother': From Seduction to Negation." Edited by John Fletcher. *New Formations* 48 (1994): 69–76.

———. *Jean Laplanche.* Paris: Presses Universitaires de France, 1997.

———. *Laplanche: An Introduction.* Translated by Dorothée Bonnigal-Katz. New York: Unconscious in Translation, 2015.

———. "Live Wires: When Is the Analyst at Work?" *International Journal of Psychoanalysis* 92 (2011): 755–59.

———. "On 'That Is Not Psychoanalysis': Ethics as the Main Tool for Psychoanalytic Knowledge and Discussion." *Psychoanalytic Dialogues* 27, no. 4 (2017): 392–400.

———. *Oublier Freud? Mémoire pour la psychanalyse.* Montréal : Boréal, 1999.

———. Preface to *The Ethical seduction of the Analytic Situation: The Feminine-Maternal Origins of Responsibility for the Other,* by Viviane Chetrit-Vatine, xiv–xvii. London: Karnac Books, 2012.

———. "Repetition: Between Presence and Meaning." *Canadian Journal of Psychoanalysis* 19, no. 1 (2011): 70–86.

———. "Sexual and Actual." In *Infantile Sexuality and Attachment,* edited by Daniel Widlöcher, translated by Susan Fairfield, 97–110. New York: Other Press, 2002.

———. "The Three Essays and the Meaning of the Sexual in Psychoanalysis." *Psychoanalytic Quarterly* 83, no. 2 (2014): 327–44.

———. *The Unpast: The Actual Unconscious.* New York: Unconscious in Translation, 2015.

Scarfone, D. Trauma, Subjectivity and Subjectality, *American Journal of Psychoanalysis,* 81 (2021): p. 214–236.

Schwartz Cooney, Amy. "Vitalizing Enactment: A Relational Exploration." *Psychoanalytic Dialogues* 28, no. 3 (May 2018):

340–54.

Solms, Mark. *The Hidden Spring. A Journey at the Source of Consciousness*. London: Profile Books, 2021.

Stein, R.. "The otherness of sexuality: Excess." *Journal of the American Psychoanalytic Association*, 56, (2008) 56-71.

Steiner, John. "Overcoming Obstacles in Analysis: Is It Possible to Relinquish Omnipotence and Accept Receptive Femininity?" *Psychoanalytic Quarterly* 82, no. 1 (2018): 1–20.

Stern, Donnel B. "How I Work with Unconscious Process: A Case Example." *Contemporary Psychoanalysis* 55, no. 4 (2019): 336–48.

Varela, Francisco. *Principles of Biological Autonomy*. New York: North Holland, 1979.

Winnicott, D. W. "Fear of Breakdown." In *1960–1963*, 523–31. Vol. 6 of *The Collected Works of D. W. Winnicott*, edited by Lesley Caldwell and Helen Taylor Robinson. New York: Oxford University Press, 2017.

Sources

The chapters contained in this book are modified versions of articles that first appeared in psychoanalytic journals, as listed below.

The conversations were never published before.

Scarfone, D. (2013) A Brief Introduction to the Work of Jean Laplanche, International Journal of Psychoanalysis, 94:545–566.

Scarfone, D. (2014) The Three Essays and the Meaning of the Infantile Sexual in Psychoanalysis, The Psychoanalytic Quarterly, Volume LXXXIII, Number 2, p. 327-344.

Scarfone, D. (2019) The feminine, the analyst and the child theorist, The International Journal of Psychoanalysis, 100:3, 567-575.

Scarfone, D. (2019) The Sexual and Psychic Reality, International Journal of Psychoanalysis, 100 (6) :1248-1255.

Scarfone, D. (2015) « Actualité de la séduction », Annuel de l'APF, 2015/1, p. 147-158.

Printed in the USA
CPSIA information can be obtained
at www.ICGtesting.com
LVHW021504280124
769707LV00015B/858